CAN'T SLEEP, CAN'T TRAIN, CAN'T STOP

MORE MISADVENTURES IN TRIATHLON

ANDY HOLGATE

Pitch Publishing Ltd
A2 Yeoman Gate
Yeoman Way
Durrington
BN13 3QZ

Email: info@pitchpublishing.co.uk
Web: www.pitchpublishing.co.uk

First published by Pitch Publishing in 2012

Text © 2012 Andy Holgate

A CIP catalogue record for this book is available from the British Library.

ISBN: 978-1909178335

Cover design by Olner Design.
Printed in Great Britain by TJ International.

Dedicated to Marie Holgate.
We all miss you Mam.

ACKNOWLEDGEMENTS

I have so many people that have helped me on my continued journey, without their help I wouldn't have made it down the correct path. I owe so many people my thanks and I can only apologise if I miss you out here. It's not intentional just a sign that as I rapidly approach my 40th year that my mind is deteriorating as fast as my body. So to anyone that has helped me, offered advice, marshalled for me, shouted abuse at me in a race, contacted me online, or just been there for me: THANKS, I really appreciate it.

Firstly I need to thank the wonderful staff at Pitch Publishing who work tirelessly to promote my writing. Paul and Jane Camillin never tire of answering my questions, offering me advice and generally making the whole process of being an author a pleasure. They genuinely care and I can't thank them enough for their support.

I'd like to thank my colleagues at Lancaster University Library who over the years must have been bored silly with tales of triathlon, and more recently tales of book signings etc. I couldn't think of a nicer bunch of people to spend my everyday life with. I'd also like to thank the ladies in the university's press office for all their support in promoting my writing. Through their work I've been given some great contacts and opportunities.

Thank you to everyone that bought my first book, without you this one wouldn't have happened. And a huge thanks to the readers of my blog, without your support I'd never have been an author. I appreciate your continued support more than you could imagine.

Thank you to everyone that has given their kind permission for their wonderful photographs to appear in this book.

Thanks to Tim for all the invaluable advice on writing. I can't wait to read your upcoming books and to help you become an Ironman in 2013.

Thank you to the wonderful triathlon community who have supported my racing and writing. I love the banter and the support that one finds on the forums of *Tri-Talk*, *Fetch Everyone* and *Runner's World*. Thank you to everyone that has sent me messages, spoken to me at races or at book signings, reading your stories motivates me to keep pushing and to keep writing.

To Greppers, Deenzy, Beebs, Broccers, Rach, TRO, Hammers, Leggers, Slogger, AJPAR, Argie, Angus, Simbers, HOD, Phew, and Stepford Wife, thanks for making this "Comfy Shoe Glassman" one of the gang and for sharing your invaluable advice laced with much p***-taking. It's been great fun.

There's not a lot I can say about the Pirates that hasn't already been said. Their advice, support and banter is second to none. Arghhhh!!!

Team Silent Assassin are a wonderful addition to my life. I love the minutes that I get to spend with them each year, few that they are, but they never fail to remind me how much fun you can have with Ironman. So a huge HUGE thank you to Q, Jo and most especially Jordy who never stops smiling.

Viking, Min and Dave, my original partners in crime and my good friends. Thanks for everything, you are not only wonderful athletes but true friends. On the rare occasions we get together it just flows and I'm transported back to the good old days of Dr Duncans. And to Loon, keep cheering from Down Under, I can still hear you pet.

I know you won't thank me for singling you out Gobi but your advice and support has really motivated me. I can't thank you enough for that mate.

Cortney, please continue to inspire, please continue to push and most of all please keep doing it with the upmost enthusiasm. Your writing and your messages have helped me out of a few dark days this year when things seemed too much. I look forward to the day when I can get out for a ride in the wonderful Virginia hills with you.

To everyone at Thurnham Cycles, I just love you guys. I don't need to say any more. Thanks for letting me be part of the team. I'm lucky to have such a great friend and training partner in Andy Holme.

Team English, Lee and Pam, Team Towse, Jacko, Richard and Lou, The Southport collective, The Toal Sisters, Taj, Kim – true friends one and all. Thank you for all your support of not only me but my family.

Simon Vaukins – thanks for the many hours spent running together, I never fail to have fun when trying to catch you. Cheers mate.

Lesley English – thanks for being so graceful in victory, one day I hope to return the favour.

Kev Foster-Wiltshire – thanks for seeing my potential, let's do this.

Mark Smith – thanks for making me a better swimmer, giving me confidence that I can push myself to be faster and go longer. Can't believe I'm saying this but I love swimming, and that's down to you.

To everyone involved with COLT I am indebted to your support, your advice and your friendship. I've found where I belong. I really do feel as if I belong to the best triathlon club in the world. I have so many to thank. Stu Foy, thanks for everything, you give me as much belief as I give you and I look forward to Outlaw training together. Jack for those miles, Podge for that curry you owe me, Andrew Mc for inviting me swimming, Big Kev for more than I could write in a blog or a book, Crazy for the pain and the laughter, Tornado for the advice and for giving me belief to better myself, Danny for the enthusiasm, Louise G for all the sensible nutritional advice, Graham H for the science and instilling a spark, Paul G and the two Tonys for some cracking Wednesday night runs and finally Team Hirst, Mick, Fi, David Patterson, Sarah Mason and Valerie for that amazing level of support in Lanzarote.

John "IronFramer" Carr – thanks for inspiring, for supporting, amusing and just being you. You are a star.

The Outlaw Ladies – Chris, Mandy and Sarah, your support, enthusiasm, laughter and friendship has been awe-inspiring. Thanks for letting me be one of the girls. Andy Ley – for being a great sport, a good mate and such a good laugh. I have loved the hours I've spent in your company even in THAT top. Kel Hirst – whether it's avoiding frogs in the dark or getting a hand from Italians on mountains, your company has been a breath of fresh air. And for teaching me "Pin Out". Chris Clarke – I would offer to buy you a beer but you'd bankrupt me. Thanks for everything mate. Pete Denness – I'll never finish in the same time zone as you, but I can't fail to be inspired by a fellow Barrow lad who beats the pros. Chris Lawson – thank you for being a crap swimmer, keep it up, it might be the only chance I have of beating you. Seriously mate, you've made the last few years so much fun. Here's to the next few. Richard Mason – thanks for all your help and advice, you are a top coach. I wish I'd been a better pupil. John Knapp – I have so many levels on which I should thank you. You are the Yoda of triathlon. One incident meant the world to me this year, the day after the Outlaw, you shook my hand and said one simple word: Respect. Chris Wild – where do I start with you? There's nothing that I can say that hasn't already been said. You sir, could headline any Ironman. Thank you for everything but especially that sweaty man hug on the prom.

I would be nothing without my family, they mean the world to me with their unquestioning support and love. So thank you to the Holgates, the Cookes, the Cubins, the Myerscoughs, and the Healeys.

Thank you to my Mam and Dad who made me who I am, and who have never stopped believing in me despite witnessing some tough moments. I love you both and can't thank you enough.

To my "Iron Widow" Em, thank you for indulging me in my sometimes selfish pastime, thank you for believing in my writing, and for all your love and support not only on race day but on every day of my life. You are the best thing that has ever happened to me, and not a single day passes when I am not thankful for that. I love you.

And finally to Charlotte, Daddy loves you more than anything. You never cease to amaze me. Thank you for enriching my life in ways I never imagined would be possible.

And now let's get on with the story, go and get a brew, get comfy, it's going to be "fun and games".

1

I HATE TRIATHLON

It had been one of the wettest summers in recent memory. Earlier that day the rain had grated at my cycle helmet like fingernails raking a chalkboard. Yet now as the sun began to slowly fall behind the horizon on the first July day of 2012 I squinted at its blinding fiery reflection illuminating the rowing basin, turning water into fire. Or maybe the fire was just in my eyes as the pain and sense of foreboding that I was a failure consumed me. It wasn't supposed to be like this, it was NEVER supposed to be like this.

The gravel path no longer crunched with every laboured foot fall. Despite my mind willing my legs to lift my feet there was no response. Come on work, you've got to move, don't let me down. This means everything to me. Nothing, no response. Just more pain as my calf contracted, shuddering like a decapitated cockroach. In a torturous duet my knee throbbed and I was engulfed with a feeling of despair.

This wasn't the fabled Ironman shuffle, hell it wasn't even a Julie Moss crawl, both of those would have been quicker. I dragged my left leg in a slow, deliberate and stunted manner. To an outside observer it must have looked like it was taking all of my brain's capacity just to instruct my body to stay upright. I was beginning to resemble a zombie from a Tim Lebbon novel, decaying and falling apart with each second that passed.

At least I'm still running I thought, trying desperately to find a shred of positivity. Just then I was aware of someone at my shoulder. It wasn't a zombie but another human being, one in a much better place than me.

"Keep going Pirate," he mumbled, his tone one of pitying encouragement. I nodded and grunted something positive about his performance as he quickly walked away from me. I focused on the heels of his running shoes, hypnotically watching the little reflective Asics signs just below his freshly shaven Achilles tendons grow ever distant.

Within a heartbeat I was once again looking at the torturous gravel that was grating the soles of my feet; my feet felt numb. I felt numb. He's just bloody walked away from you.

I stopped.

I had completed 21 of the 26 miles of the Outlaw run course, an Ironman distance race in Nottingham, England. The day had got off to a dream start when I recorded my fastest ever Ironman distance swim but now it had descended into my own personal nightmare.

I reached into the pocket in the back of my yellow and black sweat-soaked tri top and fumbled at the sticky packet with all of the dexterity of a lobster.

I ripped into the raspberry flavoured gel and slowly put it to my lips, inhaling its gloopy goodness more in a last ditch act of desperation rather than one of calorific need. It tasted so good, perhaps another sign that I was not much longer for this world?

I remembered the mantra of my COLT (City of Lancaster Triathlon) club-mate John Knapp. The multiple Kona and Norseman finisher had told me and a few other Ironman racers one night in the pub that "no matter how bad you feel keep moving forward".

If it was good enough for John then it was sure as hell good enough for me. I gritted my teeth and willed my body forward. In the distance I could hear the race commentator signalling that another person had reached their goal. "Congratulations, you are an Outlaw", was quickly followed by loud applause and cheers from the grandstand of spectators.

A grandstand that contained the source of my inspiration, the one small thing that gave me the desire and strength to continue when I just wanted to embrace the failure and quit. It was in that moment that I knew I would finish even if it killed me. There were much more important things in my life now than triathlon and Ironman, and given all that had happened on my journey since I last competed in an Ironman in fact it was almost a miracle that I was shuffling along at all.

As I approached the car park that signalled the end of the river loop for the last time I was aware of people applauding me. I raised a smile and thanked them but my main focus was on the man ten metres beyond them waiting at the side of the path. He shuffled his feet nervously as I approached, protective and concerned eyes enlarged by the lenses of his glasses refusing to look away. A face that to me still looked like the young man that taught me how to ride a bike, or who first took me running with him as he trained for the London Marathon, it was not the face of a 63-year-old grandfather watching his 39-year-old little boy destroy himself.

"Lift your head up Andrew, it'll make running easier." I knew as soon as I heard the words from my Dad that he was correct. He walked alongside me in the early evening sunshine, slowing his natural walking pace to fall in line with my running.

"I know Dad, but I just don't have the energy to lift my head," I whispered in defeat from under my sweat-stained green cap. A cap that I hoped hid my pain and disappointment. We had been here before, but unlike Frankfurt three years previously there would be no second wind along the banks of the Trent. That's the thing with Ironman, your day can go from dreams of glory to the depths of despair in an instant. I had three miles to go, I hated Ironman, I hated triathlon but most of all I hated myself for being in that moment.

Three years ago it had been so different. Three years ago I had been on top of the world. Three years ago I was in love. Three years ago I was invincible. Three years ago I had beaten adversity. Three years ago I was in my prime. Three years ago

I was me. Three years ago I deserved to call myself an Ironman.

Now I only deserved to be called "Glassman", I was so weak that I would shatter with each impact that my body took. Now the top of the world was a distant memory. Now the love was replaced with fear and loathing. Now the invincibility had dissolved into doubt. Now I no longer recognised the shadow of the man who although he had the Pirate crest emblazoned across his lycra clad chest acted like a scared little boy. Now was not where I wanted to be.

I needed to go back to 2009.

2

INTO THE DEEP

I was in what some people would call the zone, focusing on the task at hand. It wasn't one that most normal people would contemplate let alone pay to do. There was a real danger that I could be hurt but I couldn't help myself, I'd waited all my adult life for this.

The water before me glistened in the early morning dawn, a glorious azure blue enticing me to jump in. The ripples on the surface melted away into a flat calm. Raising my head to breathe in the magnitude of what lay before me I observed that the sky and the water had merged into a vast expanse of nothingness. My heart raced, it was almost time.

I shuffled on my feet, the cold slippery surface beneath them seemed to move in unison with the horizon. My right hand rubbed nervously at my left forearm, the rubber wetsuit felt more restrictive than ever. I knew it was my comfort blanket yet it seemed to squeeze me tighter and tighter as I listened to the last seconds of instructions.

A set of firm, serious words that could potentially be the difference between life and death. I exchanged a knowing nod with the rubber-suited man stood next to me, taking false reassurance from the fact that he seemed very calm. Maybe his was a skin-deep calm like mine? I looked at his mouth, careful not to stare, as the vapour escaping into the chilled morning air became more frequent. Nope, he feels just like you, and rightly so.

"It's time to get in the water." The final instruction was issued, there was no turning back.

I moved forward, placing my feet on the edge and stared down at the deep expanse before me. One final look to the horizon, now more in anticipation of what was to come rather than fear. I pulled the plastic mask down over my eyes then placed my arms by my sides and stepped forward into the abyss with one final stolen breath of air.

The azure beauty hid a desolate cold. It was another one of those testicle-retracting moments as the soles of my feet broke the surface of the water. My body and head followed suit and I was immersed in the coldest water I had ever felt. I could feel every muscle in my body tensing as I tried to adjust to my new environment. My breathing quickened and my heart rate soared as the life giving organ worked overtime pumping much needed blood to my extremities.

Suddenly that calm surface had gone as I bobbed up and down like a cork in a child's bathtub. I could feel the strong current pulling my body forward, it took a lot of strength to scull on the spot. I was aware that my legs were drifting out of my own safety space. I needed to stay in that cocoon, it was vital for what was to come. I pulled them back in and tensed in anticipation. The combination of the cold and the excitement made it feel like my heart was going to come through my chest at any moment. This was not the time for panic. They can smell your fear. Calm down.

"Here we go, down and to your right," boomed the distinct South African voice from above in the safety of the boat.

I did as instructed and immersed myself completely in the cold-temperate waters of the Atlantic. It was as clear as a swimming pool, thankfully there were no grotty used plasters floating past. This would be an amazing place for an open water swim was my first thought, which brought a sly smile to my face.

That thought was immediately rejected as my eyes refocused on what was in front of me.

I froze as the clear blue nothingness was gracefully invaded by a creature with a bigger smile than me, not to mention better open water swimming ability. *Carcharodon carcharias*, better known as great white sharks, swam silently within a couple of feet of me. Instinctively I pulled my arms and legs further into the centre of the steel cage that offered me protection. The huge conical snout lay above row upon row of bright white razor sharp teeth. Teeth that were so close I could see the striations on their triangular sides.

My vision was no longer filled with the deep blue sea but by the dark grey torso and virginal white underbelly of the magnificent fish. I finally remembered to breathe, as all 15 feet of nature's most feared apex predator slid past in tranquil silence. And in a second it was gone, out of sight but never out of mind.

I was ecstatic. It was the moment I had imagined since I was ten years old. I was an avid reader and a regular visitor to the town library. Like most boys of that age I read mostly non-fiction, books about sporting heroes, history and animals. I was fascinated with nature and devoured facts and figures in a way that only a pre-teen boy could.

I was such a geek that one of my favourite books was about rocks, minerals and fossils. I could talk about the differences between volcanic and sedimentary rocks in a manner that most triathletes talk about tubs and clinchers.

One page in my rock geek bible was stared at and pawed at more than any other. It showed a photo of a dignified looking man in a freshly starched suit sat inside a huge jaw. That man was an American scientist called Bashford Dean, and he and his colleagues working at the American Museum of Natural History had reconstructed the jaw from fossilised teeth. Those six-inch daggers had belonged to the largest fish the world had ever seen, the megalodon, the ancient ancestor of the great white shark.

I was instantly terrified at the thought of the 60-foot beast but at the same time curious and intrigued. At the library I checked out every book they had on sharks, which in Barrow-in-Furness in 1982 was two. There obviously wasn't much call for shark information in the North-West of England, where you were more likely to be attacked by a seagull than a fish when you went to the beach.

The first book was mostly pictures, with random facts written for a child, the kind I'd used on countless homework assignments. The second however was a dark, dog-eared adult paperback with a one word title, a book that would become my favourite, *Jaws*.

I still remember the discouraging look that the polyester-clad librarian gave me as I pushed it across the desk at her and handed her my library ticket. She scared me more than any scene that I would encounter in the book, with her eyes that were slightly closer together than normal and her rancid cigarette breath. She was terrifying. It's a twisted irony that I grew up longing to be a marine biologist specialising in sharks but instead somehow fell into librarianship.

It was those impressionable childhood dreams that stemmed from a book, that led me to be in Shark Alley, possibly the most dangerous patch of water on the planet. The narrow deep water channel runs between Dyer Island and Geyser Island, which are the homes to a colony of 50,000 cape seals. The sharks come for the seals, their preferred natural prey. Tourists like me come to see the sharks.

Em and I had travelled to South Africa to see our friend Michele, to go on safari and to have a relaxing holiday. OK, so while we were there we'd be conquering the world's biggest bungee jump off a bridge, feeding lion cubs, diving with Nile crocodiles, and getting a recovery run or two in, see relaxing.

The highlight of the trip for me though was the fulfilment of a lifetime's ambition to see a real life *Jaws*, but let's face it you didn't buy this book to experience my "what I did on my holidays by Andy Holgate aged old enough to know better" did you? So what the hell am I wittering on about fish for when this is supposed to be about triathlon?

Well you see it was all part of my cunning master plan to beat the post-Ironman blues. Let me explain.

Two weeks earlier I had finished Ironman Germany in a time of 12 hours 57 minutes and 21 seconds. I suffered immensely in the Frankfurt heat and saw my dreams of going sub-12 hours melt away during a particularly hard marathon run. I pushed my body and mind to the limit and as a result ended up requiring medical assistance at the finish. Despite the pain and fatigue I was very happy as I had a new personal best, my family were there to witness it and to top it all off I kept a wedding day promise to my good friend Viking.

It was the perfect end to a three-year journey that had seen me and three friends embark on our own Ironman adventure. It hadn't gone entirely to plan but me, Dave, Min and Viking got there in the end and all became Ironmen. The day of 5th July 2009 will always be one of the most emotional of my life. The memories of hugging Viking when we were reunited at the finish, both with our medals, our families and our huge grins are priceless.

The emotional highs that followed that day continued when we returned home to England. I read e-mails and texts of congratulations from friends and family and beamed with pride. My fellow COLTs gave me a round of applause at our open water swimming session, as they do for everyone that completes a race. I blushed a little as my name was read out and my achievement acknowledged with claps and cheers, it was an amazing feeling to receive that from such experienced and quick triathletes. The people that inspired me to reach further were now clapping me, that felt so cool.

My amazing month didn't stop there as a few days later I was suited and booted for a job interview. One of my colleagues had retired after almost a lifetime in the job. That's the thing with my profession; it really can be sometimes a case of "dead man's shoes".

We librarians tend to stay in the same position for years, developing our skills and expertise. I had tried several times in the past to get a subject librarian post but a combination of bad interviews, stronger and more experienced candidates and the simple fact that I was not good enough at the time had all beaten me.

In a reflection of my triathlon attitude, I'd be knocked down and p****d off but in a short while I'd bounce back and be more determined to succeed the next time. A kind of "I'll show you" type of resolve I suppose. I'd looked at where my skills were lacking and worked hard to change that by attending courses on web development, presentations and most importantly teaching skills. Most people think librarians stamp books and put them back on shelves, most people seem quite taken aback when I tell them that what I spend most of my time doing these days is teaching.

On the day of the interview I was a mixture of nerves and confidence. I was nervous because I'd be interviewed by two colleagues who knew me very well, and two heads of departments who didn't know me from Adam. I don't know about you but I always find it immensely difficult sitting opposite someone who has known you and your work for ten years and having to talk to them as if you've just met. Interviews aren't natural at the best of times but that just made it worse. I answered the questions but felt that I could have done better as I walked away.

The day was split into two parts, or three if you include lunch. Forty-five minutes of cringe-worthy awkwardness where I munched on a soggy cheese and tomato sandwich and listened to a fellow candidate tell me about all the great things he'd done. I smiled politely and nodded in the correct places, aware that all of the interviewers were assessing how we interacted with others.

Yet inside I was thinking "sorry mate, I don't care about what you are saying, I'm sure you are nice but I want this job and I don't want you to be here". Which I think is a perfectly natural reaction? If we had been open water swimming in an Ironman and he'd gotten in my way I'd have not thought twice about his welfare or his future, I'd have kept my line and done what was necessary.

The second part of the afternoon was a presentation to a room of staff and students about the library and what a subject librarian could offer them. This was the bit I felt confident about. A couple of weeks ago I'd been in the middle of 3,000 wetsuited people all trying to knock my head off, so 20 people sat listening intently to my every word was blissful in comparison. I talked about databases, journals and said all the right things. I came away feeling I'd given it my best shot. It was now a waiting game.

I had hoped to hear that night, but it was a tight decision and eventually the next morning I was called into the boss's office and given the news that I was hoping for. I was the new subject librarian for various subjects including educational research and business. I was thrilled. Like Ironman it had been a long, hard, and at times painful slog to get my career to this point but like Ironman I'd stuck at it and been rewarded.

That night Em and I celebrated with tea in the pub, sipping cider in the early evening sunshine as we talked about our "once in a lifetime" trip to South Africa. The very trip that was carefully planned so as not to interfere with Ironman training and helped to prevent 'Ironman blues'.

I'd spent the best part of a year preparing for Frankfurt. Everything that we wanted to do as a couple had to be co-ordinated with training, races etc. When your focus is one huge event be that an Ironman, a wedding or a holiday it is often the case that you can get a little down after the event has passed. After the Big Woody in 2007, I had our wedding and honeymoon to focus on, which were wonderful occasions.

Now we weren't getting married again so instead we planned the South Africa trip and my little fishy encounter as a way of keeping our spirits up and giving us both something to look forward to after a year of sacrifice. The race, the job and the trip were the perfect trilogy this side of swim, bike and run for putting a smile on my face at a time when it could have been so different.

As the second pint of cider slid down rather too easily Em asked the question, the one that she knows to ask at the end of each summer. It's on a par with the one that gets asked in November: "What do you want for Christmas?" Only the summer question comes with reserved tones and an undercurrent of polite resignation.

"So what event are you doing next year then?"

The grin formed instantly as I said cheekily: "I love you."

"I love you too. Hmmm, what's it going to cost and where is it?" was the reply, her smile giving her away as she tried to appear all stern.

"No idea," I replied nonchalantly. "But it's going to involve going sub-12."

3

RECOVERY RUN HEAVEN

After the exploits in Frankfurt my body was a bit of a mess, which was only to be expected really. I mean, 140.6 miles is a bloody long way to travel under your own steam. Add in the mental stress in the days preceding the race when you worry about anything and everything: Is my bike working? Will it be too warm for my wetsuit? Will my dodgy knee hold together? Will I hear my race morning alarm go off? Will I get the shits?

Combine that with the stress of foreign travel and it's a wonder that most Ironman athletes aren't sectioned for their own safety. Ironman is the old boxing perfect combination of the jab and powerful uppercut: the mental jab wears you down and the uppercut knocks you on your arse. Despite the feelings of euphoria that I'd completed the task that I'd set out to do many months ago I was completely knackered as a result of the Ironman assault.

Of course every one of us who takes on an Ironman is different both physiologically and mentally. Elite athletes such as Chrissie Wellington will probably recover from her Ironman race, despite being much faster, because her body is better trained and equipped than yours or mine. As a "big lad" in northern English terms or a "Clydesdale" in American terms my legs will probably ache for longer afterwards than someone whose racing weight is near 150lbs. A 2005 study in the journal, *Arthritis & Rheumatism*, concluded that if a person lost just one pound it would take away four pounds of pressure on the knee joint with each step. Over a mile of walking this would equate to a reduction of 4,800lbs of pressure on each joint.

Therefore if you were say 10lbs overweight, for every mile that you walked you'd be putting an extra 48,000lbs of pressure on your joints. Shocking isn't it? Now factor in running, which puts even more stress on the legs as the movement is more forced, and the foot falls from a greater height than when you are walking, unless you are doing the Ironman shuffle and then all bets are off! Running, if you think about it in simple terms, is a co-ordinated series of small jumps from one foot to the other. Each time one foot hits the ground our bodies are exposed to repeated impact forces estimated to be two to three times the body weight of the runner. Applying this fact to a 150lb runner, who has an average of 400 foot-strikes per foot per mile, during a one-mile run each foot would endure between 60 and 90 tons of force. If you applied it to an overweight librarian running a marathon at 210lbs, it would equate to 2,925 tons of force through each leg by the time I'd crossed the finish line. That 2,925 tons is the same weight as 16 blue whales. It was no bloody wonder that my body ached.

Other recent studies have shown that it's not only the joints that take a pounding when you complete an Ironman. Your central core temperature and rather alarmingly your brain temperature can rise to dangerous levels especially when racing in the heat. This tends to manifest itself as dehydration, dizziness and eventually collapse.

I had just suffered this to a mild extent in Frankfurt. Crossing the line I became dizzy, and I was quickly diagnosed as being severely dehydrated. Luckily, two pints of saline later I was back on my feet. I was probably also helped by the fact that my brain is quite small so it had plenty of room for expansion inside my thick skull. If I hadn't been so lucky, and my nutrition (which was by no means perfect) had been less frequent the heat may have shut down my central nervous system earlier, causing me to collapse during the marathon. Unfortunately too often we hear of this at big city marathons, and I was unfortunate enough to witness it in Hamburg, where a competitor had pushed too hard and not replenished their body with water at the very least.

Muscles also suffer as your body looks for fuel to maintain itself. The normal fuel would come from the carbohydrates in the energy gels, drink and bananas that you consume along the course. If however you don't take on enough fuel the body starts a process called catabolism, where basically it starts to cannibalise its own muscle for fuel. This breakdown leads to muscle fatigue and probably goes a long way to explaining why I for instance have to walk downstairs backwards the day after an Ironman because my quads and hamstrings are in so much pain. Just how much muscle damage does your body experience over the course of an Ironman? Scientists have conducted many studies looking into this and they use what are known as biomarkers to estimate muscle damage. Now I'm not a scientist so to get my head around the scary long words and theories I thought of biomarkers as tacks on the floor that I had to repeatedly walk over barefoot.

At a normal resting level the floor would be tack-free. As levels rise, biomarkers or tacks would be added to the floor for me to walk across barefoot. Therefore the greater the amount of tacks, the worse the damage to my feet. Still with me? Good, back to the science then. The main biomarker is creatine kinase (CK), which leaks into the bloodstream from ruptured muscle cells.

A study by Bryan Berman, PhD, showed that a typical athlete's blood creatine kinase level is approximately 125. These levels increased after exercise. Rather alarmingly the study found that 16 hours after finishing an Ironman, triathletes had an average blood CK level of 1,500, or more than ten times the normal level. That's a hell of a lot of tacks and a hell of a lot of damage!

In the days after the race your immune system is put under great pressure as it battles to keep you alive after the exhaustive stress that it's faced. Multiple cells would have been broken down and as a result you become more prone to infection and disease. It's certainly not unusual for me to find myself suffering with "Ironman Flu" in the days and weeks after a race. To try and combat it I supplement my diet with vitamin pills.

It's really good for you this Ironman lark. So for a couple of weeks after Ironman Germany I pretty much did nothing other than gently ride my bike to work and back. Which given that it was a seven-mile round trip meant that it wasn't exactly taxing having spent the last few months thinking a 40-mile ride was an easy distance.

I think though that these gentle spins helped my muscles to recover, waking them up again if you will. Feeling like I could risk running again I fired off an e-mail to my friend and training partner Andy H arranging to meet for our usual jaunt along the coastal path from Glasson Dock the next night after work.

As I pulled up outside his house I was surprised to see that the drive was missing Andy's car. Reaching to turn off the ignition I glanced in my rear view mirror just as the grey Toyota pulled past and a friendly face smiled back at me. We both got out of our cars at the same time.

"Sorry I'm late mate, bloody traffic on the M6 again. I'll be as quick as I can at getting changed." Andy looked somewhat flustered in his shirt and tie, I was only used to seeing him normally in lycra. A fact which speaks volumes about our relationship. I mean how many heterosexual male friends can say that about each other?

"I didn't recognise you with your clothes on mate. No worries, I'll just wait outside for you and make the most of the sunshine."

While I waited I did some stretching, nothing strenuous, just the usual pick my leg up, stretch the calf, and put it back down. Shake my arms, touch my toes, bring my knee up to my chest, try and push the wall down. The sort of stretching routine that you see runners doing all the time, the sort of stretching routine that probably actually does bugger all as I wasn't doing them properly. It was the stretching equivalent of Paris Hilton, all style and no substance. However it made me feel virtuous that I'd done my 'proper' warm-up before running.

A few minutes later, and now wearing an outfit of tri shorts and a running top just so I could recognise him Andy H emerged ready to plod. "It's just going to have to be steady Andy," he said as he locked up his house. "Fine with me mate, this will be my first run since Germany, so I don't even know if my legs will work again yet," was my cautious reply.

Those initial steps were quite tentative. In the first few minutes of our run everything from my back down to my toes seemed to ache. Sighing with every step I expressed this to Andy H who by comparison seemed quite sprightly, he was chomping at the bit, constantly a few paces ahead of me. "Sounds like you need a bloody good spray with WD40, you've rusted up," he laughed. He was right, I still felt very stiff, more so than at any point in the past that I could remember. Of course the passing of time makes you forget these things. I may have felt worse after previous marathons, and I'd just blocked it out. After all if all I ever remembered from doing a race was the pain afterwards then I would have retired by now and gone back to being a sofa surfer. Thankfully the stiffness wore off slightly, and I was able to engage Andy H in conversation rather than just grunting and sighing like Meg Ryan in a coffee shop. We talked about Germany, my upcoming holiday, training, gas pipelines (his work, not mine) and our usual annual favourite July topic, Le Tour.

As keen cyclists it wasn't surprising that we had both been glued to our television sets watching the coverage, listening to the dulcet, knowledgeable tones of respected commentators Phil Liggett and Paul Sherwin. I'd even managed to catch stages in my hotel room in Germany, although the commentary on RTL, the state television channel, left me somewhat confused with my limited understanding of the language. It wasn't that important though, as long as I recognised who crossed the line first, that was all that mattered. It had been a fascinating race for many reasons, notably the comeback of the seven-time champion, Lance Armstrong.

Andy H and I were both of the opinion that he should have

stayed retired, having won so many times he had nothing left to prove. Armstrong seems to polarise opinion; people either idolise him or think he's the anti-christ. Even in 2012 his transition back into triathlon (he was a triathlete in his youth in Texas before becoming a pro cyclist) has been shrouded in controversy over drug allegations that seem to follow him everywhere despite his well-publicised mantra of being the "most tested man in sport". These allegations finally caught up with him in 2012 when former team-mates, under oath at a US government hearing, testified that he used various banned drugs including EPO during his Tour glory years. He was subsequently stripped of his titles, and rightly so. Drug cheats should not go down in history as heros.

Armstrong had just finished third, behind his Astana team mate Alberto Contador in a chess-like battle. The Spaniard and the American didn't get on, and watching team tactics unfold reminded me of the famous battle in the 1980s between Greg LeMond and Bernard Hinault over the yellow jersey. The old champion holding out for one more shot at glory whilst the young pretender took the throne from under him.

Armstrong had been pushed hard by Bradley Wiggins, who would finish fourth to equal the best ever finish by a Brit, an accolade that was also owned by my idol, Robert Millar. Wiggins would cement that title by winning the race in 2012 in a display of power, speed and perfect team tactics that would also see his Team Sky 'domestique' Chris Froome finish second, further relegating Millar in the British legacy. But the thing that excited us both the most about the 2009 tour was Mark Cavendish. The Manxman was the fastest sprinter in the peloton and had just won six stages. It was great to have some British success. Watching him line up in the HTC (his team) train as the finish line drew closer was mesmerising, three or four riders all burying themselves physically to get Cav to the line.

And then suddenly Mark Renshaw would hit the front of the peloton and you knew it was all over bar the shouting. With metres to go, a white blur would flash past the Aussie at a speed of over 50km per hour and raise his arms in a victory salute. Mark Cavendish is phenomenal.

I'm 40 years old and every time I get on my bike and start to go fast, I like to pretend I'm Cav flying past other riders like they are stationary. The reality of course is much different, but even middle-aged men in lycra still have their own fantasies. As a child I'd wanted to be Robert Millar or "Big Mig" Miguel Indurain, now it was Bradley Wiggins or Mark Cavendish, the names may have changed but the fantasy never does.

Our cycling discussion took my mind off my legs, and by the time we'd got back from our four-mile social run I'd actually forgotten about them. That's the beauty of running with a great friend, you lose yourself in conversation and before you know it the miles have been banked and you are sat at home with a cuppa.

It felt great to get a comeback run under my belt. I was reassured that I was still in one piece and ready to start training again. However a couple of days later we flew to South Africa and my training was quite sporadic. I didn't have my bike with me and I certainly wasn't going to go open water swimming given the presence of sharks and crocodiles. I did manage to get in two very different runs, but two very memorable ones because of their settings.

I'd planned on running in Johannesburg, but was warned off the idea by Michele, our friend who we were staying with. I never once felt unsafe wandering around the city but she and Em thought I might be asking for trouble, being out on my own and just running around at random.

Michele explained that if I took a wrong turn I could end up in an area where because of my skin I would stand out like a sore thumb and maybe be a potential target for a mugger. This was quite alarming, as being a small town type lad I'd never even considered that on any of my travels. In the past whenever I'd travelled I'd try and run no matter what city I'd been in, just out the door, turn left and put one foot in front of the other.

It's a great way to see places. I did take on their warnings though as I had noticed that everyone in the area lived in high walled communities with armed guards on the gates. Taking in what that implied I decided that a few extra days of rest wouldn't kill me.

When I did get to run a few days later it was probably one of the most unusual and spectacular runs of my life. Michele, Em and I had driven up to Kruger National Park to go on safari. The near-20,000 square kilometre reserve is home to some of the most amazing wildlife on the planet. I had the image in my head from watching the Discovery Channel that we'd be driving to the edge of the park, leaving the car and then hopping in a Land Rover to drive around the park.

My face was a picture when Michele actually explained that there would be no safe, rugged 4x4 vehicle and in fact we would be doing our safari in her little Peugeot 206. I tell you, it's quite a surreal experience sat in a normal car while four lionesses walk alongside it, and you get a strong sense of how small you really are when a herd of African elephants stand less than ten metres away. We stayed at the Oilifants rest camp, high above the same river. Armed rangers were stationed on the gate for our protection, and at dusk the gates were closed. We'd had a long day but I just couldn't help myself, I had to go for a run. Now obviously I couldn't go out of the gates as that would have been very foolish so I basically ran loops of about 400m for an hour.

Running along the perimeter fence on the north side all I could see was the bush, an arid wasteland of vegetation browned in the sun, with bizarrely an occasional flash of green as a new plant reached for the sky. Gangs of baboons sat and watched curiously from the trees. I was obviously proving very entertaining as the crowd seemed to grow with each lap.

In the distance I heard the distinct cackle of a hyena. We had been warned on checking in that they patrolled the outer perimeter in the evening, and that it wasn't unusual to see fiery red eyes staring at you in the darkness.

The south side of the camp couldn't have been more opposite. This small section contained the most amazing view I'd ever witnessed on any run. The huge Oilifants River was below me, cutting through the bush with a gentle precision that would morph into a raging torrent when the rains came. The landscape was spectacular in itself but then I spotted a group of hippos wading in the shallows and I stopped for a few minutes, I just had to. These huge animals just looked so graceful as they moved into the water, they were one of the animals I'd most wanted to see. With each lap I noticed different animals coming to the river in the early evening sunshine; giraffes, zebras, antelopes and elephants all put in an appearance.

I actually speeded up along the north side of the loop, eager to get back to my own personal nature documentary. I usually run along singing to myself but on this occasion in my head I was doing bad impressions of Sir David Attenborough, the legendary BBC nature commentator. "And here we see the giraffe, for those watching in black and white, it's the tall one, not the grey one, that's an elephant." See, I told you it was a bad impression.

The second run that I managed on South African soil took place down near the Western Cape in a little fishing town called De Kelders. Em and I were staying in a rented home on the cliffs overlooking the sea. We had been touring along the spectacular south coast from Cape Town to Plettenberg Bay, and had stopped in De Kelders to hopefully spot a whale or two. The southern right whales come into the sheltered bay to mate in the late summer months. We didn't expect to see any though, as sightings could be quite rare. We were very lucky and from our balcony we could spot the huge barnacle encrusted snouts of the whales as they surfaced for air, and throughout the night all you could hear was the haunting calls of the sea. At first lying there in bed listening it was quite scary, it wasn't a sound we were used to, but eventually the whale song became an adult lullaby and we drifted into sleep. The next morning I was wide awake at 6am. Em was flat out so I left her in bed and put on my running shoes. The air was surprisingly chilly but oh so clean and fresh, unlike at home. I never saw another human soul as I ran along the cliff-top path but I must have seen about ten whales, sometimes I just saw the splash as they flapped their huge tails on the surface but I also saw a couple of full breaches as the 40-foot creatures flew into the air with power and something just slightly short of grace. At home on the coastal path, Andy H and I get excited about seeing a heron, so how lucky was I to be experiencing such a rare and magnificent animal on my coastal path run?

So two runs and a who's who of the animal world, it certainly made a change from the usual sheep and cows that stare at me as I run along the canal, or the shell-suit wannabe gangstas that shout "get those knees up" as I run through the grey British streets. Is it any wonder so many people run with their iPods to allow a bit of escapism? I had been lucky enough to experience that feeling in a purely natural way.

It was soon back to reality with a bang, back to Blighty, and into the new job and the steep learning curve that went with it. And also an amazing offer from out of the blue.

4

THE PERFECT END TO THE PERFECT DAY

I sat and stared at the computer screen in disbelief, reading the e-mail over and over again. This had to be a wind-up. It had to be Lee, my practical joke-loving best friend trying to get one over on me. It wouldn't be the first time that he'd done that. I was tempted to reply telling the sender to sod off but instead I paused and thought about it, could it be real? I walked away from the screen, made myself a coffee, thinking that maybe I was seeing things and that the caffeine shot would make things a lot clearer. No, it was still there on the screen in ten-point Times New Roman font, that if I'm honest with you couldn't have seemed bigger if it was on a neon billboard in Times Square.

Hi Andy

We would very much like to go ahead with a book based on your blog. With some polishing I think it will be an excellent book and one which will interest plenty of people.

Attached is a draft contract detailing our terms. If you would like to give me a call for me to explain any of it then please do on one of the numbers below. I am sure you will have various queries you wish to be answered. It's not a problem to chat them over at all. We plan to publish your book in June next year all being well and if you are in agreement.

Look forward to hearing from you soon.

Yours

Simon
Know The Score Books Ltd

Woah! I was being offered a book contract, something that aspiring writers spend years trying to achieve, and many never do. Being a librarian I read book industry literature and knew just how hard it was to get something published. Most writers needed an agent to sell them to the publishers, many wouldn't accept unsolicited manuscripts, and then an author's work had to get past the 'Gatekeepers', the mysterious people that granted a thumbs up or a thumbs down in almost Caesar-like finality. I didn't have an agent, I actually didn't have a manuscript, I didn't have a clue!

I forwarded the e-mail on to Em. She'd know what to do, she was my voice of reason, and being a city girl she could sniff out a scam easily. I knew the publishing company was real, a quick couple of minutes on Google confirmed that. Know The Score were one of the UK's leading independent sports book publishers, specialising mostly in books about football and cricket. A few minutes later my office phone rang with intent.

"Wow that's brilliant," Em said enthusiastically, the excitement in her voice given away by the fact that she'd slipped into a broader Liverpudlian accent that usually remained hidden until she got excited, tipsy or angry.

I voiced my concerns. Would anyone actually be interested in reading about me? Could I really write a book? Apart from my blog and my master's Degree dissertation I'd not written anything for years. In fact the last time I'd written a story would have been over 20 years ago at school, and if I'd remembered correctly my English teacher, Ms Davies, had returned it to me covered in red ink. Em told me to talk to the publisher and see what they had to say. "I'll ring them later, I need to clear my head. I'm going to go for a run round campus and see what Rich says." She agreed that it would be good to get my creative friend's advice.

"Seriously? Go for it, what have you got to lose?" was Richard's quizzical reply as we set off running around the university campus oblivious to the dark grey August sky. He had done a fair bit of creative writing and had a good friend who was a best-selling author, so he explained the processes of writing and marketing a book, when he could find the energy to talk in between gasping for breath.

His running had improved somewhat over the previous months but the high pollen count was destroying him. We managed about two miles of the three-mile loop before we had to stop completely, poor Rich just couldn't catch his breath. The mile walking gave us time to talk properly, until Rich asked a question that stopped me dead in my tracks. "How much are they going to pay you?" he probed. "They'll pay me?" The words were almost laughed out of my mouth in shock. It wasn't something that I'd even considered. I was so bloody naive that I thought only best-selling authors got paid, and that an unknown like me would be expected to publish their book for free. I'd actually thought that I might have had to pay the publisher a fee for doing so.

I'd later discover on reading the contract that Rich had indeed been correct and that I'd get a percentage of each book sold. This was a nice bonus that I wasn't expecting, I was just happy at the thought of people reading my story. Now I secretly hoped that I could sell about 300 copies so that I could use the money towards some nice new carbon wheels for my triathlon bike, my beloved ROO. Rich and I parted for the day, with me promising to let him know later what happened when I rang the publishers.

I nervously keyed the phone number I'd been given into my mobile phone, and anxiously waited, part of me expecting to hear "the number you have dialled has not been recognised" in that distinctive robotic voice that the phone companies seem to love. Instead I heard "Hello, Know The Score Books, Simon speaking," in a friendly Midlands accent. Taken aback I stammered who I was and why I was calling. A few minutes that seemed like hours later the conversation was over with the promise of further e-mail instructions to follow about the small details of what would be required of me.

I was potentially going to be an author but first of all I had to prove that I could actually write by sending in a couple of sample chapters proving I was more than just a blogger (their words not mine, I love blogging). They gave me a week in which to do so. I also had to write a market report showing who would buy the book, what rival publications there were and where we could try and publicise the book, magazines, websites etc. Then I had to provide an outline of each chapter, saying what the main points were. This was all very new to me and I had no idea where to start.

I e-mailed Rich as promised and Em. Both have English Literature Masters degrees, which in my mind was the nearest thing to being writers. Both of them agreed that they'd look over my work and offer advice. That was a huge relief, as this was even more daunting than standing there that day at my first triathlon staring into the cold dark pond that I'd be swimming in. At least at the Cockerham triathlon in 2006 only a handful of people had seen my efforts. With a book it had the potential to be read by hundreds of people all keen to judge me and my story.

A couple of days later I showed my friend and my wife what I'd written. I was nervous as hell waiting for their comments. I'd asked them to be brutally honest as there was no point in sugar-coating it, I had to know the truth.

They both came back to me with the same comments. It was fundamentally sound but I needed to work on describing things, letting the reader really feel like they were there with me on the bike or in the pool. I took the advice on board and made changes, I wrote and rewrote until both I and my editors were happy. The seventh day arrived and a bead of sweat trickled down my temple as I watched the cursor move across the screen of my laptop, hesitating for a few seconds before clicking on the SEND button.

It was done, Simon replied saying that they'd be back in touch in a week or so to let me know what they thought and if I would actually be getting a book contract. I tried to put it to the back of my mind and turned my attention to my other e-mails, which I'd neglected for a week.

Among the usual spam offering me a nubile Russian bride, Viagra, a Nigerian bank account, and the latest offers from cycling porn retailer Wiggle was one that made me sit up. It was from the organisers of the London Marathon telling me that I had a place in next year's race. I smiled as I'd actually forgotten that I'd entered it, having applied six months earlier. For the past few years I would religiously enter the ballot for one of the 36,000 places and each October I'd receive the magazine telling me that I hadn't got a place, but detailing the hundreds of charities that would 'sponsor' me a place if I raised about £1,000.

I understood the reasons behind the charity places but that route had never been for me. I had raised money in the past on my own terms and without the pressure of a figure hanging over my head. I was so excited.

I had previously resigned myself to the fact that I'd probably never get a place. I had applied in the past from a previous address, but the organisers had no record of this and therefore I wouldn't have qualified under the "five rejections and you get a guaranteed place next year" rule. This was great. I now had a focus for 2010, an event to train for.

My mobile phone buzzed on my desk snapping me out of my marathon glory daydream. It was a text from my cousin Mike. He was just about talking to me again after I introduced him to the suffer-fest that was the Le Terrier cycle sportive that the two of us and Andy H had limped around in June 2008. It had only taken him 12 months to stop calling me a bastard. "I'm in London. You?" the screen read. This was so cool. I had forgotten that he had entered as well, as a lot had happened since April. My thumbs got to work confirming that indeed I would be joining him in the 30th anniversary 26.2-mile run from Blackheath to The Mall. We would be second generation London Marathon runners as Mike's dad Alan had raced in the inaugural race back in 1981, and my dad Gary had raced it three times in the 1980s. I remembered those races vividly as magical affairs, which started a couple of days before the race with the expo, a circus of retailers and manufacturers all trying to entice you to spend money. My younger brother Craig and I were runners with Barrow Striders athletic club, and whenever the athletics came on the television everything stopped in our house.

The distance runners were always our favourites. Steve Ovett, Steve Cram, Peter Elliot and Dave Moorcroft were rock stars in our eyes. Sebastian Coe was deemed too posh to be liked, as we were growing up in a northern industrial town during the economic struggles of the Thatcherite era, and his sugarplum speech was just alien to our young ears.

More and more road races and cross-country races were being shown on the television as the running boom really took hold in the psyche of the general public. Suddenly the likes of Charlie Spedding, Steve Jones, Mike Gratton, Hugh Jones, Eammon Martin and the Kenyan Douglas Wakiihuri became new heroes to be admired and emulated.

Wandering round the expo was amazing, our heroes were there. They were suddenly very real. We stood in nervous awe as we managed to collect signed photos from some of the greats, who were obviously there to attract people to the stalls. One of the highlights was seeing the female legend Grete Waitz, the late Norwegian who in my eyes is still the greatest female marathon runner of all time. Race day was just as exciting, we got to go on the London Underground as we hopped around the course trying to spot Dad as he ran. The crowds were phenomenal, the sound was deafening and the atmosphere was like nothing this young lad had ever experienced before.

The highlight of the race day was always meeting up with Dad at the finish somewhere near Horse Guards Parade. Pouring with sweat he'd put his arm on my shoulder, and sweep Craig up into his arms and show us his medal. That shiny piece of metal was priceless in our eyes. We had no idea at that age that they were mass-produced. The medal would go around Craig's neck and I would get wrapped in the finishers' sci-fi looking space blanket covered in the Mars Bar sponsor's logo.

Again the irony that a healthy endurance race was sponsored by a confectionary company went completely over my head. I think that in those special moments of innocence, excitement and pride both Craig and I one day vowed that we would run the London Marathon. Craig had raced in 2009 after getting a "good for age" place, which means he had qualified with a quick half-marathon time and didn't have to enter through the ballot. He trained like a demon, the high mileage weeks supplementing his natural speedy ability. He crossed the line in a brilliant time of two hours 36 minutes, thus qualifying him again to race in 2010. So it really would be a family affair when we all lined up in April 2010.

I was so excited at the prospect of finally getting into the race that I did what any normal person did in 2009. Yes, I announced it on Facebook.   Moments later I had received messages from both Viking and Lesley, my friends and fellow runners, informing me that they too would be joining me on the start line. This was great news as Lesley being in meant that I would have a training partner for the long runs ahead over the winter and spring.

She'd beaten me in our 2008 marathon challenge when she ran faster in London than I did in Hamburg. I so wanted to avenge that defeat and now I had my chance, but the thing was Lesley knew that. We are so competitive with each other that it would make for some very interesting training runs and build- up races. Scores would be kept, it was an unwritten rule between us. Viking being in meant that we could spend the year winding each other up like we had in the build-up to Frankfurt. This was perfect.

Just when I thought the day couldn't get any better my mobile rang. The sound of Insomnia by Faithless startled me. I'd been marathon day dreaming again. I flipped it open, cutting my techno ringtone off, and answered and listened in stunned silence as Simon, the publisher, told me that they loved what I'd sent them. The blog that I'd started in 2006 as a way of communicating my training and thoughts to my friends and family was going to be rewritten and put into print. Until that point it still hadn't seemed real. Yes I'd jumped through the hoops that had been put before me but I still expected to somehow be knocked down at the final hurdle.

There was only one problem: they were running on a tight deadline. The e-mail had told me that the book would be published next June, so I presumed that I had a solid six months in which to develop my writing skills. I was wrong. Simon needed the manuscript in five weeks.

That night on the phone to my Dad I explained the tight deadline and that although I was stoked at the opportunity to become a published author I was actually flummoxed as to where to start.

As helpful as ever he simply said "start with time upon a once, and finish with they all lived happily ever after". I thought you know what, if it was good enough for the fairy tales of my childhood then it's good enough for me.

Thanks Dad.

5

MAKING STU BELIEVE

Those five weeks were some of the hardest of my life, with both the book and the new job it felt like I didn't have time to breathe. I'd be out the door before 8am to either cycle or run the three miles to work, then I'd spend all day immersed in the new job learning from my mentor Jean.

Thank God I had Jean Blanquet. She was vastly experienced and taught me everything I needed to know about the job, and she made things a lot easier than they could have been if I'd just been thrown in at the deep end. Despite the hand holding I'd still get home feeling shattered. October and November are when the new intake of students arrive at the university, and we as subject librarians were in great demand to teach them how to use and manipulate our resources. Long gone are the days when a student goes to the library and just gets a book. These days it's all about ebooks, journal citations, statistics and referencing, all of which is done electronically.

In order for me to teach these things I had to first learn about them, which was mentally tiring. Then add in the hours spent teaching and it was no wonder that my run home at the end of the day was always slower than the morning version.

Once at home it was a case of taking half an hour or so to have my tea with Em and then I'd disappear into the spare bedroom for the rest of the night. Most nights Em was in bed for hours before I fell in beside her. We might as well have been living separate lives, as the only times we would talk would be when she'd finished reading the latest chapter and she brought me her comments.

It must have been very difficult and lonely for Em in that period of intense writing but I suppose she at least got to watch *Corrie* and *Holby City* without me constantly commenting on how crap it was. Come to think of it now, she actually probably enjoyed the peace and quiet.

I was also getting valuable feedback by e-mail from the main characters in the book, Andy H, Dave, Viking and Min. All of them added their own take on events which I then incorporated into my writing. It was reassuring to read their mostly positive comments as I was so stressed about the whole thing as the deadline loomed for submission.

A consequence of the stress was that my eating habits started to slip. I was soon engulfed in old ways. In the past I'd eaten for comfort and escape as my life around me was unfulfilling and empty. The stress of a bad relationship did about as much damage to my waistline as the divorce did to my bank balance. Now thankfully I was nowhere near a divorce (or at least I didn't think I was, just check: yes, Em is still here!) and I was happy with life.

I didn't have any time to think about food, I just grabbed what was convenient. I was no longer making nice salads to take for lunch, that would mean less time writing, and I couldn't afford that. Instead I was reaching for shop-made sandwiches and wraps, and worst of all flapjacks. A tuna mayo roll could have about 600 calories, then add in the sugar and syrup-laden flapjack with over 400 calories and it is easy to see how my weight started to go back up. I was still eating healthily with Em in the evening, but the extra lunchtime calories started to take their toll as I noticed my clothes feeling tighter. I guess I was either in denial or just too busy to care as I became obsessed with words rather than food. Suddenly what I put on paper was more important than what I put in my mouth. I deliberately didn't go near the scales in those five weeks. I was scared of what I would see if I did, and besides I would have felt powerless to do anything about it as I didn't have time.

I certainly wasn't helped by the fact that I also seemed to have developed an addiction to Haribo sweets. The jelly sweets were given out at certain aid stations in Frankfurt and I'd gulped them down with a vengeance. The trouble was I continued to gulp them down while I wasn't training.

My addiction was fuelled by the campus shop, which had a buy-one-get-one-free deal that was fatal. Each night locked away with the laptop, coffee and my own thoughts, I would open a packet of sugary goodness and mindlessly eat them. Handful after handful of jelly disappeared down my throat, I wouldn't even notice that the bag was empty. I'd mentally berate myself that I'd eaten a whole bag to myself in such a short space of time but come the next day the addict in me would start the circle of abuse all over again by going and buying a packet, and getting another one free.

Those free sweets cost me dearly. The fat lad that I'd buried deep inside myself had resurfaced, and unbelievably I was powerless to do anything about it.

It has been interesting reading comments from some of our top female triathletes about their battles with eating disorders. The fact that Chrissie Wellington and Hollie Avil, two world-class athletes, both battled demons when it came to food fascinates me as I try to reason with myself for what I did to my body.

Now I certainly wasn't bulimic, there was no way that I could make myself throw up after every meal, although I had tried it in the past. I was the opposite, it was almost like my brain blocked out all advice and sense when I became stressed.

These days I don't go near Haribo, and to be frank with you I don't even think about them so why on earth did I consume them like my life depended on it? There was neither rhyme nor reason why I did it, in the same way that Chrissie and Hollie suffered for no reason. They would have been thin and athletic without the vomiting. They burned off calories with ease given the volume of training they did.

I wrote the book, not Haribo sweets, I didn't need them, but some trigger convinced me that I couldn't write without them. Stupid really, but it just goes to show that we are all human and that a normal person like me, and an elite world champion like Chrissie can make mistakes when it comes to what we need to do to get the job done.

The finished manuscript was sent off and I breathed a sigh of relief, or maybe it was just a sigh at how much my waistband was digging into me. I was informed that the book would be passed on to an editor and that he would get in touch with comments, revisions etc. It was now time to get my life back and not have to worry about writing.

Although basically I'd been sat on my arse for six weeks with little time for training I had entered the Lancaster Half Marathon, a November race that would provide a way back into the racing mentality before the upcoming London Marathon. Since September I had been getting up early on a Saturday and meeting my mate and fellow COLT (City of Lancaster Triathlon member) Stu Foy to go for a run.

I'd known the shy project manager for a couple of years. Meeting on a Sunday morning bike ride, we'd got chatting and instantly hit it off as we talked about all things triathlon. Stu was just starting out with the sprint distance and seemed a bit in awe that I'd done an Ironman. We met weekly on the COLT rides and he disclosed to me that he was struggling with his running. I instantly offered to help him solve that problem. Stu had also entered the half marathon but had never actually run over eight miles before. He certainly didn't lack ambition, just the mileage in his legs.

Despite my developing Haribo habit and jelly belly I was still capable of banging out the miles with my feet. Over the previous weeks Stu and I had slowly increased the distance we were running, starting with just an hour and roughly six miles. Each week I'd pick a different route and tell Stu roughly how far we were going to run and each week he'd look at me as if to say "I don't know if I'm capable of that".

That was Stu's problem, he lacked confidence in his own ability. On one run he turned to me and said: "You do realise if you hadn't been here I would have turned right there and headed for home. I don't need an excuse to stop or not even get out at all. I can't do that if I'm running with you."

I couldn't help but smile and agreed that it was always much easier when you had someone to train with. There had been plenty of times over the years when I really couldn't be arsed to put on my trainers or jump on the bike, usually when it was pouring down with rain, but knowing that I was meeting Andy H forced me out of the door.

I guess it's kind of a pride thing. You don't want to let your training partner down, or admit a weakness. It's harder to stay at home when you know the person you will have to keep up with next time you run or cycle is out there improving without you. Training with someone else always brings out the competitor in me, and training with me was having the same effect on Stu. As much as he wanted to stop or head home for an early shower and a bacon sarnie he wouldn't because he wanted to keep up with me.

He knew I was training for the half marathon and didn't want my running with him to affect my training, I was just happy to be out whatever the pace or distance was. He didn't know it but Stu was helping me just as much as I was helping him.

Two weeks before the race on a cold October morning I met Stu at our usual meeting point, The White Cross pub. It wasn't open at 6.30am so there was no drinking going on, it just happened to be about halfway between both our homes and easily reached by a warm-up jog. There was a distinct chill in the air and I had even broken out the running tights for their first outing of the year.

I started my Garmin GPS off as we headed east along the canal. Stu didn't wear one so he had no idea how far and how quickly we were running without my vocal updates. This was a good thing because it allowed me to set the pace and the distance. I'd learnt that if I'd said to my confidence-lacking running partner that we were going to run 11 miles he'd instantly start to worry. So I decided not to lie but to just be a bit economical with the truth.

Crossing the River Lune at the edge of the city, we descended down the aqueduct steps onto the cycle path that followed the river out to Glasson Dock. We doubled back following the path through Lancaster city centre and out towards Glasson along what used to be a railway line. We were running steadily and much to my surprise Stu didn't once ask how far we'd done.

We'd run this route before and usually we would turn left up Aldcliffe Hill. As we approached the fork in the path I asked how he was feeling. When he said he felt fine I told him we'd continue and that would give us about 11 miles at the end. Stu seemed fine with that.

His confidence was obviously high this particular morning. We talked about everything and nothing as we plodded along: jobs, family, book writing, Ironman racing, growing up in Wigan and Barrow and before we knew it we'd ran past Glasson and over the hills on to campus. We were back in the city and heading for Bowerham were we both lived when my Garmin beeped, and for the first time that morning Stu commented: "That has to be 11 miles Andy, I'm really beginning to feel knackered now. I've no idea how I'm going to do a half next month. I think I got a bit ahead of myself by entering it?" I couldn't help but smile as I replied, "Mate, for the hundredth bloody time I've told you that a half marathon is not going to bother you! Have a look at this." I slowed down and shoved my left arm under his nose. Now I'd like to be able to tell you what Stu said initially when he saw that my Garmin was telling him that we'd just run 15 miles but his wife Cath and his kids might read this so let's just say he was both surprised and very pleased.

I had never seen Stu so happy. "I don't believe it!" was all he kept saying as we ran the last mile home. We stopped outside the chemist in Bowerham, our usual finish line, and we had run 16.2 miles in just under two and a half hours. Stu took me by surprise by eagerly reaching for my hand and shaking it vigorously, before saying: "Wow mate I can't thank you enough, ha ha I've run 16 miles, I'd never have done that without you."

That run obviously had a big effect on Stu because he still thanks me to this day, and now he's not only completed a half marathon but also a half Ironman. He's even entered the Outlaw for 2013, where he'll run his first ever marathon and cycle over 100 miles for the first time. Talk about progress.

We both went our separate ways that morning with smiles on our faces, knowing that we would be able to run the half marathon without too much trouble. Running over distance had really boosted my confidence after being almost a couch potato again, I may have dented the bodywork but the old engine was still purring away nicely.

On the Thursday before the race I was reading the *Tri-Talk* forum, catching up on the usual race reports and debates: tubs vs clinchers, my bike's nicer than yours, malt loaf vs flapjack, and the always entertaining discussions about Wiganer and pies, when something other than the usual banter caught my eye.

It was a post about a new Ironman distance event that would take place the following August in Nottingham. It claimed to be a flat and fast race, something that immediately got my attention. Maybe just maybe this could be the race I was looking for, the one that would see me go under the magic 12-hour mark. It certainly wouldn't be very hot in England in August, and as the heat had destroyed me in Germany I couldn't fail.

I was really excited and sent the link with the race details round to all the usual suspects. Andy H immediately ruled himself out. I wouldn't have expected anything less, as he had no desire to go long. Dave, Viking and Min all ruled themselves out for various reasons; Min and Viking were taking a rest from going long after their immense efforts in Frankfurt and Lanzarote that summer. Dave was interested but confided that he had the desire to do an official Ironman race and not another unbranded one like the Big Woody.

So that only left my cousin Mike. I knew he had ambitions to go long but I also knew that he was concentrating on hopefully running a sub-three-hour marathon in London. So I was pleasantly surprised when he replied saying he was very interested, and if he was going to be in the shape of his life for London, he might as well carry on for a few more months and realise his Ironman ambitions. That night I discussed it with Em. She thought it was a good idea, a 'safe' race if you will because the heat factor would be removed. The fact that it cost less than £200 didn't harm either, which was very cheap compared to an Ironman branded event. Germany had cost 350 euros to enter.

A couple of months back I had a much more negative response when I'd talked about entering Ironman Lanzarote. I'd been caught up in the excitement of the discussions on the COLT forum. A big contingent of my friends would be heading to the volcanic rock in May 2010 to race. Chris Wild, Richard Mason, John Knapp, Simon Deveraux and a few others would all be facing the heat which was furnace-like in a race that held legendary status in the Ironman world for being one of the toughest races.

Em expressed her concern at the idea; she had never put her foot down with me before but told me frankly after seeing what the heat did to me in Frankfurt that she couldn't allow me to destroy myself in Lanzarote. I understood where she was coming from but I was bitterly disappointed to not be joining my club-mates, most of whom were veterans of the race. I wanted to belong. I wanted to experience what they all raved about. It wasn't to be. I promised Em that I would never consider racing Ironman Lanzarote and it was back to the drawing board in terms of my Ironman ambitions.

So I was made up when Em didn't object. I fired up the laptop and entered the Nottingham race there and then, and at that point it still didn't have a name. It would eventually be called the Outlaw after Nottingham's most famous son, the outlaw Robin Hood. Mike entered the following day to make it a second family day out after London. I was so excited that the half marathon seemed so very passé now. That feeling was to disappear though come race morning.

Some 666 runners lined up on the start line. Was the number

of the beast an omen of things to come? I felt confident as I stood there in my black COLT top. It was the first time in almost three years that I hadn't worn my well-travelled yellow and black skull-emblazoned Pirate tri top. I was in Lancaster, running for my Lancaster club, so the least I could do was wear the kit. I also felt proud to be in the black and white top lining up with my club-mates Stu, Sarah and Chris, three people that I regularly ran with.

It was a sunny, yet chilly November morning, almost perfect conditions for running. We'd been lucky really as the previous week had just been blighted by endless torrential rain. This had led to the race organisers changing the course slightly to avoid a flooded path, which they announced as we all huddled on the start line with a nervous excited energy that you only experience at races.

Moments later we were away, over a thousand feet moving along like a giant mutant millipede from a Japanese monster movie. My own two feet were moving a little faster than they probably should have been, as always when I run I'd got caught up in the moment and gone off way too fast. A glance at my Garmin when it beeped for the first time confirmed this: I had just run a mile in six minutes and 15 seconds.

Alarm bells sounded in my head. I knew that wasn't a sustainable speed but my legs for some reason chose to ignore that fact and carried on regardless. By the time I'd crossed the Millennium Bridge and turned right to head down the quayside towards Glasson Dock I was breathing out of my arse.

I'd put on too much weight and not done enough training to be running that fast. It was the equivalent of committing running suicide. Just after three miles I finally got a wake-up call that brought me to my senses and slowed me down. The unmistakable ponytail and beard of the "IronHobbit" Chris Clarke swished past me in his rather unorthodox bouncy style. He is called the Hobbit because he's about as tall as one of Tolkien's much-loved characters, and loves his beer and cake just as much.

When the Hobbit runs it's almost puppet-like. Think

Pinocchio or Muffin the Mule. He bounds up and down almost as much as he propels himself forward. What matters though is how effective it is. The Hobbit is quick and is capable of running around 80 minutes for a half marathon. So you can see why I had no business being ahead of him at three miles. I came to my senses as my hirsute club-mate ran off into the distance. Chris would go on to complete the race in one hour and 19 minutes, a long way in front of me.

I slowed down and tried to run a steady few miles, pacing myself well through the ten-mile mark. I didn't feel comfortable, it was after all a race, but I was no longer dying on my arse. That was good because the competitor in me was worried about my good friend that I knew would be gunning for me.

Lesley was running as part of her London Marathon build-up and from what she had been saying and posting on Facebook, her training had been going really well. The last thing I needed was to get "chicked" by her, as I'd never hear the end of it if she beat me in an actual race. After all, the banter had been bad enough when she'd posted a faster marathon time than me the year before.

Like Stu, I'd helped to devlop Lesley's running and she'd gone on to be faster than me. I was also aware that if I slowed down too much Stu would emulate Lesley and beat me also. Those thoughts powered my legs up the one hill on the course. I knew that both of my friends hated hills and would slow down there, I had to take advantage of any weakness I could. As much as I wanted them to do well, I hated the thought of being beaten. I crested the hill and speeded up again passing several runners getting their breath back after the short sharp climb.

Less than half a mile later I was heading down the hill from the village of Aldcliffe to the water treatment works when the road disappeared under about 18 inches of ice-cold muddy water. I thought I was doing Hellrunner or The Cross Bay again as I ran blindly through what appeared to be an open sewer with the run-off from the fields containing herds of cows. I was instantly numbed and couldn't feel my feet or ankles.

I wouldn't regain any warmth or feeling once I'd reached the dry path to the finish. Over the final three miles any momentum and second wind I'd gained just disappeared. I later learned from some other runners that they'd lost the 'will to live' at that point which made me feel better, as I wasn't enjoying it at all.

I struggled on through and despite being passed in the last three miles by everyone and their Grandma I managed to finish in one piece in a time of 1.45:23 for 315th place. I was really pleased to come in the top half of the field and I was even more pleased to have survived without being passed by my friends.

Lesley had a blinding run to finish in 345th place in a new PB time of 1.46:55. Her performance was even more remarkable given the fact that when we met at the finish she was streaming with cold. She probably shouldn't have ran but was glad that she did. I couldn't help but think when she's fully fit she'll be much faster. It was certainly going to be an interesting battle between the two of us when London came around.

Stu crossed the line with a burst of speed down the finishing straight of the track, completing his first half marathon in a time of 1.58:51. I was so pleased for him. I ran straight up to him and put my hand on his back, forcing him to abandon his bent-over gasp for breath. Once straightened out his huge grin was unmistakable despite the purple face. "I can't believe I did it, and I got under two hours. That was bloody hard," he rasped before gulping a much-needed bottle of water. "You did brilliant mate, I'm so chuffed for you," I blabbed at him like a proud father. It was a strange feeling. I felt somewhat responsible for this grown man being there and pushing himself to the limit. Yet at the same time it was a bloody good feeling to share that moment with a good friend, it reminded me that sometimes it really isn't about fast times or winning medals but about the taking part. That French bloke who started the modern Olympics might have actually been onto something, and it's not every day you can say that about the French.

6

RECOVERING DANCING QUEEN

After my half marathon efforts my legs were really sore, my muscles screamed at me whenever I moved and I was seizing up like an arthritic 70-year-old. I guess the lack of training also meant I'd not let my body get used to that feeling you get after a race, the one where it sometimes hurts just to breathe or when you have to hold on to the wall just to aid yourself with sitting on the toilet. Too much information? Just what you needed, a mental image of me on the loo.

My suffering caused much p**s-taking in our house. "You're not getting any sympathy, it's self-inflicted," was Em's take on matters as I was having to walk up the stairs using my hands as well as my feet, pulling myself up with my arms, wincing and sighing with each step. Crosby, our tabby cat, lay at the top of the stairs staring at me with a mix of disbelief and wonder, he obviously shared Em's opinion. Sometimes everyone can be a critic, even the bloody cat. That night I slept in my compression tights in an attempt to lessen my discomfort. The skin-tight garments claim to compress fatigued muscles and aid recovery. I'd started wearing them in the months before Germany and had always found that they helped with what they claimed. I could train hard on a Saturday, doing about four to five hours on the bike, wear my tights to recover and then ride again the following morning for another three hours at least without any noticeable ill effect.

It may have been a placebo effect as compression gear seems to be the sports manufacturers' marketers' wet dream at the moment, with very little independent evidence that it actually works, but I was a convert. The only downside to wearing compression tights was that Em usually laughed at me and called the tight grey leggings my "passion killers". Well at least there was no danger of me putting my back out as well.

The tights seemed to work as I woke up on the Monday morning with much less stiffness in my legs. To further my recovery I walked to work and back that day, figuring that my legs would feel better with blood circulating through them following some very light exercise. Some people would swear by a light recovery run but at that stage I didn't feel I was fit enough or recovered enough to run, so I settled for a more civilised stroll.

I stepped up the exercise regime on the Tuesday. Again I walked on to campus but I'd also arranged to play my mate Martin at badminton after work. This was my weekly dose of humility as he's very good and always kicks my arse. We had been playing together for about a year, and although I knew that the stop-start lunging nature of the game wasn't doing my knees any good I couldn't give it up.

I had loved playing badminton since school, and when I was 15 I qualified as a coach, and played in a local league. Now as an adult I wasn't as nimble around the court and my left knee groaned every time I slammed my foot into the sports hall floor, stretching my arm and racket downwards to reach the smash that Martin had just fired at me. I wore a support on my knee when I played and learnt to deal with the pain, but sometimes 45 minutes on court crippled me more than a two- to three-hour run.

This particular Tuesday my softly-spoken Geordie mate was recovering from swine flu so was way below par, which probably explains why I won the first game and was enjoying a commanding 8-2 lead in the second. I don't know what it is but I seem to surround myself with competitive friends. Maybe like-minded people gravitate towards each other?

Martin was about as competitive as anyone could get on

the court. I once witnessed him smash his racket to pieces in frustration at missing an easy shot. It wasn't bad sportsmanship, more the physical manifestation of his total desire to win. His fighting instinct kicked in and soon enough I was on the ropes, myself unwilling to give any quarter.

It became a war of attrition, sweat pouring from both of us as we put our bodies on the line, diving here there and everywhere in attempts to return the other's fierce shots. We must have looked a right sight, two blokes in their 30s thinking they were playing in an Olympic final and taking a Tuesday afternoon game of fun just a bit too far.

We were oblivious though and just lost in our own battle, a battle that I would eventually lose by two games to one. I had never beaten him and had just seen my best chance pass me by. I was so bloody frustrated but at the same time happy that we'd had so much fun.

After our epic badminton match my legs were aching. My left knee, despite the strapping, was beginning to seize up but I was determined to run home and start off my recovery, so that's just what I did. It took me a very steady 30 minutes to run the three and a half miles home, very slow but it served the purpose, my legs were working again. I actually felt better after my run than I had before I started.

The true test of my fitness and recovery came on Wednesday when I met my COLT mates for a club running session. Four of us turned up; Simon Deveraux, John Towse and a new guy who I didn't know. I'd known Simon and John since COLT had started. Simon was an Ironman veteran who was training for the club outing to Lanzarote the following May. John was training for his first Ironman in South Africa the following April.

Both of them were good runners and always ahead of me at the club training sessions which John actually organised. The session started with a two-mile warm-up which gave me ample opportunity to introduce myself to the new bloke. "Hi I'm Andy, you new to triathlon then, not seen you here before?" I started what must have seemed like an interrogation to the softly-spoken, lean and athletic shaven-headed runner. Further questions followed, the usual ones that I always tended to ask people. What's your background; runner, cyclist or swimmer? What sort of times do you do? Have you done a triathlon before? What are you training for? I asked more bloody questions than a toddler.

Granted I also answered quite a few, and got the standard response when I said I'd done a couple of Ironman races and explained that the 2.4-mile swim, 112-mile bike ride and the 26.2-mile run were done consecutively, and not days apart. "Bloody hell, that's nuts. I could never do that," came the newcomer's response. "Don't rule it out, you keep training with us lot and I guarantee that one day you'll be an Ironman. This club has that effect on people," I quipped back at him. I don't think he believed me.

And that is how I met Chris Lawson, a man who would go on to be a great friend, training partner and of course in this competitive domain, rival. It turned out that Chris had also run the half marathon, although much faster than me; he'd finished in an hour and 39 minutes. Male ego kicked in as we started the session proper. Simon and John were a class apart but I was determined to show Chris that I meant business. The session was a tough one: three one-mile fast runs with a two-minute recovery in between each mile, and a two-mile warm-down to finish.

I really had been in two minds whether to go along or not as my legs were still sore, especially my hamstrings. I'm really glad that I did as the session was hard work but fun. I was over-cautious on the first rep and ran a mile in seven minutes and 45 seconds. Nothing pulled, snapped or broke down so I thought sod it and ran properly on the next two. Miles of 6.45 and 6.50 followed.

Chris beat me on the first mile but I edged ahead of him on the second two. We were both really pleased with our efforts along the promenade, with the wind blowing in across the sea, and thankfully it had been with us and not against us making the session slightly easier. But the best thing was that my legs felt perfect the next day so maybe the key to recovery is a hard session a few days after a tough race.

I ran a couple more times that week and had every intention of running at the weekend when we went up to visit my parents. However the weather in Cumbria put pay to that. The wind and rain on Walney Island was coming in horizontal bursts that actually saw my car rocking on its wheels parked on my parents' driveway.

I wouldn't have lasted five minutes out there, which was a great shame because Biggar Bank, the beach there, is one of my favourite places to run in the world. I love running by the sea, the rhythm of the waves numbs out any pain you may be feeling and I find it almost therapeutic.

Living away from the sea now (granted it's only about six miles away) I really miss it. Growing up with the constant sound of the waves, so much so that you channel it out, you really do notice the lack of that when you move away. As much as I love Lancaster I consider myself an Islander, a Walneyite, and a large part of me will always feel nomadic when I'm away from my small island.

This got me thinking about some of my other favourite runs, and they all seem to be near the sea or water. Running along the cliff tops that summer in De Kelders, South Africa, watching the southern right whales and their calves has to be the most spectacular training run I've ever done.

Running along Crosby beach as the sun sets and the tide comes in covering the iron men of Andrew Gormley's *Another Place* is another sight to behold. Sunset on Treasure Island beach in Florida makes you feel alive as you run along trying to avoid the waves chasing your feet while dolphins breach just metres away. Running along the tree-lined Canal du Midi and through the deserted vineyards around Beziers in the south of France was amazing, going for ten miles without seeing another soul.

Running across Sydney Harbour Bridge at sunrise feels like being in a dream, I had to pinch myself that it was real. I've been extremely privileged to run in some awesome places.

I never travel abroad without my running shoes and always try to run wherever I go. I've ran in Asia, Africa, Europe, Australia, and North America. I just need to run in South America and Antarctica and I'll have the full set, although it's highly unlikely that I'll ever achieve that one.

Back to reality though, and the following week was spent running around the rain-drenched streets of Lancaster. I was surrounded by a soul-sapping gloom that only a British town can give you in the height of a miserable winter. I imagine only a wet Wednesday in Warsaw could be worse.

Shutting out the meteorological misery I managed to complete a 45-mile week running twice a day over four days. On Wednesday the rain was so bad and the path to work so flooded that I had to pour water out of my shoe into the sink at work when I arrived. I was soaked to the skin, and the irony was that I'd been listening to the MP3 player and Sunshine on a Rainy Day by Zoe had come on. P*****g it down on a stormy day would have been more apt.

During the rest of the week I got two further runs in of five miles without any pain or incident but it wasn't all just about running. Now that I had the Outlaw to look forward to I decided that I'd better get my bike roadworthy. I'd not actually ridden my Giant road bike for about six months as I'd constantly been on the ROO in the build-up to Germany. I'd needed to get used to the aggressive riding position of the carbon speed machine and as a result my old trusty aluminium first love had been relegated to a corner of the cellar, not quite abandoned but certainly not given the attention she deserved.

The ROO wasn't a winter bike. It was a thing of pure beauty. I couldn't risk getting it dirty, which would be as inappropriate as wearing Jimmy Choos to Glastonbury. Bet you didn't realise I was so in touch with my feminine side. Good job I'm not telling you that I read my wife's copy of *Cosmo*, own a couple of pink shirts, like Disney movies, sing along to Abba in the car and have a collection of Barbie dolls. The ROO would be put on the turbo trainer for the winter months and the Giant would be my wellies, an appropriate choice for the winter conditions ahead. In preparation I'd ordered a new chain, brake callipers, pads and cables. I told Em that I wouldn't be too long and headed into the cellar full of confidence in my bike mechanic skills. The chain came off in seconds, the holding pin was taken out and it fell to the floor like a mechanical snake. I picked up the oil covered rattler and put it outside in the dustbin.

Removing the old cables was easy and the callipers came off with some expert wielding of Allen keys. I was on a roll. The new brake callipers were fitted in a matter of minutes.

It was at this point that I consulted my Haynes manual of cycle maintenance and realised that I'd made a mistake. Yes, I had the correct components that I needed but I'd made the rookie mistake of not having the correct tools. I didn't have a cable puller or indeed any wire cutters, I'd just presumed that ordinary kitchen scissors would do the job. What a numpty. I discovered the scissors were about as useful as me when I tried cutting the old cable and failed. It was like trying to saw through a tree trunk with a bread knife.

There was only one course of action that could save me. I picked up the phone and called the cycling equivalent of the Batphone, only my caped crusader was Andy H, CEO and chief mechanic of Thurnham Cycles. OK, so it's not really a company, just what we call Andy H's garage where he does all his bike fettling. It's an Aladdin's cave of bikes, parts and tools that he's collected over the years. If Andy doesn't have the tool for the job then either the tool doesn't exist or the job doesn't actually need doing.

He listened and laughed at my best pathetic voice on the phone and told me to come down. Ten minutes later the Giant and I were heading down country lanes in the car, on our way to be educated and improved. Andy clamped the bike in his work stand and laid out the new cables on a bench ready to fit them, placing them carefully next to the cutters and the cable puller, the vital missing ingredients in this mechanical cake. He'd also offered to fit the new chain whilst we were fettling so I handed him that as well. He put it to one side while he made light work of my cabling.

"OK Holgs that's the cables done, let's sort your chain out.

Where is the chain you took out, we are going to use it to make the new chain to the correct length," Andy asked with an air of the inevitable. He knew me and my bike maintenance skills too well. I looked at my feet like a schoolboy in front of the headmaster when I realised that I'd cocked up. "Err I didn't think of that, I've thrown it in the dustbin."

My chief mechanic just shook his head and started wrapping the chain around the chain set and cogs, the drivetrain of the Giant. "We'll just have to estimate and break where we think is best, it won't be perfect but hopefully it will do. We might have to adjust it after you've ridden it. Never throw anything away until you are certain the job is finished in future, you never know if you'll need it," he advised.

Nothing had changed. I was still bloody useless at bike maintenance. Soon enough Andy had finished the chain. He span the pedals to listen to it whirr a mechanical tune and when he tested my brakes, they were tighter than a pair of Mick Jagger's pants.

I loaded the bike back into the car and thanked him again. Being a Scouser he couldn't resist having the final word. "Now are you sure you know how to fit your mud guards Andy," he laughed. I've never had the heart to tell him that it took me almost two hours, a lot of swearing and the liberal use of a hacksaw that night to do so.

Reading this now I'm sure he'll be sat shaking his head in disbelief. Maybe I should just leave bike maintenance to the men and stick to doing what I know best, like seeking out that elusive 1998 Happy Holidays limited edition Barbie, while singing Dancing Queen.

7

FROM TOP BANANA TO FROZEN PEAS

As 2009 came to a close thoughts turned to social matters rather than just training. Even Ironmen have to have some downtime. I didn't make it to my work's Christmas party as I was actually at work. It was a complete waste of time though as we had about six customers all night. And none of them needed my help. Still, I took comfort in the fact that me being at work meant that at least one of my colleagues didn't have to miss out, and besides I had two social engagements to look forward to within a week. And that for an unsociable sod like me is unprecedented. I was the London bus socialite: not going out all year and then two come along at once.

First up was a meeting with some old friends, well Dave is old at least. Em and I drove down to deepest, darkest suburban Cheshire to meet up with my Pirate buddies for a meal. Whenever I venture into Cheshire I always feel like if the police stopped me they'd ask to see my bank account balance rather than my driving licence. "I'm sorry Mr Holgate, but we'll have to escort you back to common old Merseyside as you have less than £100,000 in funds." It's not like that at all but it always feels that way, all no knickers and fur coats and that's just the blokes. Social inferiority aside it was great to see Viking, Dave, Min, Loon and their partners. We'd not all actually been together since the previous Christmas. Two or three of us would meet at races, but such were our busy lives that the whole gang got together as much as Jools Holland and his clock-watching mates. The wine flowed, stories were told, the p**s was taken, and friendships came alive like they should when they are perfectly true.

There was much talk about my upcoming book. Viking wanted to know if he would be getting any money for his image rights, so I took two pence out of my pocket, slid it across the table and told him to keep the change.

Dave wondered who would play each of us in the film adaptation. Maybe it was the drink but we decided that Robert De Niro would make a great ex-Spartan, Angelina Jolie if she slimmed down could be Min, and I would be played by either Will Ferrell or Jack Black. Neither were known for their athletic physiques.

That only left Viking. We couldn't decide between Mini-Me from Austin Powers or the guy who played Phil Mitchell in *EastEnders*. However in the end we decided that he'd have to play himself as no actor could do him justice, he's that bloody unique. We ended a great night with a great comment from the ever observant Loon: "Guys, you do all realise the progress we've made here?" She paused as we all looked quizzically at her in the lamp light of the dark pub car park. "Three or four years ago we used to meet in Liverpool city centre, get hammered and go clubbing until 4am in the morning. Now we're meeting in a Cheshire country pub for a meal and we're saying our goodbyes and heading for home and bed just after 11pm. Such is the rock and roll lifestyle of triathletes!"

I didn't actually enhance my inner party animal a few days later when I attended the COLT Christmas party and awards evening. Over the course of the night I drank three pints of Erdinger (the German beer that I got after I completed Frankfurt) and I was a bit drunk. I wasn't slurring my words, falling down nor doing the two things that I only do when p****d – dancing and singing karaoke – but I could feel the room swaying.

I was officially a lightweight; well not literally, it was only applicable when it came to alcohol. Despite the fact that as the night progressed the gaudy wallpaper seemed to move more I had a great time catching up with club-mates and just having a laugh. I'd worked myself to near exhaustion with the book and my proper job over the previous few months and it was such a mental release to be letting off steam. The highlight of the night wasn't the beer though, it was the prize giving and I almost did nearly fall over when I heard my name called out. I was very honoured to win the Captain's Prize for Outstanding Contribution to the Club, a reward for my work on designing and maintaining the COLT website. I hadn't won anything for a long time, not since the school needlework prize in 1986, but the less said about that the better. It really isn't something you want to win as a hormonal 14-year-old boy trying to impress girls. Needless to say I saw more cotton thread than knicker elastic.

This however was a real honour, of which I'm very proud. Did I receive a medal, a shield perhaps, or even a silver cup to take away and engrave for all eternity? Well no not exactly on account of the fact that the club captain, Richard Mason, having a wicked sense of humour. He said I was "the top banana" and that's exactly what I received, a cuddly banana from a funfair in Blackpool. We don't take ourselves too seriously in COLT, and some people may have been disappointed at receiving such a prize, but as the banana was won the previous year by John Knapp for his achievement in Kona qualification I knew I was following in illustrious footsteps.

Em was fast asleep when I rolled home in the early hours of the morning, and she got a bit of a shock the next morning to wake up next to her husband grinning in his sleep and hugging a huge yellow banana. It's a good job she's used to me.

I woke up with a fuzzy head, not banging but more of a slight tapping on the inside of my skull. It wasn't surprising really. In one night I'd consumed more alcohol than I had all year. I'd not drunk until that celebratory beer was consumed in Frankfurt, still flushed with colour from my efforts, and I hadn't drunk since.

Through the mental fog I decided that I'd better go for a run. I don't know about you but on the rare occasion that I drink,

I usually find that a run the next morning brings me back to life. This routine always reminded me of a poster I had on my bedroom wall as a kid. I was a massive fan of Garfield the cat, the orange sarcastic lasagne-loving fur ball that was a 1980s icon.

Among the posters of Debbie Gibson, Tiffany and Molly Ringwald was one that showed Garfield before and after his morning coffee. On the left of the poster he was grumpy, bleary eyed and dysfunctional. On the right he'd had his coffee and was transformed into an alert, smiling, fully functioning cat. I was Garfield in that poster when I was hung over, only my pick-me-up to make me functional again was my run. The perfect cure for my below-average excess was a five-mile run on a beautiful crisp and clear winter morning. I love running when the air is that clear and cold that your cheeks get a warm blast as you run through the air you've just breathed out, resulting in a warm glow. I was careful to avoid the patches of ice as the frost on the ground crunched under my feet. A sound that I loved as it meant I was the first and only person to hear it, as once I stepped forward that particular crunch was gone forever.

I felt so alive, it was a joy to be running and it made a bloody nice change from all the wet weather we'd been having. I was buzzing when I got home, and after my shower I refuelled in the best way possible with a bacon sarnie and a cup of Garfield's strong coffee.

On the last Sunday before Christmas I had planned to go and run in the Ulverston 10km road race but unfortunately it was cancelled due to bad weather. The heavy rains had flooded the course and the high winds that had been swirling around Morecambe Bay had uprooted a few trees on the course. I was bitterly disappointed as the fast and flat course would have given me a perfect fitness marker to end the year on and take forward into 2010 and the year of London and the Outlaw.

I completely understood though as the organisers, Hoad Hill Harriers, had to think about the safety of the runners and the other road users. If anyone had been seriously hurt they no doubt would have been sued and all subsequent events would have never taken place. It pained me, and it still does that some idiots were online moaning about their decision. Come on people get a grip on reality here, it's only a bloody race.

I see people all the time on internet forums slagging races off for this, that and the other, and I'll be the first to let them have their opinions. After all they are paying customers and freedom of speech is essential in a fully functioning society. But they have to realise that if a race is cancelled or shortened or lengthened even, for health and safety reasons, then it's for their own good. Why take a risk, when there will be other days, other races in perfect conditions? Some people just need to "chillax" as my friend Louise would say. Running is supposed to be fun, yes races are serious business but we aren't pros, it's not our livelihood at stake, it's just a hobby.

So instead of pounding the streets of South Cumbria's quaint little market town I enjoyed a glorious Sunday morning on the bike with Andy H. One door of opportunity had been slammed shut but another one leading to a cycling catch-up with my good mate had been opened. It was the first time we'd been out in ages due to work, family commitments, writing commitments and the bloody awful November weather.

It was very icy and bitterly cold, the full winter gear was on, but it was one of those early starts when the heat of your lingering breath six inches in front of you kept your spirits up. It was one of those mornings where the sunshine is blinding, more so than on a summer's afternoon.

I was smiling away, riding alongside Andy as he hugged the grass verge, constantly keeping one ear out for an approaching vehicle from behind on the narrow road. It was extremely quiet, the odd call of a sandpiper or a gull across the estuary were the only sounds that interrupted our conversation. It felt great to be back out on the bike after a run-heavy few months.

Cycling as a sport is a time-consuming mistress. In order to get the benefit of a good workout you have to be out for at least an hour or two. Those hours were a luxury I hadn't had of late.

Running was simple; throw the shoes on, go out the door,

beast yourself for half an hour and the job was done. Cycling in bad weather was even more time inefficient as I took ages just to get ready to go out in full winter gear.

Here's the routine. From a naked start, I would lather my undercarriage in cream to stop any unnecessary chaffing and discomfort. My weapon of choice was called Udder cream, and yes it was developed for use on cows. You really couldn't make this up.

My heart-rate monitor strap would go round my chest, and then my wind-resistant bib tights would be pulled up over my legs and secured around my shoulders. Standing there in front of the bathroom mirror I'd look like an American wrestler from the WWE. "Whatcha gonna do bruther when the Holgster runs wild on you? Grrrr."

Arm-warmers would then be pulled tightly up from my wrists to my armpits, and a merino wool base layer would complement the sexy look before a long-sleeved cycle jersey would be zipped up to complete the outfit. If it was a particularly cold or wet day I'd add on my waterproof jacket making me a hi-viz version of the Michelin Man. I had more layers than an onion.

Then I'd start on my feet. Merino wool socks enveloped my toes, waterproof seal-skin socks were added on top. I could just about squeeze my cycling shoes on over my feet, which now looked like comedy clown feet with all the padding. The final touch was pulling on my neoprene, waterproof overshoes, a wetsuit for my feet if you will, that kept them totally dry.

A balaclava that made me feel like a terrorist was placed over my head, with only my eyes showing, and these were then covered up with protective sunglasses. Goretex snowboarding gloves were the final addition before the helmet was placed on my head. I not only now weighed several pounds more but had wasted half a day just getting dressed. Cycling must be so much simpler if you live somewhere nice and sunny like Florida or Australia.

Andy had just finished telling me about his encounter with the pop star Alexander Burke (he's a big *X Factor* fan; I worry about him at times!) up in Peterhead. I joked: "It's a wonder you still want to ride with me after rubbing shoulders with such a famous karaoke singer," showing my disdain for manufactured talent show 'superstars'.

I'd just finished laughing at his description of Peterhead (unrepeatable here) when disaster struck. We were approaching the village of Nateby and the road surface beneath our wheels changed noticeably from the usual grippy, bone-shaking, weather-beaten track to a perfectly smooth, black and glistening piece of newly laid tarmac. Andy H, ever alert to danger, said that we should slow down.

It was a warning that came a fraction too late as suddenly I felt my world start to spin. Going into a blind bend I'd fallen in behind Andy's rear wheel, conscious that we couldn't see oncoming traffic. It was a good job I had or we could have both been in serious trouble. In an instant my back wheel just disappeared from under me. I had hit a patch of black ice. I hit the tarmac hard, the brunt of my body weight crashing on my left elbow and hip. I slid uncontrollably around the bend on the wrong side of the road.

It all happened so quickly, I didn't even have time to make a sound. Thankfully there wasn't anything coming the other way or I would probably have been killed. I was floundering helpless in the middle of the road like a goldfish whose bowl has just been dropped.

Thankfully changing my riding position from Andy H's side to his rear meant that there was enough distance between me and Andy that I didn't take him out as well. My fast-moving bike actually slid past him and seeing the Giant prone on the road without me alerted him to the fact that I'd crashed.

He found me lying in the grass ditch at the side of the road. My momentum and the slippery surface had carried me straight through the bend and dumped me unceremoniously on the wet grass. Before Andy could reach me, a car passed by from the other direction. Less than 30 seconds earlier it would have hit me. That really brought it home to me how lucky I'd just been.

I thought that I'd broken my elbow or wrist as the pain was

quite intense, but thankfully I hadn't. I was shaking like a leaf, a combination of pain and shock. We were about ten miles from his house and neither of us had any signal on our mobile phones. Once I felt up to it I got back on the bike and we rode gingerly back to Andy's where he put my bike in his car and got me home.

Stripping off the protection and the torn jacket I discovered that despite three layers I'd taken about six inches of skin off my left arm from my elbow towards my wrist. I also had a sore wrist, road rash on my knee and a deep purple bruise on my hip. I dressed my wounds with antiseptic, swearing as it stung my damaged skin, and covered it with a dressing to help it heal.

I spent most of the afternoon lying prone on the sofa with a bag of frozen peas held firmly against my bruised hip, replaying the incident over and over again in my mind. Trying to find a reason, some human error that had led to my spill. I drew a blank but the more I thought about it the more I realised I was very glad that I'd taken ages to get ready, layering up, the damage would have been much worse if I hadn't. It was all such a shame as the ride had been so much fun up until the crash.

Subsequently, with sore legs and arms, that was my training for the week gone. I don't know how the hell the professional cyclists get back on their bikes and cycle through massive distances and altitudes at the likes of the Tour de France. I could hardly grip my car's steering wheel the next day and it hurt like hell changing gear.

Andy H and I did plan to get out for a ride on Christmas Eve morning as after having a week off I'd recovered enough to feel like I could pedal again, and more importantly actually grip the handlebars without wincing in pain. However we woke up to a generous blanket of snow. There was no way I was going to risk riding in those conditions. The fact that the powdery snow had frozen solid meant it wasn't even safe out for a car let alone a bike.

I rang Andy and he was in total agreement, adding that he was heading into the garage to do an hour on the turbo trainer. Putting the phone down I considered heading into the cellar to jump on the turbo like my conscientious mate but the reality was

I couldn't be arsed. I decided to save my energy for my traditional Christmas morning run instead.

The next morning I was up and out early, kissing a half-awake Em and leaving her to snooze under the warm duvet while I ran a gentle five miles. It wasn't quite like the scene in *It's a Wonderful Life* where George Bailey wishes the world and his wife a merry Christmas but I did pass one old lady walking her Yorkshire terrier and wished her "all the best". She reciprocated my greeting with a smile and that put me in the Christmas spirit.

I always love to run on Christmas day. It allows me to indulge in the culinary excess of the day without worrying too much as I've already burnt off the calories from at least two potatoes. Unfortunately the other half-dozen, and the mince pies, more than damage the good I've done. Oh well, sod it, Christmas only comes once a year and I'm sure we all kind of over-indulge a little.

I also secretly hope that Alberto Contador's climbing ability has been bottled up and is waiting under the Christmas tree. Yes, that's the one in the snowman wrapping paper sat next to the bottles containing Alistair Brownlee's running strength, Michael Phelps's power in the water and Chrissie Wellington's enthusiasm. Or is that just me?

The period between Christmas and New Year seemed to be so busy, visiting various family members. I also finished editing the photos and their captions for the book, and I did my first interview with a national magazine about the book. It was an e-mail interview with *Runner's World* magazine, designed to give them some background information for an article that they were planning to run in June to coincide with the book's publication.

The whole world seemed to be planning ahead. There must have been something in the air in those final days of December as two of my mates committed themselves to massive events in 2010.

First of all Dave the ex-Spartan signed up for Ironman UK. When I'd entered the Outlaw he'd expressed a desire to do a branded Ironman race and now he'd be fulfilling that ambition by strutting his stuff around Bolton the Sunday before the Outlaw. And Andy H, Thurnham's answer to George Hincapie, told me that he'd be battling his way around one of the Belgium classics. He had signed up for 140km of cobbles, hills and drunken Belgians at the Tour of Flanders Cycle Sportive. I admit to being a little bit envious of his planned trip but I couldn't justify the cost to go and ride with him.

As the year drew to a close I was in both a reflective and hopeful mood, which is why in the spirit of all the TV news programmes that were showing I did a kind of review of the year on my blog. It summed up my highs and lows of a very eventful year and outlined my dreams and aspirations for the coming one. I'm sure that a lot of athletes do this in their training dairies or on their blogs.

There are certainly plenty of internet forum threads each December and January about this sort of thing. It's a great way of getting perspective on what you've actually achieved, and what is attainable moving forward. Below is what I wrote on my blog as I reflected on 2009.

2009 Low Points

Falling apart in the marathon at Ironman Germany – getting off the bike I felt confident that with a steady run of four hours I would go under 12 hours for the event. The excessive heat and to a certain extent my mental state as a result of it saw me run the slowest marathon of my life.

Missing a 10k PB by just ten seconds in April in Lancaster – if I'd known how close I was I'd have found 11 seconds from somewhere.

Newcastle United being relegated from the Premiership, a sad day indeed...but we were crap!

Andy H getting injured and not training together as much.

2009 High Points

Ironman Germany – For many reasons: seeing Viking complete his IM dream, meeting Macca and Faris, new PB, awesome experience, the pain and the emotion has made me stronger. I've learnt from my mistakes and will be back stronger. Ending up on a drip showed I'd pushed myself to the very limit, I couldn't ask for more.

Family – Once again the amazing support of my "IronWidow" Em. None of what I do or achieve would be possible without her: from getting up at daft o'clock to watch me race, listening to geeky stuff and most importantly proof-reading. She's a star. My Mam and Dad – I've never been so proud as I was in Frankfurt when they 'finally' got to see me finish an Ironman race.

COLT – The club just went from strength to strength in its first year and it was a massive honour to win the award for outstanding contribution to the club for my work on the website.

PBs – I recorded personal bests in every triathlon I raced in during 2009, I can't ask any more than that.

Non-triathlon – Got an amazing new job. Achieved a lifelong ambition to dive with a great white shark (several of them actually). Also dived with Nile crocodiles, raced a cheetah (and lost) and did the world's highest bungee jump (216m).

So all in all not a bad year – and there was one other high. Writing a book.

2009 was a year of highs for me, but I was determined that 2010 would eclipse it. I was full of confidence when I made public my ambitions for the year.

2010 Goals and Wishes

A new PB at the Outlaw Ironman in Nottingham in August. Breaking 12 hours 30 minutes will be a great day at the office, 11.59 will be an amazing day. Watch this space.

Finally getting my hands on a London Marathon medal in April.

To finally go under 40 minutes for 10k. Hopefully I'll be able to carry my IM fitness through until December where I'll hope to record a new PB on the fast Ulverston 10k course.

To sell a few books, and hopefully have people enjoy what they read.

To hopefully come across as down to earth, yet fiercely ambitious in any interviews I give.

To improve my bike climbing ability.

To shift the extra weight that I'm carrying. Lighter = faster – SIMPLES!

I ended the last blog of the year with a statement of intent: "So have a great 2010, I intend to have the best year yet. 2010 The Year of IronHolgs!"

I'd have to wait a whole year to discover if it really would be the Year of IronHolgs. One thing I did know though, if I was at the centre of it then it certainly wouldn't be boring.

8

CRACKING UP

The Year of IronHolgs couldn't have got off to a worse start. I had two weeks with plenty of running and a few trips to the gym to try and work off the yuletide excess, trying to find space among all the newcomers with their sparkly new kit and trainers. I guess gyms must love New Year's resolutions because if you attend in January, it's as crowded as Linford Christie's running shorts, and if you go in March, as much as it pains me to say it, it's as empty as Newcastle United's trophy cabinet.

It was great that all these people were enhancing their lives by working out. I wondered to myself if the ones in full make-up and those not really sweating wouldn't be there before too long, their membership fees being easy profit for the gym owners. But the reality was these new gym-goers were playing havoc with my training. I was wasting too much time waiting for machines to become available so I reluctantly decided that I'd just have to head outside and train in the harsh winter conditions.

The morning after I had decided to temporarily abandon going to the gym I was about a mile into my commute to work, running well despite the melting snow on the ground. As I approached the sharp downhill of Bowerham Road I instinctively slowed down. Suddenly both my legs whipped up from under me and I had one of those slow-motion moments. I was falling for what seemed like an eternity, yet in reality it was a fraction of a second before I collided with the unforgiving pavement.

Thankfully the well-packed rucksack that was strapped to my back took the brunt of the impact with my rolled-up work trousers, shirt and towel providing a buffer that meant that my head didn't bounce off the pavement too badly. It still hurt though, resulting in an egg-sized lump on the base of my skull.

Instinctively my hands went out to protect myself, which was a big mistake. A fire-like pain shot through my left hand and I swore aloud. Embarrassed more than anything, conscious of the busy school run traffic, I got to my feet like nothing had happened. Brushing the dirty slush from my now wet backside and legs, I set off rather aggressively on the final few miles to work, wanting to distance myself from the embarrassing scene as soon as possible.

At work I ran my hand and wrist under the cold shower and the bruising started to come out instantly. As the day went on the pain got worse. Stubbornly I ignored colleagues' and Em's advice to go to the accident and emergency department at Lancaster Royal Infirmary. I was doing the man thing of openly saying: "It'll be alright" while internally thinking "s**t this hurts a little too much, I hope they don't have to amputate". Eventually after not being able to sleep I admitted defeat and went to see the campus nurse the next morning. Understandably there wasn't a lot she could do except send me to hospital. So a day later than advised I walked through the doors of Lancaster's A&E department.

Actually technically that's not true. It was so busy that I had to queue up outside waiting to register before I could get in. I may as well have walked into a war zone as the place was in total chaos. All the chairs were occupied and every bit of wall space was being leaned against by a person in some form of distress. The receptionist taking my details looked like she was about to snap at any second. She was obviously having one of those days when she earned her money and then some. The sort of day when you just want to go home and collapse with a glass of wine in front of the telly, watching intently as your winning lottery numbers are displayed on the screen.

The three people in front of me in the queue were all cradling one of their arms, victims of the ice. One poor bloke had blood covering his scalp and forehead. Having a head injury he was understandably taken away by a nurse within minutes of arriving, causing mutterings and tuts from people that had obviously been there quite a while. Surveying the distress in the crowded waiting room I knew that I was in for a few uncomfortable hours while the overworked doctors and nurses tried to clear the backlog of the sick, the lame and the broken.

Eventually I was assessed by a triage nurse and sent for an x-ray before returning to the slightly less crowded waiting room. Unfortunately a couple of hours into my wait the gobbiest, most common, foul-mouthed woman the city had to offer came and sat next to me. Why do I always attract the weirdos, the unclean and the downright dregs of society?

It was one of the reasons I refused to use public transport any more. I'd spent many painful hours over the years on my commute listening to some nutter or other who decided to sit next to me and talk at me. Maybe I have a welcoming face, I don't know. It even used to happen though when I had my earphones on and my head buried in a magazine.

On one such occasion as I got the train home from work, an old drunken dishevelled man actually put his arm on my shoulders and removed my headphones for a chat about life. I was that shocked I just let him. Sometimes I wish I wasn't so polite, it must be the librarian in me.

Back in the waiting room the vile witch proceeded to have an hour-long domestic with her husband about how much agony she was in and how it was his entire fault because he didn't bring her to hospital the night before. I pretended to be asleep.

Later when she got back from x-ray she again sat next to me and threw a total toddler paddy, and stormed out after waiting ten minutes for her crutches. Her limp had miraculously disappeared. Everyone in the room gave a collective sigh of relief as her poor sod of a husband smiled at no one in particular and dutifully followed her. You would have thought she'd been dying given the noise she was making but she can't have been in that much pain if she left without completing her treatment, could she? What a prat.

Moments later I was called back through the double screened doors to the treatment area, only there were still no free cubicles so I was treated in a side corridor. I was given the news that I'd managed to crack a small bone in my wrist. I must have looked mortified as I was quickly reassured that thankfully it was "the best possible break" by the stressed-out-looking doctor. I was given some painkillers and told to use my own at home if I felt I needed to manage it further.

My wrist was placed in a splint and then wrapped up in a sling, pinning my damaged limb tightly to my chest for protection. I was sent on my way some five hours after arriving with instructions to keep it immobile for two weeks, and then to just wear the splint for a further week. I wasn't to go back to the hospital unless I felt like it wasn't healing.

I was shattered. The walk home up the hill finished me off. I must have looked so pathetic as I walked through the door because Em spared me the "I told you so" lecture and instead just kissed me and made me a brew. Sometimes that's all you need when you've had one of those days.

I had a couple of days off work while the pain and stiffness settled. It wasn't like I was much use to anyone in my condition. When I did get back to work after the initial sympathy had been expressed, my colleagues were quick to question my sanity for running in such treacherous conditions.

It was actually hard to defend my corner because to a certain extent it was my fault. I had figured that the pavements were safe and put my normal running shoes on. Until that morning I'd been running in my off-road shoes with the extra grips. I'd done over 30 miles in the icy conditions without incident, but as soon as I became overconfident and changed my shoes that all ended.

I quite surprised myself that I didn't descend into a "woe is me" type funk that I'm sure all athletes experience when they are injured. I had done so in the past when what I loved was taken away from me. Perhaps my spirits were kept on a level just the right side of divorce by the fact that I was walking the seven miles to work and back every day and fitting in a sneaky one-handed turbo session in the cellar whenever Emma was out with friends or working late.

I'd remove the sling and rest my splinted wrist on a cushion that I'd laid across the tri-bar extensions on the ROO. I'd taken my inspiration from world Ironman champion, Chrissie Wellington, as millions of people around the globe do. She had recently broken her arm after a bike accident and had posted a photo on *Twitter* of herself on her turbo trainer pedalling away, flashing her trademark smile, and wearing her right arm in a bright white cast. I figured if it was good enough for Chrissie, it was good enough for me.

Four long weeks later I tentatively took my first steps back into training after my unfortunate fracture. To say that I was nervous would be a gross understatement, in fact I'd pretty much lost all confidence in my ability as an athlete.

I was nervous about getting out on the bike; what if I fell and re-injured myself? I couldn't face swimming; the thought of putting my wrist through that kind of workout left me in a cold sweat. I was down about running because I had become so unfit. Daily walks and occasional turbo sessions couldn't make up for the decent mileage weeks I'd been doing prior to my fall.

I felt sluggish, fat and completely useless. My psyche had suddenly gone dark as I considered my return to training. I guess I knew it would be like starting from scratch again; a position I couldn't afford to be in with a marathon only a couple of months away.

So with my confidence at an almost all-time low I picked myself up and forced myself to join Andy H out on the bike. It actually felt like a momentous decision that I was making. I was worried that I wouldn't be able to grip the handlebars (especially on the hills) or that my arm would ache, but the fear of falling was at the forefront of my mind.

After an hour or so of that first ride I began to relax. On the descents I'd hang back just in case there was any ice, and in places there was, but thankfully I stayed upright. I definitely wasn't myself, and I think Andy could tell by the way I was unusually quiet. I just listened and nodded in the right places, with an occasional flash of the real me as I laughed at one of his stories.

By the end of the ride I was knackered and sucking Andy's rear wheel like my life depended on it. We had ridden for a solid three hours without incident, or pain. I was so relieved that I really felt like hugging my lycra-clad chaperone but instead I just offered a simple "thanks for the ride mate" after he made sure I got home safely, riding out of his way in doing so.

Supping my post-ride recovery drink I reflected that I'd gone further and longer than I was wanting but that for the majority of the ride I felt comfortable. Maybe I wasn't as unfit as I thought, or maybe Andy H had just been taking it really easy with me? I concluded the latter.

I was cycling again and my confidence was growing. The following weekend I again joined Andy H for a two-hour ride, and felt so much stronger. I even did a few turns on the front, pulling him along for a change. I hadn't dared do that the previous week for fear of blowing up.

In a true test of my nerve I cycled 24 miles after work in between the rides with Andy H. That doesn't sound like much but I deliberately headed out on the deserted unlit lanes around Dolphinholme and Quornmore, two local villages joined by winding, technical roads that really test a person's bike handling skills. I knew that I needed to ask myself some serious questions if I was going to feel confident on the bike again. If I could ride well in these conditions then I could ride well at any time.

It was freezing but I managed to navigate around any ice by the combination of moonlight and my high powered Ay-Up lights and sheer good fortune. My ploy worked. As the ride progressed, my skills and confidence returned in unison. I was in love with the bike again, having so much fun. I actually felt like heading up into the Trough of Bowland and on to some of the tough fells but then I remembered that I needed to re-index my gears, one bike maintenance job that I knew I could do without a trip to Thurnham Cycles. I'd discovered on the latest ride with Andy H that I couldn't change into the granny ring – an essential for a climber like myself. I headed home with a smile as bright as the moon above.

Hidden behind that smile though, I knew that cycling wouldn't get me through a marathon. I had to start running again, it wasn't a choice it was a necessity. I started tentatively in my lunch hour, running around campus gently. It wasn't quite the run three lamp posts and collapse scenario that had started me on this path many years ago but it was just as difficult. Every other day I'd run but it just left me flat. Running for one of the few times in my life felt like torture in those couple of weeks. The confidence I'd regained on the bike just wasn't forthcoming. I don't know why but since my fall I seemed to have been mentally scared to put a foot out of the door. Maybe it was because I was carrying a little extra weight, unfortunately making every stride just a little bit harder than it should be. Maybe it was the aching knees that constantly plagued me post-run or maybe I'd just burnt myself out.

I finally decided that my problem stemmed from a fear of the upcoming marathon. Yes I knew I'd run them before, and yes I knew I was an Ironman BUT at that moment I had a mental block against running in the London Marathon. I just didn't see the point when my training had been disrupted, and I wasn't in the shape I needed to be in.

So I'd completed a few shorter runs including the first head torch outing of the year with Andy H but in the back of my mind I kept hearing "you have a 20-mile race in March and a marathon in April". My longest run since November had only been eight miles, how was I going to cope with the massive distances ahead of me?

In the end there was no magic cure, no moment of

enlightenment. It was a combination of things. Thoughts that actually came to me during a wet run home from work. I'd paid for the hotel, the train tickets and the entry fee. I've never been one for wasting money and I decided I wouldn't start now. I decided that I just had to suck it up and get on with it.

I was running now and actually it didn't seem so bad. Yes the marathon was going to hurt. Yes I wouldn't perform as well as I expected. Yes I probably wouldn't enjoy it. But let's face it, if you can't get excited for possibly the biggest race on the planet then you have no business calling yourself a runner. I was proud to be a runner, and there was no bloody way I was going to quit now.

People who had suffered a lot worse than me would be running, and taking a lot longer than me. Who the hell was I to bitch and moan about it, and to duck out in a funk of self-pity? My nickname was IronHolgs not TamponHolgs, I was made of stern stuff. It was time to man up.

The next night after work I just set off and ended up running ten miles in 85 minutes. My longest run of the year and apart from being drenched to the skin, it felt comfortable. I wasn't on my knees and I certainly wasn't breathing out of my arse. My mind was racing, if I could run that and then could keep it up then I'd survive the Trimpell 20 and London and be able to move towards the Outlaw without much damage. My mood lightened somewhat.

The big test came that Saturday. My 'other' training partner Lesley, who was also doing London and Trimpell, e-mailed to ask if I fancied a long run. With my confidence just returning I wanted to say no, but I knew I had to say yes and really test myself.

Andy H's son Gareth would also be joining us as he prepared for the Bath half-marathon. As Lesley and I got out of the car we were met by a smiling Andy H and Gareth. Andy H wasn't joining us, he was setting out on his bike getting some crucial miles in before his upcoming race in Belgium. Gareth however was obviously very keen as he was ready to run in his shorts in the sub-zero conditions.

I on the other hand had tights on, a compression base layer, a thermal cycling jersey and a Goretex running jacket, oh and gloves. Lesley was also wrapped up from head to toe with no bare flesh exposed. Gareth took one look at us both and headed back into his parents' house to cover up his legs with a pair of tracksters. We drove back to my house and set out on our run. Even as the sun rose over the River Lune I didn't regret my clothing choice, and I'm sure my companions didn't regret theirs either. It was colder than a skinny-dipping eskimo.

The pace was steady and the three of us chatted about all sorts of topics; work, holidays, football, what I'd said about them both in my book, you know the usual sort of subjects. We headed out along the frozen canal before reaching the village of Halton. Crossing back over the river we followed it all the way to the end and to the sea at Glasson Dock. The salt water in the dock basin had also frozen, providing a different experience for the ducks and seagulls that were pretending to be penguins sliding around ungraciously on the ice.

Despite the cold, Lesley upped the pace in the last mile. It was still massively within Gareth's comfort zone given his usual speed but I was flagging, determined however not to slow them down. We reached the car park at Condor Green and said goodbye to Gareth as he headed home while Lesley and I doubled back to add some extra miles on.

We eventually made it back to my house and had covered just shy of 16 and a half miles in two hours and 19 minutes. My confidence was renewed; if I could keep that pace up I'd get round the marathon in about four hours. I figured that the Trimpell 20 would take me approximately three hours and then as Andy H always says: "The last six miles of the marathon will always take an hour at least."

Thanks to a successful run I'd come out the other side of my mental fog. I knew I wouldn't set the world on fire at London, but I felt more confident that I would finish without disgracing myself, and in all honesty that's all I was bothered about. It had been a dark few months but I'd emerged ready to push myself to the limit once more all in the name of fun. As Dave the ex-Spartan is so fond of telling me: "You have a twisted idea of fun."

With the challenges that lay ahead I couldn't argue with that.

9

ALMOST A MARATHON MAN

My legs eventually recovered after my long run with Lesley and Gareth, and my mileage for the week just seemed to grow and grow. For the first time in a long time I put over 50 miles into my legs, something that a few weeks earlier I wouldn't have even contemplated. Isn't it funny how a couple of good runs can get your mojo back?

Several weeks ago, feeling bloated and unfit, I hated running and could never see myself getting around Trimpell or London. Suddenly it was like I was a born-again runner, no longer apprehensive but instead looking forward to that time each day when I could lace up my shoes and head out the door for my running fix.

Several friends had asked how I was feeling in the build-up to London, to which I'd replied that I was OK but not expecting great things of myself. I think this must have shocked a few of them, as I was normally bouncing before a big race and talking up PBs etc. A quietly subdued and pragmatic response from me was, well, totally out of character.

It initiated a very interesting response from all of them, something that I certainly wasn't expecting: "You'll be alright, it's only a marathon." It was a response that really got me thinking. They thought that because I was a multiple Ironman that doing a marathon should be easy.

I could see their logic. After all if you can run a marathon after already swimming 2.4 miles and cycling 112 miles then surely a marathon on its own should be easier. I didn't think any of them fully understood the amount of effort and training that it takes even for an Ironman to run 26.2 miles. In my opinion anyone that says marathon running is easy obviously hasn't pushed themselves hard enough to finish one. I decided though that the response was actually a compliment. They believed in my ability, they knew I'd been there, done that and got various t-shirts – it was another confidence boost.

With any endurance event it is the mental aspect of the competitor that leads to success as well as the physical. You need to have strength of both kinds. Self-belief, or the lack of it, can destroy you. When you have it though it's like taking a minute a mile off your time. In those final couple of weeks before London, I had both and loved it.

Just how much I loved it was brought home to me on a midweek run after a tough day at work. I ran for 14 miles.

All day I'd been feeling completely wiped out, my original plan had been to just run the three and a half miles home and collapse in a heap. It was a glorious day. The sun was shining, burning up its last rays of light by the second as I left work. It was crisp but not too cold. My gloves were on my hands more for wiping sweat from my face than for keeping my fingers warm.

I could feel my 16-mile run in my legs from two days before hand as I set off so I was conscious of running relaxed and not overcooking the early pace. I'm a big fan of training to my heart rate and was periodically checking the screen on my Polar watch as I put one foot in front of the other.

I find that reading your heart rate is a great way of keeping yourself reined in, noting that mine said 135 beats per minute as I plodded down the hill into the village of Galgate. That number told me that I was running sensibly. Anything below 122 was too easy and anything above 160 beats per minute was getting into tempo running, so at 135 I was bang on.

Feeling good I didn't make the usual turn for home but instead

I crossed the busy A6 and headed for the canal towpath. Being a history buff, I loved running along this marvel of the industrial revolution.

During my undergraduate degree in social and economic history at Hull University I'd studied the impact of the canal system on the British economy. Canals in their day were the backbone of the country, a vital network that transported everything including cotton, food, coal and livestock. Eventually of course with the coming of the railways they'd be made redundant, in the same way that roads would make rail redundant.

The Lancaster canal had been built in 1797 and connected the market towns of Kendal in the north and Preston in the south. In 1826 a 'branch line' was built from Galgate, connecting with the sea port at Glasson Dock thus allowing the import and export of goods by sea. It was on this branch line that I was running, heading towards the once busy port that now is more of a place to stop on a weekend for an ice cream and a walk.

I loved this run because people were always a rare sight and there were no traffic fumes to breathe in. I passed fields full of sheep and cows, geese and swans swimming in gangs avoiding one another in an act of avian segregation. My heavy breathing and footfalls on the gravel towpath disturbed a magnificent heron that hard been lurking in the reeds. It took to flight, my eyes following with admiration as it headed up the canal to another safe haven away from the lycra-clad lout that had destroyed its peace.

A mile or so later I was snapped out of my enjoyment of nature's tranquillity as the towpath was reduced to ankle-deep mud. My shoes lost all traction causing me to slide from side to side. I looked like an awkward speed-skater, without the speed naturally. Eventually I made it down to Glasson, my mud-caked running shoes now bearing no resemblance to the white pair I'd laced up an hour earlier.

Emerging on to solid tarmac I worked hard going up Tithebarn Hill, but it was worth the effort as I was rewarded with the most spectacular view. The sun was almost setting and its vivid red and purple hues made the waters of the River Lune glow in a tie-dye fire of colour that would have made any Grateful Dead fan happy.

I took a moment, thinking that I was just admiring the view. The reality was that I was getting my breath back after the climb, before dropping down on to the coastal path for the long run into Lancaster. Once on the path I never saw another soul, not surprising because by the time I'd emerged at the other end of the unlit, wooded path it was pitch black.

I was worried about my footing. I could just about see where I was planting each foot but if the light had been any worse I'd have been in trouble. Given how accident-prone I am I made a mental note to keep my head torch in my work backpack for any future such detours home.

By the time I stopped at the bottom of our street and called in the corner shop for a well-earned chocolate milkshake, leaving a pool of sweat on the floor in the chilled aisle, I'd ran for two hours. Which considering I'd only intended to run for about 30 minutes was an indication of how much I loved my running again.

That run actually surprised me because I'd had a hard week's training, including a total of 18 miles the day before. I'd got up early and ran ten miles before work and as the day wore on I still felt good so I went along to the COLT running session where I proceeded to push myself through eight miles of interval training, a leg-sapping session if ever there was one.

But the main reason for my surprise was because I'd done a fairly hilly 16 miles again on Saturday morning with Lesley, and every run with "Little Miss Competitive" is a tough one.

My heart rate on that particular run had been 156 beats per minute, a marked difference between the two runs. The extra beats were the result of a combination of the hills and the trying to keep up with the speedy brunette. Most men when they have their heart rate raised by an attractive woman have a pleasurable experience: breathing heavily, sweating, going weak at the knees and ready to collapse when they finish...oh hang on a minute.

I began the taper week for the Trimpell 20 in bed with a raging sore throat and the sort of headache that makes you want to hit your head against a wall just to make the pain go away. I didn't make it into work on the Monday or the Tuesday as I lay shivering under my duvet. Now it wasn't a case of full-on man-flu, more just a virus giving me a swift kick in the b******s to remind me that although I like to imagine myself as invincible I'm not.

By Wednesday I'd improved enough to go back to work, although I felt very stiff walking in. My whole body felt heavy on my legs. I should have paid more attention to what my body was trying to tell me but I ignored it. As the afternoon drew to a close it was pouring down. I had originally planned to walk home but the deluge changed my mind. I decided to run home, figuring with twisted logic that I'd get less wet that way. What an idiot.

The warning sign was there when I was getting changed at work. My heart rate monitor was showing me a rate of 172 beats per minute, and I was sat down putting my socks on. That was a racing rate BUT I wasn't racing, I wasn't even walking, I was sat down. I should have thought sod it and caught the bus home but being a man I figured it would calm down, so on went the running gear and off I set.

Within seconds my heart rate was 202, and I was moving slower than the cogs in Viking's head. In a eureka moment of unusual clarity I came to my senses and I stopped. I must have looked a bit of a prat walking home in shorts and a t-shirt in the middle of a thunderstorm but it was much better than the impending heart attack I was heading for.

Scared by what had happened I wore my heart rate monitor all that night, probably causing Em as much concern as myself. It was probably an over-reaction as I'd had no chest pains, tightness or tingling limbs and my heart rate steadily dropped as the night wore on. On waking the next day I felt much fitter and my heart rate was back within its normal parameters.

Eager to put the sorry incident to bed I decided to again attempt to run home. I had three days before my race and I needed to test myself. Thankfully my heart didn't scare me as it stayed around the 140 mark. I took it as a sign that I was over the short-lived virus and ready to race.

Trimpell 20 was a race of, go on have a guess at the distance. If you said 20 miles, give yourself a pat on the back, if you said three miles are you related to Viking? It wasn't a race I had been looking forward to at all. I didn't feel that I was in racing shape but racing 20 miles is kind of an essential test for an upcoming marathon.

On the morning of the race, like any race, I was itching to go. I couldn't wait for the starter to unleash the gathered throng of runners onto the course to do battle. No matter how the preparation had gone I was, and still am, ready to give it everything on race day. If they could bottle race day adrenaline I'm sure they would be able to cure most of the world's depression sufferers. It wasn't the perfect race morning but it was manageable. It started off cool and sunny. It would however warm up after the 11am start when myself, my cousin Mike, Lesley, a few people from COLT and about 500 others reacted to the klaxon and surged forward for the initial lap of the running track.

I didn't really have a game plan and didn't concentrate on pacing. I just went for it in an attempt to get round as quick as possible, and hopefully under three hours and 15 minutes. From my limited marathon experience I knew that if I wanted to crack London in less than four hours I'd need to set a decent benchmark at Trimpell.

I felt good through the first 12 miles or so, running what seemed like a steady and manageable pace. For some reason I wasn't paying attention to the pace on my Garmin. I'd set it to 'virtual partner' so the screen showed two digital stick-men racing each other. One was me and the other was the virtual time that I'd pre-programmed.

Ambitiously I'd put in a finishing time of two and a half hours and I was a few minutes ahead of this. My little pixel man was hammering the pixel man from Team Garmin. I still felt OK at 11 miles when I saw my parents and Em, and managed a little banter as I ran past.

But by 12 and a half miles I could feel myself slowing drastically. Lesley came past me at this point and quickly disappeared up the road after we panted a brief greeting to each other. I'd been telling her for weeks that she'd finish ahead of me but she wouldn't have it. Unfortunately for me it looked like my prediction was coming true.

My slowest mile came at 15 miles when it took me over 17 minutes to cover the distance. Mind you I'd calculated at that stage that barring a disaster I'd finish in less than three hours. I wasn't running that poorly, I'd just stopped to walk with my Dad for a bit and then had a chat with Em and my Mam. All very sociable for a Sunday by the river, but it played havoc with that particular mile split.

Coming into the last mile I was passed by my mate Chris Lawson from COLT. Since our initial meeting we'd run on a weekly basis and become quite pally. I initially tried to run with him but hit a brief bad patch and he pulled out a gap of a couple of hundred metres between us.

I dug in and chased him, he was slowly getting bigger in my sights as I started to reel him in. We hit the running track for two torturous laps, as Chris also speeded up, sensing that I was catching him. We really went for it as the family and COLTs cheered us on. Unfortunately I was ten seconds too late to catch him. Later on checking the data from my Garmin it would emerge that I'd run the last mile in six minutes and 50 seconds, the fastest of the day. I would be over the moon at that but as I crossed the line all I could think was "don't throw up, don't throw up".

I finished in 2.55:30, which I was very pleased with. Reflecting on my performance I knew that I could have run faster with a bit more pace intelligence, something that I knew I lacked. I needed not to go off too fast but rather run like a metronome, in a well-balanced rhythm. This would allow me to conserve energy for the later part of the marathon. I decided that I would try to employ that strategy in London.

It would be interesting. I don't know if you are the same but I'm great at the theory of running, swimming and cycling but once I get caught up in the atmosphere of a race the theory seems to go the way of the Dodo.

Mike had an amazingly strong race to finish in 2.15:14 which he hoped would see him get around London in around three hours, or under. Lesley too had a great race, running with strength and determination. She crossed the line a full 11 minutes ahead of me in 2.44:25.

Talking after the race I told her that she would run 3.45 at London easily. "If you have a good day you could even get close to 3.30," I said with a sincerity that brought a smile to her still-flushed face. But I couldn't leave it at that and added: "Which would give you a good for age place the year after, being a female veteran and all." I tell you if looks could kill, Trimpell would have been my last ever race.

I had a four-week gap in between Trimpell and London. I was not looking forward to running in the capital. My feeling was that I'd be glad to redress my training balance. It would be good to ditch the pavement pounding and burn some rubber on the road. I'd be glad to get it over with and move forward towards August and the Outlaw.

I started my recovery from Trimpell with a couple of short runs during the week, nothing strenuous. That Friday night Em had gone out with her friend Sarah and I was a bit bored. I'd already run home and felt strong so decided to do two hours in the cellar on the turbo trainer.

Now two hours on a turbo trainer is no mean feat. As any cyclist/triathlete will tell you, turbo training is dull, the scenery doesn't change, and I always seem to ache more than I do when I'm out on the roads. I passed the time watching a DVD on the old TV that I'd set up down there for nights like that.

Watching a DVD always made the time pass much quicker, whether it was the latest box set of *Lost* or a Spinervals custom cycle workout. Spinervals were the turbo trainer equivalent of the exercise DVD that people jump up and down to in the privacy of their own living room.

My viewing choice on this particular night was the 2003 Ironman World Championships from Kona. Pedalling away I got inspired watching Peter Reid storm his way to his third championship. As I left a small pool of Andy accumulating on the floor under the bike I felt very sorry for Tim DeBoon who was rushed to hospital in immense pain while in second place during the marathon. It turned out that he was passing two kidney stones!

How unlucky is that? You train all year, and that happens. How p****d off would you be? I'd be livid. It just showed that even the pros experience huge amounts of bad luck. As I jumped off the bike at the end of a leg sapping session I secretly hoped that I never experienced such a fatal blow to my race day ambitions.

That weekend the clocks jumped forward an hour in the early morning dawn of Sunday. That single movement of the clock hands signified the official start of summer here in the UK. Unfortunately the weather gods didn't get the memo. Biting winds and heavy snowfall were still the order of the day.

So with summer comes the triathlon season, and lighter nights mean more training. I love the fact that in summer you can get up and get out the door for a couple of hours of riding in the morning before work on deserted roads, listening to the dawn chorus. And after work we have light until about 9pm, giving a full four hours for some big cycling miles and the occasional brick session.

Summer is so much better than winter with long hours spent pounding the dark pavements or locked away on the turbo trainer in the cellar. Yes, you build your base over the winter, but come on, do any of us really enjoy, and I mean REALLY enjoy those long dark runs or the hamster ball-style cycle training?

Getting out on the open roads in sunshine is what it's all about for me. Struggling up some hill and then enjoying the view before descending at lightning speed to repeat the process over the next lump in your way. Even open water swimming beats swimming lap upon lap in a pool. Granted, when it starts again in May it's always frighteningly cold. Once you get over the initial shock though it's great fun.

I must have had open water swimming on my mind because I actually went swimming in the week after the clocks changed. It was April and I'm almost ashamed to admit this here that it was my first swim of the year. I was doing an Ironman race in less than four months and I hadn't even got my toes wet all year, unless I'd been running or cycling in bad weather.

I kind of had a valid excuse, or at least that's what I convinced myself. I had been really apprehensive after injuring my wrist in January. Thankfully though there were no ill effects and I actually could remember how to swim. At 7am that Wednesday I had the whole pool to myself as I swam 2,100m in just about 43 minutes. It wasn't fast, it wasn't pretty, but it was a start and one that I intend to build on as I started my three key sessions in each discipline. I just needed to get this pesky marathon training out of the way.

With two weeks to go until London I received two pieces of news that would leave me with very mixed emotions. On a sad note, my partner in crime, Viking, had to pull out of the London Marathon. He'd developed a bad back in the months after Frankfurt and never really hit any of his training goals, in fact he could hardly run at all. It was a decision that he didn't take lightly but it was much better for him to take time out and get his injury sorted out. It would actually be almost another 12 months before he was able to run again pain-free, which shows that if he'd attempted to run the marathon he'd have maybe done some permanent damage. I was gutted for him but totally understood.

The second piece of news was much better. On the Wednesday my publisher told me that my forthcoming book had gone to the number one spot in the UK pre-order chart for sports biographies. What's more I was the only non-professional sportsperson or journalist in the top 100. How surreal was that? I couldn't believe it. Little old me, a normal working bloke from a small town in a small corner of northern England, whose English skills leave a lot to be desired, was outselling global superstars.

I was amazed that people wanted to read my story when there were so many great sportspeople out there. I was more made up by this surprising turn of events because I knew that

I'd put as much time and effort into writing as I ever had with my training. I knew that books like a good album are very subjective. For every person that loves it you'll find an equal amount that hates it.

In the pub on Saturday night my mate Richard warned me to be prepared for the first negative review along the lines of "can't swim, can't ride, can't run, can't write". It was the perfect anecdote that I needed to bring me back down to earth.

That Sunday was unusual. I was having a rest day, something that my wife, Em, will tell you that I don't do well. I pace, I tut, I get restless and I drink way too much coffee. I'm not wired up to just sit around and do nothing. I suppose I could have gone to the small Yorkshire town of Skipton to watch my friends and COLT team-mates compete in the opening triathlon of the season. However I knew spectating would have given me itchier feet than resting.

So why was I doing nothing? It was seven days until the London Marathon, a race I would be competing in for the first time. I was resting my legs as in the previous week I'd trained every day, albeit lightly as I tapered for race day. The previous weekend I'd given my legs a good work out with a hilly 35 miles on the bike and a 15-mile run.

The run was only supposed to be a ten-miler but I got a bit carried away. I was visiting relatives in Crosby near Liverpool, and taking full advantage of the surrounding countryside for a run. It was one of those runs where I just felt privileged to be out there. The sun warmed the back of my neck as I ran through a meadow at the edge of a small wood. No aches, no pains, I felt strong.

Each stride being driven by the carefully chosen music in my ears. Faithless, Green Day and the brilliantly uplifting Popiholla by Chicane. I know that running with an mp3 player isn't everyone's cup of tea, but I find that on long runs mine really helps to keep me both sane and motivated. I'd never wear one in a race as I like to feel the atmosphere, and be aware of approaching footsteps chasing me down, which unfortunately happens a lot.

My Garmin told me that I was running at bang on eight minutes per mile pace, much faster than my intended marathon pace but my heart rate monitor told me that I wasn't particularly pushing myself. I turned on to the beach path instead of heading home. I had run nine miles and by turning the wrong way had just committed myself to another four at least.

Running along the beach was amazing. I could smell and taste the salt in the air as the cool breeze chilled the beads of sweat running down my face. I used to live on a small island and experience the sea every day, and this run reminded me how much I missed it. I completed my 15 miles in one hour and 56 minutes, almost metronome-like in my pacing. Something that I promised myself I'd work on since my run at Trimpell, my pacing was coming together nicely and at the ideal time.

That run however couldn't have been further removed from what was supposed to be my last long run before the race. It took place the week before and I was running 16 miles with Lesley. After about 13 miles I was really struggling and feeling wiped out. We were only running about nine minutes per mile pace but my heart rate was about 20 beats per minute higher than it should have been. All I could do to lower it was to stop and walk, but as soon as I started to run again it shot up and I felt light-headed.

I think poor Lesley thought she would end up carrying me home, which given she's about 80 pounds lighter than me wouldn't have done her back any good. Luckily for her I made it home without her assistance. Once at home I started to throw up, and when I went to the toilet I was peeing a brown-coloured liquid. I instantly realised that I was dehydrated and spent the afternoon rehydrating carefully with sports recovery drinks.

The worrying thing was that while I had been running I didn't feel thirsty, and it wasn't particularly hot. I had run longer and harder before without suffering, however I'd had a virus earlier that week and it must have taken more out of me than I realised. So I was really glad of the Liverpool run as it raised my spirits going into London.

However there was another significant event that happened on that final Sunday before the marathon. One that would change my build-up in those final few days, one that would change my preparation for the Outlaw, and ultimately one that would change my life forever.

10

FOUR LITTLE WORDS

Isn't it funny as we go through life that sometimes the shortest of sentences can have the biggest impact? I love you. I'm leaving you. You're hired. You're fired. Guilty. Not guilty. I'm sorry. I'm not sorry. You've won. You're disqualified. Congratulations. Commiserations.

All of those and many more can be life-changers. Sometimes they are good, sometimes they are bad, but all of them have a profound effect on the recipient. I got one of those sentences just after I'd returned from a leisurely ride with Andy H on the final Sunday before the marathon. I thought something was amiss as when I got back Em was awake and washing down her toast with a cup of tea.

I sat on the edge of the bed and said, "Didn't expect to see you up, I thought you'd be having a lie-in?" Swallowing some toast she smiled and said: "I'm late."

"Late? Late for what? Where are you going...oh...LATE!?" It suddenly dawned on me that I was hearing one of those sentences. I reached for her hand, my mind was racing, and I had so many questions. "How long?" was the first one that sprung to mind.

"Just a few days, might be nothing," was her cautious reply.

We sat in silence nervously grinning at each other. "Do you think I should take a test?" Em asked, squeezing my hand. I agreed, after all there was only one way to find out. We stood up and embraced. It really felt like the next chapter of our lives was about to begin. Em grabbed the pregnancy test kit out of her drawer and kissed me before heading to the bathroom. "Next time I see you you might be a Dad," she said excitedly as she closed the door behind her.

I couldn't sit still. I paced the bedroom like a caged tiger. I quickly threw on a clean t-shirt and some jeans, it just didn't seem appropriate to await the most important news of my life in sweaty lycra. When we had saved up to go on our South African trip we had known that it would be our last 'big' holiday because we wanted to start a family. On returning Em had gone to see her doctor and told him of our plans, and he referred her to the consultant at the hospital.

When she was a child Em had emergency heart surgery to save her life. She got breathless one day and was taken to the doctors. Her regular doctor was off sick and a stand-in who happened to be a heart specialist treated her. He suspected that she had a major defect known as a hole in the heart. She was admitted to hospital and operated on, and the doctor had been right. A hole was discovered that if left untreated would have been fatal by the time she matured. The surgery was successful and part of a pig's heart was used to fill the hole.

Thankfully Em made a full recovery and apart from the 12-inch scar that often attracts the stares of strangers on the beach or in the pool you'd never know what she'd been through and how close to death she'd come. The problem was that at some of the check-ups she attended as an adult she was given conflicting advice from the different doctors she saw about getting pregnant. She'd been told "having children will be fine, it's nothing to worry about". Yet in stark contrast she'd also been told "your heart wouldn't take the strains of pregnancy, I'd advise against it".

We were desperate to have kids but we needed to know that Emma would be safe. A whole raft of tests was done and the heart surgeon gave us the news that we longed for, it would be safe to start trying for a family. The hospital did add that if Emma fell pregnant they would monitor her a lot more given her medical history, and that given that her heart condition was hereditary there would be a slightly heightened risk of the baby's heart being affected. Being positive people we decided that we just couldn't see lightning striking twice and started trying, which wasn't exactly a hardship.

I just kept pacing the bedroom, waiting for Em to emerge, thoughts racing in my head.

Wow I'm going to be a dad. S**t we are going to need a bigger house. How are we going to afford that? I'll be gutted if it's negative. When do we tell our parents? I wonder if it will be a boy or a girl? Please let it be normal and healthy. What's keeping her in there, surely it doesn't take that long to pee on a plastic stick. Maybe she's nervous and can't go, like me at a race just before the off, I know I need to pee but I just can't. Don't be daft she'll be fine. Isn't it weird how new life is confirmed by going to the toilet. What will we call it? I can't stop shaking. She's been five minutes, that can't be good. I need a coffee. What do you do with babies? Am I too old to be a dad? Am I mature enough to be a dad? What do I say to her if it's negative? Please be positive. Please be positive.

The creaking bathroom door that I'd been meaning to oil for months opened with a sound that magnified the importance of the moment. That creak sounded like a 12-gun salute from the Royal Artillery at the Edinburgh Military Tattoo. Startled, I turned and stared at my beautiful wife stood in the doorway, the light from the window behind her making her look like she was blooming. She was glowing. She was wearing a bloody poker face.

I threw my arms around her shoulders and looked down into her eyes for any sort of clue. She gave none. Feeling like I was about to burst, I said probably too abruptly: "Well?"

Em smiled, rose up on her toes and kissed my lips firmly. Was it a kiss of reassurance or one of regret? I just couldn't tell. In a heartbeat she moved her head and whispered in my right ear, the teasing was done. "We're having a baby," she giggled.

Four little words that stopped the world as I picked her up in my arms and spun her around. We both couldn't stop laughing, it was the news we had hoped for. Suddenly I realised that I was carrying a pregnant lady in my arms and given how accident-prone I am I promptly set her back down on her feet before I dropped her. We sat on the bed and babbled at each other like excited kids for ages, lost in our own little bubble of happiness.

"I can't believe we're going to be parents. You are going to be an amazing mum, I can tell. I mean you already mother the poor cat to death. And isn't it great that I've got strong little swimmers, it must have been all the practice I've done this year in the lake and the pool."

I laughed before being battered with a couple of pillows.

11

A VIRGIN AT THE LONDON MARATHON

I lay there staring at the ceiling, just staring, thinking about the weekend that had just gone. It was 5am the day after the marathon and I was shattered. I hadn't slept that night as every time I moved in bed the pain in my legs reminded me of what I'd put my body through earlier that day.

I was feeling every inch of the 26.2 miles that I'd run through the streets of London. My left Achilles felt like someone was sticking hot needles in it, it wasn't happy with me for what I'd put it through. I lay there feeling a burning thirst rising in my throat, but I couldn't bring myself to move and get a drink, as the kitchen was downstairs. At that precise moment stairs were just terrifying. Anyone who's ever ran a marathon will understand what I'm on about.

That pain that I was feeling just lying there on that particular morning meant as much to me as the medal that a nice volunteer had put round my neck the day before because it proved that I had given my all. I didn't run as fast as I would have liked BUT I couldn't have run any quicker, so in my mind I can't say fairer than that. Let me talk you through my one and only experience of the London Marathon.

Em, myself and my cousin Mike travelled down together on the Friday before the race. I was possibly more nervous about the journey than I was the race. I'd been fussing over Em and her condition, only to be reminded once more: "I'm pregnant, not ill you know!" Thankfully the three of us managed to get seats as the train seemed fairly quiet.

I hated travelling by train. I'd spent seven years commuting with up to two hours a day on the cattle trucks that passed as public transport. It always seemed to me like they were either breaking down or didn't have enough seats forcing me to stand all the way home. I had also concluded that outside every station was a big sign saying "weirdos not only welcomed, but encouraged especially if you sit next to that Holgate bloke". Even writing about trains just made me shudder.

Anyway, my irrational phobias aside we all survived and arrived in the big smoke, checking into some dive near Paddington Station that might have passed for a hotel in the 1960s. Paper thin walls, psychedelic wallpaper, a TV with a coat hanger aerial, soap on a rope complete with complimentary pubic hair attached, and they were the positive points. It was the sort of hotel, and I use that word loosely, that even *TripAdvisor* wouldn't have a low enough rating for. As I'd been in charge of booking the accommodation I only had my penny-pinching self to blame. Thankfully my understanding wife and cousin didn't seem that bothered, after all it was only a place to kip. After we dumped our bags Mike and I headed off to the Excel conference centre to register and Em headed off to Covent Garden for a latte, some cake and a spot of people-watching. I was disappointed in the Expo, it no longer seemed to have the captivating allure that had held me as a kid when my Dad did the race. It was just stall after stall of people trying to sell me things, which in reality was what it was back in the 1980s as well.

Back then I was probably just too innocent to notice, and saw it as a place of running stars and freebies. Now as an adult I saw the reality of what it was: a way to get runners to spend more money. I usually have no problem parting with money for running gear but I left with nothing that afternoon. My Expo expectations just go to show that if you give a kid a free trinket you've got them hooked for life. I guess some would call it the

"Happy Meal principle". I must have spent thousands of pounds over the years on Asics trainers because someone gave me a pen and a balloon as a kid at the Expo.

On the night before the race we decided that we'd just eat near the hotel and then fall into bed early. We wandered around aimlessly looking for somewhere to get pasta and failed. We actually ended up in Subway eating sandwiches, not the ideal preparation but we figured there would be some carbs in there somewhere. The drinks machine had broken so after we'd finished eating we decided to pop across the road to the Golden Arches to grab a latte to take back to the room.

At this point poor Mike didn't know that Em was pregnant, as we'd only told our parents and both our brothers. His face was a picture when she declared she was hungry and ordered large fries, a filet of fish and a milkshake. He'd just watched my petite wife polish off a foot-long tuna sub and two cookies not ten minutes earlier. I think he thought that she had worms or something. To top the night off as we walked the hundred metres back to the hotel, Em declared that she "needed" chocolate and dived into a shop to buy a couple of bars. Eating for two had begun with a vengeance.

My race day started at 6am when Mike and I got up to eat breakfast. I had my usual race day breakfast of porridge and he had a tuna sub sandwich, trying to convince me that it was a great choice. There was no way I could have stomached that at that time of the morning. I already knew that Mike had an asbestos stomach as he always sought out the hottest and spiciest food he could find. His favourite dish at the local curry house was something called the "Cinderloo" which we joked caused him to "singe-the-loo" the next day.

He wolfed down the sandwich and started to munch on a couple of bananas as I went to say goodbye to a sleeping Em. In a couple of hours she would be jumping on the Tube to meet up with Lesley's family: Richard, Jake and Charlie. Together the four of them were going to dash from point to point on the course trying to spot Lesley and me among the thousands of runners. I felt reassured that I wouldn't be leaving Em all alone and pregnant in London. I kept forgetting that she is a city girl and as such she has more streetwise smarts than I have bikes.

Mike and I headed towards Charing Cross station to catch the train up to the start at Blackheath. Runners seemed to come out of every doorway and side street as we approached the station. The concourse was in total chaos as thousands of tracksuited nervous people were herded on to a couple of trains by half a dozen transport workers. Their shouts of direction were tinged with stress as they tried to organise the chaotic throng.

The train was so crowded that I couldn't breathe out without my chest touching the person in front of me. Just when we thought it couldn't get any worse, ten more people were physically pushed on to the train. All of a sudden my nose was touching the wicking fabric of another competitor's armpit as he hung onto the overhead handrail.

Anyone with claustrophobia would have been in hell. The heat on that train was horrible, not to mention the smell, thousands of nervous stomachs didn't make for a very pleasant journey. Mind you it must be a logistical nightmare to try and get almost 37,000 runners and their supporters from central London out to Blackheath, and I can't help but admire the organisers for their efforts.

Half an hour later we were at the start. It was the usual pre-race chaos but magnified one hundred fold. Bin liner-clad runners joined queues for the Portaloos that seemed a mile long, some annoying bloke was talking nonsense on a PA system, a chorus of Garmins beeped as satellites were found through the rain clouds, and lines of trucks as far as the eye could see were being filled with red kit bags.

One thing that I'd never seen before was a sign saying "Female Urinals". Mike and I stood there trying to figure out just what they entailed as we stripped off down to our race gear. By the time I shook his hand and wished him luck, and headed for a slower pen, we still didn't have a clue. And that is probably for the best.

The start at London is a precise logistical affair with three different starts and various pens for athletes to line up in. When we'd registered for the race the year before we'd had to put down our expected finishing time and as a consequence we were allocated a coloured start and a pen number. This was all indicated on the numbers the runners wore on their chests. Then within each pen attached to the lampposts were signs indicating the estimated finishing times, for instance 3.15 to 3.30, 3.30-3.45 etc.

Mike was at the front of pen two, looking for a time just under three hours. I wasn't as good as that so I lined up in pen three at the blue start, just below a lamppost sign saying 3.45-4.00. I stood for several minutes staring at my shoes, wiggling my legs and arms, trying to keep loose.

As TV helicopters swirled overhead, loudspeakers announced "five minutes until the start" which was the cue for the officials forming barriers between the pens to move out of the way. It was like a sluice gate had been opened as the thousands-strong pack of runners surged forward along the road, jostling for position. I was a bit slow off the mark, not expecting that, and hundreds of people shuffled past me before I came to my senses and moved forward myself.

Naturally we all came to a stop as the space in front of us was swallowed up. I looked to my right and couldn't believe my eyes, there was my friend and training partner, Lesley. What were the chances at a start line that contained over 20,000 people of accidently standing next to one another? In those final minutes we chatted and wished each other luck. Then it started. A voice from above: "Ten, nine, eight...three, two..."

The noise of all the runners was deafening, so much so that I didn't even hear the starting gun/siren, I only knew that the race was underway when I saw the crowd in front of me start to move. There was only slightly more room than there had been on the train earlier. I quickly lost sight of Lesley as in the final surge across the line she had gotten a few yards ahead of me and was swallowed up in the crowd. I secretly hoped to pass her later, but I had a sneaky suspicion that such a move would be difficult given her form going into the race. All I could do was run my own race and see what the outcome would be in a few hours' time.

The first mile went by in just under ten minutes. I wasn't deliberately running slowly, I just couldn't physically move any quicker. The pattern was set for the rest of the race as my eyes focused on the six-inch space in front of me, and I kept altering my short stride pattern to avoid tripping over fellow runners' feet.

Feed stations along the route would become a nightmare as the race went on as discarded gel wrappers and bottles became tricky obstacles to avoid. Later as I slowed down it felt like I had to almost jump over each one, rising higher and higher making me feel like Mario jumping over barrels in a video game.

Disaster almost struck me as I passed through the first aid station. Runners were throwing their discarded bottles of water to the side of the road. One such bottle landed under my left foot and I went over on my ankle resulting in instant pain. Luckily I didn't hit the floor where I would have been trampled.

For a second or two I thought my race was over. The heat and the pain in my ankle were annoying but grimacing I managed to run it off. I spent the rest of the race taking extra care and watching where I placed my feet, jumping barrel after barrel.

In the build-up to the race I'd been worried about the heat and becoming dehydrated, but thankfully on race day the sun didn't come out until the final few miles. It was however pretty humid all morning. Since waking up that morning I'd consumed a cup of coffee and two pre-race bottles of Powerade in a bid to stay hydrated. I know coffee dehydrates the body but I just don't function without it.

I'd obviously hydrated too well before the race because at three miles I had to stop for a 'comfort break', dashing off the side of the road into a portable toilet block. It was a huge relief to empty my bladder as I'd pretty much needed to since the gun went but there was nowhere to go. If you could actually find a way through the rows of spectators the only options were the gardens of some very nice-looking houses. I didn't fancy getting arrested on my London debut for peeing in a plant pot.

I felt so much lighter as I waited at the side of the road trying to find a gap in which to jump back into the race, and luckily in seconds I'd re-joined the masses en route to The Mall. The race seemed to be going by very quickly, although I seemed to be running well within myself.

It was strange, I expected to see lots of landmarks that I'd watched on the TV for the last 30 years or so, but as I was actually running these were very difficult to spot. Even the famous tea clipper, *The Cutty Sark*, whizzed by without me realising I'd passed it. It was only on the journey home discussing the race with Mike that I realised where it had been. OK, it was shrouded in scaffolding for essential repairs but I'd missed it because I was consciously looking at the runner in front of me, trying not to catch their heels.

At the Expo I'd picked up a pace band from the *Runner's World* stall. These simple, free, and yet very effective plastic wristbands were designed to help runners pace their perfect race. There were 26 individual mile time splits written on them, so that you could work out at what time you should reach each mile with the ultimate goal of getting to the finish in the time you wanted.

I was wearing a pace band for a finishing time of three hours and 45 minutes, which if I had a great day I felt I could achieve. Going through every mile I was about ten to 20 seconds behind the pace. I was pleased with this because I have a tendency to go off too quickly in races. I felt comfortable at that pace, my breathing wasn't laboured and my legs weren't grumbling. I was running along smiling to myself.

Just after passing the 11-mile marker I got a boost as I managed to spot my wife Em in the crowd. Or rather I spotted Lesley's husband, Richard, who happens to be about 6ft 4ins and Em was stood next to him. I would never have spotted Em if she'd been on her own. Richard's booming voice alerted me to "look in that direction" and he actually pointed to Em stood below him, blending into the crowd. Later I would also spot them at Canary Wharf and on the Embankment, and each time I couldn't help but increase my speed in response to their enthusiasm.

Just before the halfway point I crossed Tower Bridge. I just turned the corner from a street full of kebab shops and there it was looming ahead of me in all its majesty. It was a welcome sight because I knew it meant I was almost at the halfway point, which gave me a good feeling. To me it seemed that the bridge was straining under the weight of all the people on it.

The level of the support on the bridge was overwhelming. Deafened by the shouts, cheers and blasts from various air horns I couldn't actually hear my own breathing. Halfway across the bridge between the iconic towers there were strips of timing mats, which we had to run over to get our race splits, and more importantly to prove that we'd actually done the race.

In the past at London and various other marathons around the world people had been disqualified after running amazingly quick times. What was their secret? Diet? Training? Shoes? No, they took the Tube and didn't actually run the whole way. Perhaps the most famous example of this type of cheating took place at the 1980 Boston Marathon. Rose Ruiz came out of nowhere to win the most prestigious marathon in the world at that time.

People were instantly suspicious that in doing so she had recorded the third fastest time ever by a woman, running 2.31:56. Bill Rogers, the legendary distance runner, had won the men's race and in talking to Ruiz afterwards found it incredible that she didn't recall some of the course landmarks, especially the tough hills. Officials and rather more damning the TV cameras had missed her on the course as they focused on the lead group of female athletes. Where had Ruiz been?

Witnesses eventually came forward to say that they had seen her on the underground and she was disqualified and banned. Ruiz to this day maintains her innocence but has never even come close to running that sort of time again. It was as a direct result of the Ruiz incident that development started on eradicating cheating in races with the use of closed circuit TV and an RFID chip timing system. So next time you race and get accurate splits when you finish you can thank Rosie and her cheating.

At least some good came of it. As we approached the bright

orange timing mats that would talk magically to the chip attached to our shoelaces some poor guy in front of me was too busy waving at the TV cameras. He didn't spot the mats. He tripped and landed face first on the tarmac. I winced as I passed him, but medics were already at his side.

Passing over the bridge the course swung to the right and I headed out through the Isle of Dogs towards Canary Wharf. At this point the elite runners were on the other side of the road and heading for home. Like gazelles they looked amazingly graceful as their effortless strides carried them past me in a heartbeat. It must be nice to be able to run like that I thought to myself as I plodded along, more of a hippo than a gazelle.

As I passed the 17-mile marker I was consciously aware for the first time that I was slowing down. Glancing at my wrist, I was now a minute down on my pace guide. I got a much needed boost from my fellow Pirates at the Mudchute feed station but despite their support I found the whole Canary Wharf section of the race to be difficult with its twists and turns. It felt like I was just running in a never ending maze.

Before I knew it I was back at Tower Bridge and my legs were about to get a shock. There was a short sharp hill down into an underpass, the scene of one of the race's iconic moments. In 1985 my hero Charlie Spedding was running neck and neck with Steve Jones, the Welshman who remains Britain's fastest marathon runner. The helicopter filming them lost the duelling pair as they went undercover. Moments later only Spedding emerged.

Surely it was a winning move, he had a large lead. Jones came out of the tunnel going like a steam train and against the odds caught the Geordie and went on to win the race in 2.08:16. It later transpired that Jones had stopped for a pee while the cameras were out of range, something Paula Radcliffe failed to do almost 20 years later on her route to victory. How the times have changed! The descent into the underpass hurt me, the change in running stance and the extra pressure on my quads took away all my leg strength, and that essentially was my race over. I tried to pick up my pace but it was like I was running along dragging someone holding my ankles. My head was fine but my legs just wouldn't listen.

I knew as I emerged out of the tunnel on to the Embankment that my pre-race goal of going under four hours was beyond me. There was still a chance that I could beat my stand-alone marathon PB (my quickest was in a triathlon) of 4.17 but it wasn't looking good as I was passed by a rhino, a Mr Man and a woman in a wedding dress. I hope she made it to the church on time.

With just over one mile to go I was joined by a fellow Pirate, "Hess", and together we kept each other moving along to the finish, rounding the corner and passing Big Ben and the Houses of Parliament. As we approached The Mall, Hess moved ahead. He had more left in his legs and quickly opened up a large gap on me.

The imposing sight of Buckingham Palace was most welcoming as I knew that as I turned the corner into The Mall the race would be almost over. I had enjoyed the race but I had suffered towards the end. There were no excuses, I'd just run out of steam. Maybe I was undertrained, I was certainly carrying too much weight, but I'd done it. I'd followed in my Dad's footsteps and finally completed the London Marathon, albeit in a much slower time than him.

I crossed the line and managed a smile for the cameras, a mixture of pleasure and relief, and a nod to those watching at home that I was OK and in one piece. I had finished in a new personal best time of 4.13:05 and on checking the results later it would transpire that I had finished in the top half of the field (just) in 14,222nd place.

I was filed through the efficient finishing system: chip removal, medal collection, kit bag collection and goody bag collection. The poor guy trying to direct me to the finish photo opportunity area looked dismayed when I told him "I can't be arsed with that". I just wanted to meet Mike and Em at our designated meeting point on Horse Guards Parade and get out of London as quickly as possible. The race was done, it was now time to go before the transport system ground to a halt.

I managed to meet Mike straight away. He'd finished in 3:45, and he was quite pragmatic about his performance, initially disappointed in his time but still pleased to get his first marathon done. Mike sat on the floor in the early afternoon sunshine as I wandered around trying to spot Em or the English family. Growing more p****d off with each passing minute, I ached, I needed the toilet, and I just wanted to go home.

Upon retrieving my mobile phone from my kit bag my mood wasn't helped when I discovered that in the middle of the busiest city in the country I had no bloody signal. Unfortunately Em was trapped on the Embankment with no way of contacting me and it would be over two hours before she made it to Horse Guards Parade and the athlete meeting point. When we finally did meet up poor Em looked more knackered than me. She'd been on her feet all morning and as the temperatures started to rise she understandably began to flag. I instinctively gave her my bottle of water, which she gulped down having drank all of her supplies while trapped amongst the Embankment crowd. I thanked Richard and the boys for looking after her and we were just heading for the Tube to Euston when Lesley came through the crowd. She had a beetroot-coloured face but she was grinning like a Cheshire cat. She had finished in a new personal best time of 3.53:55, some 5,000 places ahead of me. I'd once more been well and truly "chicked" by my mate. It was unfortunately becoming the pattern of the year after Trimpell. I was really pleased for her though as I knew just how hard she'd worked for it.

The journey home was more harrowing than the last few miles of the race. As we limped towards Trafalgar Square station to catch the Tube up to Euston Station, and the train home, Mike's legs seized up. He had to hold on to the wall as we walked along the street. He just managed to descend into the underground station, wincing aloud with each painful step.

What greeted us there was a scene from hell. Thousands and thousands of people were crowded into the access tunnel to the platforms below. It took us nearly an hour from crossing the ticket barrier to actually getting on one of the trains. The heat in the tunnel was unbearable and even the hot air of a passing train was a welcome relief.

Eventually we made it to Euston and on to the platform for the Virgin train home. Virgin were the company that sponsored the marathon, so you'd think they would have laid on extra carriages that weekend knowing that thousands of people would be flooding the rail network. The train we boarded was almost as packed as the one that Mike and I had taken earlier that morning. Em managed to fight her way through to a seat but unfortunately Mike and I could only find a space stood by the doors.

Unsurprisingly for me it was the only space that some drunk could find as well. I spent the next three hours on my feet being serenaded with a drunken out-of-key version of Oasis's Wonderwall and listening to his life story, which thankfully for you I won't share here. Once again I found myself cursed on a train.

And to make matters worse every time I looked over at Mike supping his cans of celebratory Guinness he was trying to make me laugh. Years of working in a public library had taught me never to laugh at a drunk, as things might turn ugly. Just like during the marathon I became very familiar with my shoelaces as I stared at my feet, wishing for the journey to end.

As I stood there trying to ignore my surroundings I reflected on my day. At first I was a bit disappointed as I didn't get the time I wanted. However I'd got a PB, I'd ran quicker than I had at Hamburg. I couldn't help but be pleased with my performance.

My build-up hadn't been perfect having lost all of January to a broken wrist. Those weeks without running were probably the reason I'd run out of steam in those final miles. There was also the fact that this race wasn't my 'A' race. I needed to peak for the Outlaw and this had been part of the journey, it wasn't the destination.

That night, finally sat with my feet up, I spoke to my Dad on the phone. I learned that my brother Craig had ran brilliantly to finish in 2.36:08, and we both joked that he didn't beat my Dad's time, as no matter how fast either Craig or myself ran, we still weren't quick enough.

Even Haile Gebrselassie and Patrick Makau wouldn't beat my Dad's time and they were the quickest in the world. It was an unwritten rule. When my Dad asked for my thoughts on the race I'd had a while to think about the day and replied honestly.

"I'm pleased with my efforts. I really enjoyed the actual race, I didn't enjoy all the chaos that went with it. In terms of atmosphere and enjoyment I don't think London is a patch on the Hamburg Marathon, maybe just being abroad made that feel special. And neither of them compare to the magical experience of Ironman Germany.

"I don't think anything will ever top that. That's not me being critical of London, I'd recommend that everyone does this race at least once. I've done it now, I loved it but I really have no desire to do it again."

I could tick another one off my bucket list, and start concentrating again on Ironman training, once I got back from holiday.

12

SICK AS A PARROT

When I finally did drag my sorry carcass out of bed on the day after London, it was for a very good reason. It was to drive to the airport, as Em and I were due to catch a flight to Munich in Germany for a few days of rest and relaxation.

Even getting dressed that day had been a struggle as my body seized up but it had also given me a strategic opportunity. I made sure that I wore my bright red marathon finishers' t-shirt in a vain attempt to explain to passers-by why I was limping through the airport like a 90-year-old with gout.

My legs were mostly fine, it was just my left Achilles that was really painful. Earlier as I'd lay in bed too scared to go and get a drink because of the evil stairs I'd surmised that the pain near my ankle was a direct result of standing on a discarded water bottle in the first few miles of the race. If I'd been on a training run I probably would have walked and then given up, headed home and iced the affected area. However you just can't do that when you are in the first mile of the world's biggest race, and now I was paying the price for that.

As we passed through the duty free shop I had to ask Em to slow down and wait for me, and this role reversal amused her no end. Flying with a budget airline meant that there was no air bridge so instead I had to limp up the stairs. As I boarded the plane the stewardess inspected my boarding pass and then noticed the t-shirt.

"Excuse me sir, did you do the marathon yesterday?" she

enquired. When I told her that I had, she quickly grabbed the intercom and told the whole plane, prompting the passengers and crew to respond with polite applause. It was a wonderful touch, and utterly unexpected. I blushed like a schoolgirl on a first date as I limped down the aisle thanking people as I passed.

On the Tuesday I limped around following Em as we explored the ancient Bavarian city. We enjoyed a bit of shopping, well she did, I mostly sat outside, grateful for the opportunity to get off my feet. We found a wonderful ice cream parlour just opposite the infamous Beer Keller and I indulged my sweet tooth in apple ice cream. It tasted divine and I'm convinced that it had medicinal qualities. Why? Well because on the Wednesday morning I woke up, I was pain free, and felt like I could run again. It must have been the magical healing powers of the ice cream. Unfortunately that morning was when Em started to be ill.

I was happy that I could walk down the stairs and not have to use the lift as we headed into the hotel dining room and the breakfast buffet. Em was in good spirits and looking forward to her breakfast. I was tucking into my scrambled eggs when she went deathly pale. She'd just taken her first mouthful of cereal when she kicked her chair back and fled the hotel breakfast room at a speed that would have impressed Usain Bolt. What the hell?

I shot after her wondering what was wrong, really quite concerned. I'd never seen her act like that. I found her outside the front of the hotel. She had made it out into the street and was violently sick right in front of the dining room window. The poor French family sat in the window gazing on the technicolor display from Em instantly put down their cutlery and left the room. I smiled apologetically as they left, hoping it wouldn't start a chain reaction of vomiting.

A few moments later Em righted herself, her grey cheeks now flushed with colour, and said: "At least I managed to be sick down a drain." She was partly correct. "Err pet, that's not a drain it's the air conditioning vent for the hotel's basement kitchen!" Thankfully we weren't booted out on to the street by the understanding hotel management, and the next morning the French family still spoke to us after I indicated that Em wasn't just hung over but actually was pregnant.

In a complete flip of the first few days of the holiday, I was the fully fit one and poor Em was struggling. She was having a torrid time, and whatever she ate just came back up a couple of hours later. In a desperate attempt to help I rang my Mam at home and got her to find out what was supposedly good for morning sickness. I went to the supermarket and bought ginger biscuits, lemons and dry crackers, all of which seemed to go down well and the vomiting eased a little. The magical ice cream also seemed to help and each night Em looked forward to her lemon ice cream. It was the one thing she didn't throw up while we were in Munich.

Em survived the flight home without being sick. I'd never seen her so worked up before as we waited at the airport, which was about the only good thing to happen that week. Alarmingly Em got steadily worse and was admitted to hospital after a few days back in England with severe dehydration and sickness. Things had got so bad that she couldn't even keep water down. She ended up losing over a stone in a week, and she's only slightly built anyway.

She was seven weeks pregnant and being fed through a drip. It was such a worrying time. One of the doctors said that the severe sickness was more common when twins were being carried. We both laughed and said they didn't run in our family, only to find out later that day from both sets of parents that they did. We weren't ready for twins, we'd only just started to think straight about one baby let alone two.

The doctors decided that because of the family history and the sickness they needed to check the condition of our baby – or babies. Our concern was starting to grow. A hastily arranged ultrasound scan took place which at first was terrifying, sat there in the dark not knowing if what we would see on the grainy monitor would lead to heartache or joy. You could cut the tension in the air as the radiologist moved her magic scanning wand over Em's gel-covered belly. I gripped my wife's hand tighter than I ever had before, I couldn't look at the screen.

"There's the head, and an arm, everything seems to be OK," said the reassuring voice. I could have kissed the radiologist, however I came to my senses and kissed the hand that I had been holding so tightly. I looked at the tadpole-like figure on the screen and was hit with an instant tidal wave of joy. It took all my self-control not to cry, and suddenly the room seemed very smokey. "Are you sure there is only one?" was Em's nervous response to the radiologist. In my moment of joy I'd forgotten about the prospect of twins, and suddenly my attention was peaked again. "As far as I can tell, there is only one heartbeat." Em and I breathed a collective sigh of relief.

It was so good to know that our baby was fine. I think the news certainly started to help Em recover. She'd been more stressed out about it than she'd let on. Eventually after a week Em was well enough to come home, but she was to have total bed rest. I took a few days off work to play nurse maid and Em started eating again properly. The sickness never left and she would have good and bad days for the rest of her pregnancy, resulting in further hospital stays, but for now she was doing OK again.

While Em was so ill I didn't want to go out and leave her, so my planned marathon recovery went on a little longer. When Em was taken into hospital there were set visiting hours, so I managed to get a little training done. Some running was done between hospital visits and phone calls to worried friends and family but no more than three miles, there just wasn't time.

I was knackered. I wasn't sleeping and was extremely stressed and worried. Sat at home on my own I sought comfort in the wrong foods again, I had no time or energy for cooking and became a ready-meal addict. The salt-laden pasta dishes and breaded chicken burgers became my staple diet, topped up with chocolate bars. Things were not going well, all I cared about was being there for Emma, and I paid little attention to my own well-being. It would be almost a month before I felt like I could leave her to get out on the bike for more than an hour. Preparing for an Ironman that was 14 weeks away was pretty low on my radar to be honest.

Once I felt like she was strong enough to be left alone I did venture out on my bike, adjusting my routine and comfort zone to head out at 6am on weekend days. That time shift allowed me to get back in time for the patient to wake up. I had a couple of good strong rides of 45 miles and one of 60 miles which I was very pleased with.

I certainly wouldn't have scared anyone with my time of three hours and 40 minutes for the shorter ride but it served as a strong confidence booster. I was seriously lacking 'bike legs' as I edged closer to the Outlaw but I felt comfortable and could have kept going. It is those sorts of rides that you need when you are preparing for Ironman. Confidence is a great tool.

With me, whenever things seem to be going well again I always hit another speed bump in the road. I punctured on my ride over the May bank holiday weekend and despite the factor 50 sun cream that I thought I was lathered in I got badly sunburnt. I'm blaming the puncture.

The tyres on my road bike were Continental Gator Skins, and they were a total nightmare to get on and off. I can understand why people refer to them as being "bombproof". That particular morning my riding partner Andy H could see the frustration setting in and stepped in.

"Let me have a go before that wheel ends up being thrown into the field," he said. I happily stepped out of the way. One snapped tyre lever later he had the tyre removed. A new tube was placed onto the wheel and the tyre put back in place, a process that was only slightly easier than taking it off.

I decided to try my CO_2 cartridge for the first time. I had no patience for the traditional pump. WOW! The little sealed gas canister inflated the tyre in seconds and it was at full pressure. I was very impressed and decided there and then to always carry cartridges with me in future when I rode.

My running post-marathon was limited to short bursts fitted in around hospital visits, or half-hour breaks in patient care. Over a month had passed before I could run any significant distance. I ran for 12 miles on a Wednesday night including the COLT club interval session after 45 minutes of hard steady running. I was the slowest in the group and struggled to hang on as we did two pyramid sets of one, two and three minutes, then back down with two and one minutes, all with one minute of recovery.

My legs hurt, my lungs hurt and I felt a little despondent that people I'd been beating pre-London were now a good 50 to 100 metres ahead of me. At least I had people to chase, and that probably made me work harder than I would have done on my own. I had to try and find the positives out of those sessions or I would have just quit in my Outlaw attempt.

My swimming had also suffered as I missed my two club open water sessions. The first one was when I was visiting the hospital and for the second one I had an eye infection which stopped me swimming full stop for a week. The infection was probably caused by the stress I was experiencing.

Suddenly there were only 11 weeks to go until the Outlaw and I was seriously undertrained. I didn't have enough time to make up for all the training hours I'd lost, and given that in the run up to the marathon I'd neglected the bike in favour of running I knew that I was on a hiding to nothing really. I would be racing on adrenaline and experience, not miles and miles spent in the saddle, a factor that is an essential ingredient in a successful Ironman race.

I was giving serious consideration to quitting before I started, feeling I wouldn't do myself justice come race day. I was beginning to feel down about the whole thing when my friend Anna sent me an e-mail that changed my mood.

The bubbly Yorkshire lass had attended a training weekend put on by the organisers of the Outlaw and only had great things to say about it and the course. I couldn't help but be excited about that. Unknown to her, she had just stopped me from being a quitter. Thanks Broccers, as I look back now on that time I know I would have hated myself if I'd quit. I'm stronger than that, and your little nudge pushed me back from the edge. I owe you one.

Just when I thought nothing else could come along and kick me in the b******s I got blindsided with more testicular bruising stress. Ironically the day had started off brilliantly. That month's edition of *Tritahlete's World* magazine had just been published. It contained a nice article about me and my soon to be published book. I had been at the newsagent's on campus at 7.30am when they opened so that I could buy two copies. One copy was for me and the other for my proud parents, as it was the first time I'd appeared in a national magazine and we all wanted a copy. I walked around work that morning like the cat that got the cream. I shouldn't have been so smug. What's the phrase? Ah yes: "Pride comes before a fall." I was in for the mother of all falls.

I returned from my lunchtime run and started reading through my e-mails, and noticed that there was one from my publisher. With the publication date just over a month away I was eager for news. I excitedly opened it and read the words below:

Andy

> *Sorry not to have got back sooner to you but as you read on you will understand that I was preoccupied with other things over the last week, which all came to a head yesterday.*
>
> *Very sadly I have to tell you that Know The Score Books went into administration yesterday.*
>
> *It's been a terrible time and I have tried everything possible to keep us going, but we could not cope with the slump in sales and general depression of the industry.*
>
> *As you are not a creditor you will not receive formal notification from the administrator, but as you are a future published author the administrator is aware of your book. He is currently trying to find another publisher for you and will*

no doubt be in touch once that process has borne fruit.

    I am very sorry about what has happened and sorry that it may affect you. All the best and I hope the book makes it out there as it deserves to.

Yours
Simon

I couldn't believe what I was reading. I could feel tears welling up inside me as it slowly dawned on me that my book wasn't going to get published. I'd worked so damn hard and now it looked like it would come to nothing. I felt like such a fraud because I'd told all my friends, my family and numerous strangers online about the book. I'd created quite a buzz, and many people had paid out for a pre-order copy on the likes of Amazon. They were going to be disappointed.

I felt like one of those dodgy salesmen you see featured on *Watchdog* or similar consumer rights programmes. The sort of scum who go to old ladies' houses and con them out of their life savings, promising to deliver windows or a conservatory and then disappearing into the night without doing the job. Granted no one had forked out their life savings for me but the principle was the same, I'd promised something and not delivered.

I felt numb over the next few days as people contacted me to let me know that Amazon and others had sent them cancellation e-mails. All I could do was apologise publicly on my blog and Facebook.

It had been a horrible month and this just capped it all. I felt as sick as a parrot, but still not quite as sick as poor Em. I eventually got a little bit of perspective lying on the sofa at home massaging Emma's bump. "I'd love to be an author, it would be so cool to walk into a bookshop and see my book on the shelf in front of me but I'm going to be a Dad, and that is so much better. It's upsetting but there are bigger things out there for us."

"That's quite profound for you love. Keep positive, I'm sure that a new publisher will take it on. Anyway on to more important things, can you rub my back now please?"

I couldn't resist that smile, it was a smile that seemed to make even the darkest moments that much brighter. Surely I was due a few bright moments?

13

THE ANSWER IS YES

On the second Monday evening in June I managed to fit in my first open water swim since the previous September, and although the water was cold it wasn't freezing which was a bonus.

I had missed several of the COLT swimming sessions at the lake because of the way things had been at home. The sessions took place every two weeks and I'd just dropped unlucky with circumstances on those particular nights. But the fact was that since I'd cracked my wrist in January I'd been really neglectful of my swimming.

I only had myself to blame for that. I think it may have been psychological. Fear of aggravating my wrist played a part. However I think it was more a case of "well, no matter how hard I train I'm not going to make significant time gains like I would on the bike or the run". I'm sure that I'm not the only triathlete that thinks that? I kind of see swimming as a necessary evil, something that just gets me to the bike in one piece. Maybe I should take up duathlon?

I spent the first lap of the lake helping my mate, Chris Lawson. We'd arranged by e-mail that I'd swim with him because in the previous session he had panicked and had to be rescued by the safety boat. Apparently he'd clung to the canoe like glue, paralysed with fear. I promised Chris that I would stay with him, he could set the pace and together we'd get round.

I knew what he was going through. Your first ever open water swim never leaves you. Mine was cold, dark and scary. If human beings were meant to swim in deep dark bodies of water evolution would have given us webbed feet or flippers by now.

I had grown in confidence since my first swim and now felt at home in the open waters of a lake or a river. I'd not swum in the sea yet but that would eventually happen. I actually preferred swimming in the fresh water of the lake to the tepid heated artificial water in the pool. It felt natural, invigorating and most of all fun, something that one day just clicked into place in my head.

I had explained all this to Chris, and reassured him that in a year or two we'd look back on this and laugh. I knew Chris was destined to do an Ironman, he asked too many questions on a Wednesday night when we were running. He couldn't hide his interest or desire. I don't think he believed me when I had told him that one day he would swim under 90 minutes for 2.4 miles in an Ironman race. I think he thought it was just macho bravado that I was spouting to stop him from panicking but I saw a lot of myself in him and I knew that if I could do it then he certainly could.

As we walked down to the water's edge I could actually hear his breathing quickening. He looked really pale, his face a monochrome stark contrast to the matt black of his wetsuit. "Let's just stop, let everyone go. Just relax, concentrate on breathing easily because if you get in like this you'll panic. I'll be on your left within touching distance. If you stop, I'll stop." I hoped I'd reassured him as he just nodded at me in acknowledgement.

We waited a few moments and then waded in up to our waists, feeling the water and getting used to the temperature. That initial moment out of the zone seemed to work as I could see the determination rising inside my nervous friend as we stood there alone. After a moment of thunderous silence between us Chris moved his goggles into place, his eyes now a mirrored mask of plastic mystery. I could no longer read his thoughts, but I didn't need to.

"Come on let's do it," he said calmly and dove into the water. I quickly followed suit with a broad smile that dissipated as I held my breath into the first stroke of the swim. During our 500-metre loop Chris stopped a few times to gather his breath and his thoughts. We didn't speak other than a cautionary "you OK?" from me and a positive "yep" from him. It was one of those occasions where actions really were a lot louder than words.

He completed the lap and headed to the shore, swimming the 50 final metres on his own while I turned to swim a few more laps alone. Surprisingly I felt strong. Maybe I was on a high after what had just happened and I felt that I could have swam further but the fading light and the growing cold meant I headed for the shore after 1,600m. As I walked up the beach I was met by Chris, now dressed and drinking coffee. He looked like a different person to the one I'd seen not an hour earlier in the same spot. His grin said everything as he shook my hand.

It was one of the best moments I've experienced in triathlon. I knew in that moment that I'd actually made a difference. We would continue to swim together and we still do to this day. Chris is considerably quicker and more confident these days though. I'm proud to say that I played a minute part in that. On your own triathlon journeys if you get the chance to help a newbie as they seem to be referred to these days, just take a moment out of your training and lend them a hand. Remember where you once were and the people that helped you, and I guarantee that you'll feel brilliant about it, even when they eventually beat you – but more about that in future chapters.

As the Outlaw loomed on the horizon I continued to build up my bike and run mileage which led me to put in a 75-mile brick session one Saturday morning. I took the ROO, my TT bike, out for its first real long ride of the year. All of my longer rides had been done on my road bike up until that point. The weather had been less than ideal and the road bike with its slightly wider tyres and more forgiving geometry led to a more comfortable ride in harsh conditions.

I'd learnt in the past that if I went out on the ROO on

the exposed country roads around Lancaster I tended to have to battle to keep upright. The aerodynamic, lightweight frame seems to fall victim very quickly to crosswinds, and it makes for a very unpleasant ride. To me training is also about having fun, and those rides when I actually feel for my safety are never fun. The counter argument would of course be that if you ride the ROO more in harsh conditions it will become easier to handle. I understand that but for now I'd just rather feel safe. I was eager to get out early, wanting to spend the afternoon with Em. We had a trip planned to Mothercare to look at travel systems, which when I was a baby were known as prams. I was out of the door just before 7am without any breakfast, in an attempt to burn off some fat. To be honest it wasn't really the wisest nutrition decision I've ever made. I now always make sure that I eat something before heading out the door. Being properly fuelled is an essential part of any training and racing programme and back then I was stupid.

I guess when I looked in the mirror I could see that my body was slowly heading back to the bad old days when I'd weighed more than the entire cast of the Oompa-Loompas in *Charlie & The Chocolate Factory* and I panicked a little. I now firmly believe that for the fire to burn you have to feed it more fuel. Starve it and it will peter out.

I did eat however while I was cycling. I had three fig rolls, one every hour. I'd not eaten those things since I was kid, but had rediscovered them recently when Em started eating them. Their biscuit and fruity goodness were what she craved, along with fruit teacakes and vegetable ravioli.

We had stockpiles of the stuff. The fig rolls were easy to use on the bike but I didn't fancy carrying a can opener for the ravioli so knocked that idea on the head. Fig rolls became the new bike food of choice, although the existing champ, malt loaf, was still a firm favourite.

It was a really good ride around the lanes of Lancashire, taking in a few hills, but nothing too taxing. My legs felt fine. I wasn't in the form of my life but I had gradually come to terms with that. I knew that I might have to rethink my whole sub-12 hours ambitions given where I was but I was still confident that I could better my 12.57 PB in Nottingham. None of this the glass is half empty approach, just refill the bloody thing.

Arriving back at home I quickly changed from my bike shoes into my running shoes and headed out for three laps around the local park, a hilly run of five miles. The jelly legs appeared for a couple of minutes but I was soon into my running and again felt like I could have gone longer. The whole session took me five hours and two minutes, granted it was no Ironman but it was a good endurance session and one that I knew I needed.

Later on in Mothercare we ended up spending hundreds of pounds on the travel system which incorporated a pram that looked like an extra from a *Transformers* movie and a car seat. Adding in a few other 'essentials' there wasn't much change from a thousand pounds.

"That could have bought a really nice set of carbon wheels for the ROO," I half-joked as we got back into the car. "Andrew!" was the short reply. My Sunday name made me make a mental note of not to push my luck too much with the pregnant one, after all couldn't they get away with murder?

Pleased with how I had been progressing in training and keen to get that race feeling once more, I decided to enter the Cockermouth Sprint Triathlon, getting my entry in on the closing date. I don't know quite how it happened but this low-key, beginner-friendly Cumbrian event was my first triathlon since the behemoth of Ironman Germany the previous year.

The day before the race I laid out my gear that I would need for the event, and was confused. Surely I'd forgotten something? I stared at the items on the bed and went through them all again in my mind for the third time, checking for any obvious omissions. I couldn't think of any. All that I had was a tri top and shorts, running shoes, bike shoes, helmet, number belt, goggles and a bike. The last time I'd packed for a tri it was like a military operation, this really was getting back to basics.

The next morning I met up with Sarah Patterson, my COLT

club-mate who I'd be travelling north with to the race. The early Sunday morning traffic on the motorway was a breeze and we arrived in Cockermouth with plenty of time to spare before the race got underway.

Sarah had taken part in the race a few times over the years and talked very enthusiastically about it as we drove along between the beautiful Cumbrian hills. It had been her first sprint triathlon and as such it held a magical place in her heart.

You never forget your first triathlon. It's a bit like your first kiss, it might not be what you expected, you might get it wrong and you'll move on to much better ones but you'll never forget it. My first kiss was in the cinema with a girl called Vicky. Funnily enough I don't remember it quite as well as my first triathlon.

We registered and racked the bikes in a torrential downpour. My own personal raincloud seemed to be following me again. I'd not brought a plastic box or any cover for my shoes unlike the well-organised Sarah. Her cycling and running shoes would remain dry inside a covered plastic box while mine ran the risk of being swept out to sea. The rain would only get worse as the day went on. In fact the driest part of the day would be the swim.

It was a pool-based swim, with athletes in each lane, all setting off together. On poolside my two fellow swimmers and I chatted and watched as those before us set off open water-style with arms and legs churning in all directions in a bid to gain a territorial advantage. We quickly decided to be more civilised and worked out among the three of us an order to swim in, with the understanding that if we got it wrong we'd tap the swimmer in front's foot and change position at the end of the pool.

The race started and I was the slowest in my lane, which I had predicted. No foot-tapping was needed as the three of us in our wave stayed in the starting order throughout the swim. This was my first competitive pool swim for 13 months and I was surprised at how well it went. I had expected to be a little bit winded, as racing is a different animal to training. In the pool when I race I tend to get overexcited and forget the theory of breathing, and the mechanics of the stroke, basically just blasting it. On this occasion I seemed to be more mature about my swim, the technique stayed with me and my breathing wasn't laboured. I wasn't quite dolphin-like but neither was I a rock. Granted it was only 500m but I felt relaxed and strong.

Exiting the pool into what could only be described as a monsoon, I ran barefoot along the grass picking up a layer of loose turf on my exposed feet as I reached my bike in transition. I took a moment to try and claw away the lawn that was prospering between my toes but it was no use. I stuffed my green feet into my flooded cycling shoes. It felt horrible, like walking on mulched up soggy newspaper. As I pulled on my helmet I discarded my cycling glasses. I wouldn't be able to see clearly through them and would be constantly trying to wipe them clear.

It was raining that hard that the foam on my aerobar arm rests had soaked up lots of water resulting in a pool lying on top of them. I brushed it away with my hand and ran gingerly in my cleated shoes across the wet tarmac towards the bike mount line.

The bike course was tough, very hilly and the elements certainly didn't help. I felt good but I rode very conservatively as there was so much water on the roads, and combined with mud being washed out of the fields it felt like a lethal combination especially on thin racing tyres. Every time I feathered my brakes I was holding my breath that I would stay upright, fully aware that the Outlaw was only weeks away.

I passed one guy on a mountain bike and was really quite jealous of his thick, wide, knobbly griptastic tyres; he obviously wouldn't be worrying about the slippery road surface. Two people passed me on the bike and I passed three including the aforementioned Mountain Bike Man, so I pretty much held my position as I headed back towards town and the run section of the race.

By the time I got back to T2 I was wetter than when I'd gotten out of the pool, and my calves were caked in mud and other farm-associated goo. Racking my bike I wiped my hand across my face and discovered that I had mud on my face as well. In essence I looked like I'd ran a cross-country and not just completed the bike leg of a triathlon.

The run was tough, an out and back course with 2.5km straight up a long hill and then back down again. My legs didn't feel jelly-like at all and as I climbed the hill I started to pick people off. My club-mate Sarah came steaming down the hill on her way to the finish. I'd tried to catch her but her wave had too big a lead on me, and she was running strongly.

I ignored the water station at the turn round point and focused on a guy about 100 metres ahead of me, he would be my target for the last part of the run. When I run I always like to pick a target in the distance, another competitor as it gives me a hare to chase I guess.

Sometimes it works, other times this slow old tortoise just plods a bit too slowly to catch the hare. On this occasion despite my grumbling knees – they hate running downhill – the tortoise caught the hare. I powered past my target with about half a mile to go and offered encouragement: "Well done mate, dig in." "Alright lad, good running," came the broad Cumbrian response. Turning back into the leisure centre I crossed the finish line in 1.16:52. I was over the moon with that time as I had hoped to finish in about 1.20. I met up with Sarah and waited for our young club-mate Alasdair Grubb to finish. At this race the faster athletes set off in the later waves. We didn't have long to wait as he was flying, recording a performance of 58:24 which was good enough to win the event.

So it was good to be racing again, and it didn't really take too much out of me. The day after the race I swam 1,700m in the local lake in 34 minutes, which for me was pretty quick, and I followed that up the day after with a seven-mile run along the canal. The race and those training sessions showed me that I was on track with only a few weeks to go until the Outlaw. Things felt like they were starting to come together at the right time.

I received the news that I'd been waiting for about the book. Ironically it came just days before it was due to be published originally. An e-mail arrived from Paul, the boss at Pitch Publishing. They had bought the rights to Know The Score Books and its book catalogue.

Hi Andrew

Yours is one of the titles we wish to proceed with, do you know what stage the production process is at? Has the book been laid out etc?

Paul

I breathed a sigh of relief as I read the simple message and immediately rang my parents and Em to share the good news. I felt so relieved that Pitch was giving me and my book a chance. It felt amazing to have this particular monkey off my back. I had no idea about the answers to Paul's questions but after several e-mails and phone calls we decided it would just be easier if I resent them the manuscript and let them work their magic. I was assigned a new editor who was great to work with and we would work hard that winter getting the book ready for a January release. It was only six months late but it was better late than never.

I'd targeted the weekend three weeks out from the Outlaw to be my last big training weekend before I started my taper, the period just before a race where you ease back a little on your distances if not your intensity as you ready your body for battle. Unfortunately on the Thursday I started with a cold. I'm not going to say it was "man flu" because that would be too much of a cliché. How does "Ironman flu" sound?

So I spent those last few days in an enforced state of lethargy. In all honesty I had to rest because doing anything else would have been risking setting myself back. I found myself gasping for breath after walking the 200m to get the Sunday morning newspaper. Some Ironman eh, I was in worse shape than my pregnant asthmatic wife! Not wanting to dwell on the negative, life's too short and as I said earlier the glass can be refilled, I found some positives in my enforced rest:

1.   It was better to get the germs over and done with than have them infect me in three weeks when I would be racing.

2.   I got to watch the live coverage of the Tour. The weekend

stages were two great races but it was hard to get excited about Alexander Vinokourov winning. Maybe that's just me being too harsh, but in my opinion if you get caught doping you should be banned indefinitely. The Kazak was a cheat, and I could never bring myself to cheer for one. I still can't.

3.   I also got to watch the internet coverage from Roth, the legendary iron-distance race in Germany. It looked like a cracking race, I added it to my list of future things to do. Chrissie Wellington smashed the world best and beat a shed-load of male professionals in the process. She is an awesome and inspiring athlete. I wondered how quick she could actually go. Is a sub-eight out of her reach? On a good day I think not.

Until I caught the lurgy I'd had a great few weeks. My long rides had gone well, no punctures, no dramas, just hours and hours of solid, steady riding. The week before the onset of the germs I was lucky enough to be on holiday in Palma, Spain. We'd gone there for a few days to help Em's mum celebrate her 60th birthday and of course I couldn't resist the opportunity to get some warm weather training in.

Our hotel thankfully had a proper shaped pool that was twenty metres long, so I swam a mile every day. I followed this up with 90 minutes of spinning while watching World Cup football games in the deserted hotel gym. Finally I also managed to run a few 10k stints on the hilltop trails in the mid-afternoon heat. This was a deliberate ploy because I don't run well in the heat, and I wanted to prepare myself in case it turned out to be hot at the Outlaw. Granted Nottingham shouldn't be as hot as Majorca but stranger things have happened to me in the past.

Still recovering from my "Ironman flu" I attended the Business Librarians Association conference in Liverpool. As the first day drew to a close we all headed to the Albert Dock for a meal. Walking along the side of the dock I was chatting away to some of my fellow delegates whilst keeping an eye on the 50-odd red silicon-headed bodies swimming in the dock (an organised open water swim training session). "Look at those nutters," one of the women said to me. "Err, actually that's what I do in my spare time," came my amused response. There followed a quizzical look and then an hour or so of questions as she and a few other colleagues wanted to know more about me, triathlon and why anyone would want to do an Ironman. It was an interesting night and I think I educated a few of them.

While at the conference I took the opportunity to get a couple of early morning runs in along the Mersey. There weren't many people around on the windswept river bank and certainly no fellow librarians. I ran eight miles each morning along the mighty river and felt fresh-legged, in stark contrast to my final pre-race long run when I returned home.

I made the rookie mistake of skipping lunch and then trying to run 15 miles. Needless to say I bonked, it was very warm and I'd taken on no fluids or food on the run. Will I ever learn? By the time I staggered through the front door I was out on my feet. Once I recovered I was so angry with myself, I really should have known better. Two days later I ran 11.5 miles fully-fuelled and felt great – it just goes to show how important good training and racing nutrition is.

Apart from the illness, everything seemed to be falling into place at the right time. The last week before the race was crucial as I mentally prepared for the big day. I re-read the Outlaw information pack over and over again, my bike went into the shop for a full MOT, I inspected all my other gear intently, and I watched a few inspirational films and Kona DVDs to get myself in Ironman mode.

The build-up to the Outlaw seemed to have gone on forever but the final few weeks just flew by. I desperately wanted to get in the water and get going. I'm sure anyone who has ever done an Ironman or spent hours training for a triathlon or a marathon will know that feeling. I'm not sand-bagging when I say it had been the worst year I'd ever had in terms of preparation for an Ironman – mostly because of all the winter months I dedicated to writing my book, followed by a cracked wrist and the major distraction of marathon training. I sat doing nothing except writing and rewriting for a couple of months, which saw me put on over a stone in weight, ironic really.

Then the enforced inactivity in January didn't help but that was in the past and couldn't be changed. I'd made my choices and I would live with them. I was positive though that taking away the excessive heat from the previous year's marathon section that I'd be able to beat my time of 12.57. I HAD to believe that, or else there was no point starting. There is no room for negativity when it comes to racing Ironman. Negativity will eat you up, spit you out and leave you wondering what could have been. That's not for me.

Everything I'd done over the past year in terms of training had all been for Sunday 8th August, it was time to prove myself once again. It was time to step up, it was time to answer the question. People had asked me: "Are you ready?" There was only one answer: "YES!"

14

PROUD TO BE AN OUTLAW

I sat there in our lounge propped up on cushions and feeling like a truck had hit me. To look at me I could have been the poster boy for not racing long-distance triathlon. The pain however I knew would eventually fade the memory of finally crossing the finish line and becoming an Outlaw will live with me forever.

Twelve months ago I was high on my personal success at Ironman Germany and an adrenaline-fuelled day of supporting my COLT club-mates at Ironman UK. I wasn't inspired to enter the Bolton event, it wasn't a course that played to my strengths, but when news broke of a new event in Nottingham called the Outlaw, I signed up straight away. My cousin Mike also signed up for his first crack at the distance, meaning it would be a family affair. In the weeks that followed many Pirates also announced that they would be racing. This really would be one hell of a weekend.

I drew final inspiration for my race from pulling a 13-hour shift the previous Sunday watching my club-mates and friends compete at Ironman UK. The race in Bolton had seemed to grow and develop since the previous year. I had goosebumps as I watched many people realise their dream of becoming an Ironman. I stood in the same spot that I'd stood in at the previous year's race in the little village of Addlington at the start of the bike loop.

We'd nicknamed that stretch of road "COLT Alley", as a meeting point for the Lancaster faithful. I was shouting encouragement as the first riders came past just after 7am and I was still stood there at gone 3pm when my very good friend Dave the ex-Spartan completed his last lap.

Learning from the previous year I was wearing my gel padding cycling gloves, as clapping for hours had left the palms of my hands red raw last time. I couldn't afford that with my own 140.6-mile adventure to come in seven days. I obviously wasn't as quiet as I thought I was because by 8am the man who owned the house at the heart of COLT Alley came out and said, "I thought I recognised that voice," and said to the missus "he's back again this year," before handing me a mug of coffee. What a star. It was an amazing day out and I was inspired and a little envious watching all the bikes whizzing past, standing there thinking: "This time next week that'll be me." OK, maybe I would not so much be whizzing as rolling.

It was a great day out for COLT as all six team members finished the tough, hilly race in less than 12 hours and one of them, John Carr, qualified for the Ironman World Championships in Kona, Hawaii. We joked that this made the young dairy farmer the quickest "IronFarmer" on the planet.

I was made up for him as he always raced with heart, and dedicated each of his enthusiastic finish line celebrations to the memory of his mother who he'd lost at a young age. I'd been lucky enough to get quite friendly with John over the previous year and being a good 15 years younger than me I found his enthusiasm to be infectious. After talking to him I couldn't help but feel good. If a pharmaceutical company could bottle his enthusiasm and blend it with Chrissie Wellington's smile and release it into the atmosphere then I'm pretty sure that world peace would be achieved and every Miss World and beauty queen would see their wildest dream come true. My mate Dave put in a very brave performance to finish his race in less than 16 hours despite losing the contents of his stomach. He'd achieved his goal of finishing a branded Ironman race. In the days that followed he claimed to be officially retired, something that I didn't quite believe. So as you can see I had a very high standard to maintain to keep up with my friends when I competed the following Sunday. That motivated me immensely as I surveyed the lay of the Nottingham land.

In a blink of an eye, an extremely eventful year had passed and it was time for me to join almost 900 other triathletes in our quest to become an Outlaw. Mike and I arrived at the race venue Holme Pierrepont, the national watersports centre, on the Friday to register and were both instantly blown away by how long the swim was. Now that might seem strange but most open water swims I've ever done had involved swimming laps. This being in a rowing basin the swim was a straight out and back, if I squinted then I could just about make out the final turn buoy. It was a hell of a long way.

We both stood transfixed, laughing with a nervous fear I guess at the enormity of the task that we'd face in a couple of days' time. "S**t. Nothing has prepared me for that," said Mike, incredulously. I couldn't help but agree. "Me neither, I've never seen anything like it before. Bloody hell it goes on forever, 2.4 miles is a hell of a long way when you look at it in a straight line."

We were back at the lake the following morning to rack our bikes, and that vast expanse of water unfortunately hadn't shrunk overnight. Wheeling our bikes towards transition it was a boost to see my COLT team-mate Chris Wild doing the bike check-in. Like many of the volunteers that weekend he worked tirelessly for the success of the event. The "IronHippy", so-called because of his long hair and vegetarian lifestyle, had been the first person to speak to me when I came out of the closet and attended my first open water swim. I had the highest respect for him as an athlete and a person, and it was great to have him witness me race.

I don't know where he found the energy from as it was only six days since he had finished Ironman UK in ten hours and 54 minutes. What made his performance even more incredible was that he'd travelled through the night having been at the Monsters of Rock concert at Knebworth, had a couple of hours' kip in his car and then raced.

Not content with that, immediately after the race he jumped back in his car, getting back to Knebworth to watch his beloved Iron Maiden perform a killer set. I can't imagine being in a mosh pit immediately after an Ironman race would have been the most comfortable of experiences. For me being in a comfy bed is bad enough.

The man is a legend, and a little bit of a nutter, which I suppose helps in our chosen sport. After all we must all have a little bit of loose wiring to want to push our bodies and minds to hell and back over the course of 140.6 miles. It's not exactly normal behaviour. Wouldn't you agree? Racking my bike was where it all started to go pear-shaped for me. I couldn't get my bike sensor to talk to the computer. I'd decided to remove the computer and the sensors for the journey to Nottingham as the ROO was on a cycle rack on the roof of my car. I had been fearful that driving down the motorway, even at a somewhat sedate 60 miles per hour, might cause the cable ties holding the sensors to snap. The last thing I wanted was to arrive at the race without a working bike computer. Stupid really as I could have ridden without one, using my heart rate. This was just another example of how maybe we as triathletes have come to rely a little too much on technology.

I spent a very frustrating 40 minutes bent over fiddling, making minute adjustments to the magnet and the senor. Each time that I thought I'd cracked it, I'd stand up and spin my wheel looking at the computer display hoping that the sensor on the spinning wheel would talk to the receiver on the bike frame and then transmit the data to the tiny screen on my handlebars. Each time the screen registered a blank I swore under my breath as I felt my blood pressure rising. This was not what I needed the day before the race when I was supposed to be relaxing.

Eventually the computer picked up a reading but as I stood up something in my back just went. I had to grab the heavy steel bike rack to stop me from falling over. It felt like someone had just punched me as hard as they could in the kidneys, and I felt winded. After a few minutes I tried to walk it off and it did ease somewhat. On returning to the hotel I took a few painkillers which seemed to make a difference and I settled into the mindset of nailing it the next day.

I was half awake before my alarm went off at 3.30am, conscious as ever of sleeping in. I'd had a recurring nightmare over the previous few weeks which saw me do just that. In my nightmare I would arrive at the lake two hours late, running through the streets in my wetsuit, dive into the lake and start swimming. A safety boat would block my path as the two hours and 20 minutes time limit for the swim expired and I would be hauled out in a trawler type fishing net. I would be left swinging from the boat's crane for all to see and that was usually when I woke up in a cold sweat.

One morning I'd actually shot out of bed and had my running shoes on before I realised that it was 2am and about four weeks until the race. I crawled quietly back into bed and was asleep again in minutes. I had my usual breakfast of porridge and coffee, with a precautionary couple of Nurofen painkillers. A quick good luck kiss from a half-asleep Emma and I was away. Mike and I were up at the venue for 4.30am and preparing for the race. In no time at all the wetsuits were on and we were herded out like sheep to the swim pens. Much like the London marathon there were graded ability start pens, and due to the fact that it was a rowing basin there were start pens for boats which made ideal pens for triathletes.

I headed for the third pen of the four, for those hoping to swim between 80 and 90 minutes. The idea was that the quickest swimmers would be long gone from the first two pens by the time the slower swimmers like myself had swam diagonally across the lake to get on to the straight for the next mile of swimming. As I paddled towards my pen I saw a couple of people lose their footing on the concrete slipways leading down into the water and decided to just go to the end of the jetty and jump in. As a result I was on the front line, not good if you are a bad swimmer like me.

As I treaded water waiting for the gun to go off I composed myself and engaged in positive thought. I'm not nervous, I've been here before. I respect the distance but I don't fear it anymore. I will experience pain, I will experience very dark points but in the end I will finish and I will achieve what I set out to do 12 months ago when I entered. I will be an Outlaw. Come on Andy it's time, make it your day.

The hooter sounded at 6am and the inaugural Outlaw was under way in a maelstrom of splashing limbs and white rubber caps. The first half of the swim until the turn was the usual bun fight, hands and feet delivering blows of varying intensity. If violence of this nature took place on dry land it would be called wrestling. Despite the constant jostling I managed to find a comfortable rhythm and swam comfortably watching the crowds walking and cycling along the towpath trying to spot their loved ones in the water.

I could also spot the huge signs that marked off every 100 metres of the lake. These acted like mile markers in a marathon so I could work out where I was in terms of distance, and gauge how I was feeling. Just after I passed the 600 metres sign I hit a very dense patch of underwater grass. It was quite unnerving as it made me feel quite claustrophobic, I couldn't see or feel clear water. It was like I was lying in a freshly mown field trying to crawl through grass cuttings. The grass was hanging off my goggles and actually tore off my nose clip.

I never swim without one and it felt awful for those first few strokes as water gushed into my sinuses, but the clip was gone and there was nothing I could do about it other than swim. Every time my hand came out of the water I had a fistful of grass, and I also had to check that my timing chip was still on my ankle because grass was hanging off my lower limbs as well. That was the worst part of all because my mind played tricks on me, telling me that someone in the deep was pulling my ankle down. Those thoughts were bizarre because the reality of the situation was that I could have actually stood up on the grass and walked.

As I swam around the turn buoys at the halfway point I managed to catch a decent draft for a while, and swimming in the near wake of another competitor allowed me to conserve energy as they did the hard work of cutting through the water for the pair of us. With each stroke my fingertips were just centimetres from his feet, almost like playing a cat and mouse game of "tickle me if you can". This combined with sighting off the bright red rowing lane markers that were situated every 20 metres meant that I was probably actually swimming in a straight line in an open water swim for the first time ever.

Before I knew it I was back at the start being pulled out of the water by Chris Wild, who was part of a wetsuit-clad team helping swimmers to their feet and up the ramp into transition. "Going great Andy, see you later. Have a great bike," he said enthusiastically as he patted me on the back. I removed my goggles and cap while running up the ramp and looked at my watch for the first time, fully expecting a slow time. I was quicker than expected, 1.25:02. That was my quickest ever Ironman swim and I was elated.

Distracted by this revelation I wasn't watching my footing as I turned the corner on the slippery mat, my left foot slipped and I hit the concrete hard on my left knee. Two other competitors stopped to pick me up, I thanked them and walked gingerly into the transition tent. I didn't feel like I was damaged as I faced the rows of plastic kit bags and semi-naked athletes.

I'd had so much stick that year over my shameful T1 performance at Germany when it had taken me 14 minutes to get out on my bike. Theories as to my performance offered by other triathletes included that I was doing *The Times* crossword, having a quick nap or drying my hair and putting on make-up. Here I was determined not to give my friends any more ammunition and got out on my bike in as quick a time as I could.

I stopped only to put on socks and shoes. My gloves, helmet and glasses were put on while moving forward, once again taking on the expert advice of John Knapp who was fond of saying: "Keep moving forward." I paused as I exited the tent to have sun cream applied and I was off and running through the bike racks to my machine. I was on my way cycling around the lake, out of transition in five minutes and 35 seconds. I was grinning, as I was so pleased with myself. I couldn't have done *The Sun* crossword in that sort of time let alone *The Times* one.

I took my time in the first few miles of the bike section, eating and drinking in an attempt to fuel the efforts that were to come. Once away from the crowds that had gathered around the watersports centre it was a quiet course through the open Nottinghamshire countryside with not many spectators until we reached the spectator hotspots of Oxton and Southwell.

My knee that had taken the impact of my transition fall was a little sore with the pedalling motion but thankfully my back felt OK. The bike hummed along underneath me as I was riding on a set of very nice and fast borrowed Hed Jet wheels.

One of the Pirates, Bassy, had been very trusting to send me his very expensive wheels to use. I couldn't believe what a difference the deep section carbon wheels seemed to make. They felt so much faster than the standard issue Alex wheels that had come with the ROO. I'd never upgraded my wheels because of the expense but the performance of these ones was slowly turning my head.

The bike course was a quick one, there were a few hills on it but nothing significant. The highlight for me came on each of the three laps as we passed through the Pirate feed station. Each feed station on the course was manned by enthusiastic volunteers from triathlon clubs. The noise was uplifting as my yellow clad Pirate friends shouted encouragement. I already had a huge smile on my face as I rode away from the feed station but a few hundred yards down the road was a bright Pirate yellow sign with the skull and crossbones on it. Emblazoned in bold black writing was the proclamation: "SUNDAY AFTERNOON: BIKE SALE HERE." I almost fell off the ROO laughing. At the bottom of the loop I saw my family, and their encouragement was a welcome lift after a particularly hard section into the wind along what seemed to be a never-ending dual carriageway. They also gave me an update on Mike, who as expected was a good few minutes ahead of me. When you are racing it is very difficult to ascertain how your friends are getting on. You have no idea where they are in relation to you, especially in a field of almost a thousand athletes. I was pleased he was going well. Mike had trained like a demon and thrown himself wholeheartedly into his transition from runner to triathlete. He deserved to have a successful day.

My chain had come off on the first loop when I changed gear. It didn't cause me concern as I'd had a similar thing happen to me in Germany. It was frustrating that it slowed me down but it wasn't fatal like some mechanical issues. However I almost suffered a mechanical fatality on the third and final lap. I had 92 miles on the computer when another gear change went wrong. I heard clanging and looked down expecting to see that my chain had come off again, what I wasn't expecting was that it had snapped. Oh bugger!

I got off the bike and my first instinct was to pick the bike up and throw it in front of the passing traffic. If it wasn't for the very expensive borrowed wheels I might have done. Somehow, and I don't know how, I managed to compose myself. I guess it was the realisation that it was a freak accident and out of my control. I could have a tantrum or laugh it off and remedy the situation.

I leant the chainless ROO against a wall and reached into my saddle bag, pulling out a chain splitter tool and spare chain links. Ironically I'd removed the tool the day before, deciding it was too heavy and unnecessary, but thankfully something made me repack it. I was also very grateful at that point that my training partner and bike guru, Andy Holme, had actually taught me how to fix a chain earlier that year on my other bike. That lesson in the garage at Thurnham Cycles just saved my race as without that knowledge I would have recorded my first "DNF: did not finish". My hands were covered in oil. I had lost about 15 minutes in time, I'd been passed by what seemed to be every other competitor but as I got ready to remount the bike I was just happy my race wasn't over. As I attempted to swing my leg over the bike, pain engulfed me and I swore out loud. Being bent over trying to split and reattach the chain had aggravated my back again. I couldn't believe how stiff I was. I wouldn't have expected to feel like that until an hour or so after I'd completed the race. It was almost like rigor mortis had set in.

I had to lay the bike almost horizontal to be able to get my leg over the top tube. I managed to remount my steed but the final 20 miles of the bike ride was slow and laboured. I somehow managed to raise a forced smile as I passed my family on that final lap, and headed towards the second transition. The ride was done in a very disappointing 6.46:06. I had been hoping with the faster wheels to be somewhere in the region of six hours. Looking at my watch though as I pulled back into the watersports complex I quickly calculated that if I left the pain on the bike I could run well and scrape a PB. I felt confident.

Into T2 and I managed to get off the bike without embarrassing myself. I sat down on a chair to put my running shoes on. Big mistake. I had to be pulled to my feet by a race official as my body just seemed to seize up. Within the first 800m of the run I knew any thoughts of a PB had to go as every time I planted my left foot my knee and back exploded in pain. If it had been a training run I would have stopped immediately but it wasn't, this was a race, so I had to man up and run/walk/shuffle/crawl a marathon. It wasn't going to be pretty.

The laps around the lake felt like they would never end but the out and back legs along the River Trent were uplifting because of the support, especially from my fellow Pirates. There was also the support of the fellow athletes on the narrow path. My brother Craig and his family had come up for the day to watch and hearing my young nieces, Georgia and Eloise shouting "go Pirate go" with an innocent enthusiasm that only children can generate brought a smile to my face.

Just after I passed my mini supporters and heading towards the river I saw Mike running back the other way. "Never again" was his comment as the temperatures soared. He was grimacing but still moving at what looked to me to be a decent pace. I was slowing with each foot fall. I was above the legal limit of painkillers, having popped a couple more that I'd picked up in transition. I'd placed them there that morning in case they were needed. I wouldn't normally advocate their use and Em usually has to force me to take any sort of medication as I'm of the attitude "I'll be alright in a bit."

But I was desperate by then, I would have gulped down a whole packet if I'd had one to hand. I was knackered, in pain and not thinking rationally. Viking and Dave were there as spectators and both of them walked with me on the side of the path at various points, their words of encouragement keeping me moving. I was slightly embarrassed that they were witnessing me in such a state but they were both Ironmen and fully understood what the race could do to you.

They had both suffered vastly at the Big Woody and Ironman UK. I'd seen them when they were struggling and now it was their turn to witness my anguish and pain. "We've all been there mate, one foot in front of the other and you'll get there Holgs," offered Viking. I managed to half-smile in agreement at the simple description of what I had to do.

On the final lap my Dad joined me like he had at Frankfurt the year before. He encouraged me to run between the floodlights that had been set up for the stragglers on the riverside. They hadn't been switched on yet, which I took encouragement from, as at least barring a disaster I would finish in daylight.

His encouragement kept me going, as did fellow Pirate Silent Assassin before storming away from me. The ex-chain smoker was just about to complete his first Ironman and was telling me how excited he was at the prospect of crossing the line in celebration hand in hand with his son Jordy. It was wonderful listening to him talking with such pride about his family, and I only hoped that I would be able to emulate his enthusiasm for fatherhood when my time came later that year. His enthusiasm was infectious and it lifted me when I didn't think it would have been possible. I suddenly seemed to have maybe not a spring in my step but less of a limp.

Then I crossed the meadow leaving my Dad to head to the finish line. I shuffled through the car park and crested the small hill and suddenly the lake glistened like glass in front of me. With the final river path section done I had a two-mile lap of the lake to do and I would be an Outlaw. It felt like the longest two miles of my life as I could see and hear the finish but I was continually running away from it towards the far end of the lake.

It was a blessed relief when I turned at the end and had a mile in a straight line to run. I wasn't even remotely interested in the Hooters girls who were looking after the feed station at the turning point. Their skimpy hot pants, tight white vests and unnatural breasts held no interest as I just stared at my feet as I waddled past, edging slowly closer to salvation. I wanted to finish so badly, I wanted the pain to stop.

From somewhere deep inside my pride kicked in because I knew that three friends, Lisa, Anna and Dan, were chasing me down. All three of them had made significant gains into my lead on each lap. Each time we passed one another they were further down the river path and on the last lap I knew I was in real danger of being caught as the three of them were moving much faster than me.

The competitor in me wanted to finish ahead of them. I looked behind and Lisa was less than 400 metres behind me, I recognised the familiar yellow and black vest of the female Pirate. She was moving fluidly and I cursed under my breath that she was making me work hard in the final mile. I dug deep, my Dad shouting encouragement, his booming voice seeming to carry further than the race commentator's on the public PA system.

Soon enough the finishing chute came into view on the horizon. With a hundred metres to go I was met by fellow COLTs Chris Wild and Rob Sellers who escorted me to the carpeted finishing chute. That was a great feeling, sharing an Ironman finish for the first time with a couple of my club-mates. Having first looked behind and made sure that my gap over Lisa was large enough I milked the finishing chute for all I was worth, high-fiving the crowd and applauding them all.

Suddenly among the Pirates, there was Emma, my wife, in floods of tears. I embraced her, kissed her and reassured her I was OK. Being heavily pregnant she had stayed on the grassy knoll near the finish, sheltered and rested. We had only exchanged shouts from a distance as I passed with each lap. She'd slowly watched her husband deteriorate on each of those laps and the tension and worry had built up inside her.

That moment of release as she cried into my sweaty shoulder was captured in a photograph, and although you can't really see our faces it remains one of my favourites of Em and I. To me it illustrates the pure raw emotion of love, and the drama and intensity of an Ironman.

Having reassured Em that I would indeed live, I kissed her goodbye and ran the ten yards that were left of my race. I crossed the line and punched the air in sheer delight. The hardest 14 hours 17 minutes and 48 seconds of my life was over. I was in agony but my pride at being an Outlaw drowned it out. Seconds later Lisa crossed the line and we hugged in a Pirate celebration. She had just completed her first Ironman and was rightly elated at her achievement.

After passing through the medical tent and being given the all-clear I went into the food tent. The smell was amazing as huge pans of pasta, chips, curry, meat stew and other dishes were served up to the ravenous triathletes. Unfortunately I just couldn't stomach anything, and rather meekly opted for a plain white roll with butter.

As I limped onwards to transition to pick up my kit bags and my bike I munched on that roll like it was the last meal I would ever consume. The starchy goodness tasted divine after 13 hours of consuming sugary gloop in the form of gels and energy drinks.

My Dad met me just outside transition and took my bags and bike from me and went off to put them in the car. I was reunited with my family on the grassy knoll and discovered that Mike had finished in 12.43:51. He seemed to be moving OK. He'd hit a bad patch just after I'd seen him but he kept focused on my time from Germany and decided that if he moved quickly on his last lap around the lake that he'd beat it. He had done and already while the sweat was still drying on his face he was talking of a sub-12 attempt. I'd warned him that Ironman racing was addictive.

The Outlaw was a great event, and one that everyone should consider doing. If a Kona slot isn't your objective you'd be mad to dismiss the Nottingham race. I can fully understand why it has gone from strength to strength and won national awards. I knew that one day I would be back, I had unfinished business with a course that although fast had kicked my arse.

As always I learnt a lot about myself, particularly about my resolve, my weaknesses, my stubbornness and my desire to complete the task. The tough days make the good ones that much sweeter. We all need a tough day sometimes.

15

FOOTBALLERS, MIDWIVES AND DRUGS

We limped in to the supermarket cafeteria, two ravenous and battered warriors resplendent in our black Outlaw finisher polo shirts, our pace quickening to a crawl as we smelled the intoxicating aroma of bacon. The morning after the race Mike and I were both craving food, and specifically high-calorie, high-sodium and high-fat goodness in the shape of a good old fry-up.

After I had finished the race I couldn't stomach anything to eat and Mike had also struggled to consume food. A few hours later it was time to replenish what we'd lost in those long hours of racing. We both ordered the biggest breakfast they had: bacon, sausages, beans, fried eggs, hash browns, tomatoes, mushrooms, toast and coffee. We attacked the food like lions on a fallen gazelle. It was wonderful. I can still close my eyes and taste that bacon.

In Ironman racing your body can lose a lot of salt and minerals and in the days that follow you just crave it, or at least I do. Normally I wouldn't put salt on my food but I always add it in the days afterwards or seek out salty food. It's also a release I guess after spending months being strict with your diet as you prepare for your race. We sat there scoffing and talking about the race with our family and it caused great amusement that we had to get my Dad to go and refill our coffee cups because we'd stiffened up and were welded to our plastic chairs.

"Alright Holgs!" came the booming voice from across the cafeteria, a voice that could only belong to Silent Assassin. Never has the term "silent" been so wrongly used. A T-Rex would be stealthier hunting prey on London's Oxford Street. He weaved through the tables like Lionel Messi through an opposition defence as he came over and hugged me. "Bloody hell mate, you don't look like you raced yesterday the way you shot across there," I managed to croak as the burly contractor squeezed me. Introductions over with he, his wife Jo and son Jordy joined us. They ordered the same and the whole competitive eating display started again while we supped our coffee.

It came up in conversation that Silent Assassin, or Q to his mates, did a lot of work in the Stoke area, and on hearing that my Dad couldn't resist sharing with him the tale of our journey to Nottingham. We'd travelled down in two cars, me and my family in one and Mike and his Mam in his car. We drove through Stoke and then stopped at the services for a comfort break. Now Mike is an avid Stoke City supporter, having fallen in love with the club when he studied sports science at university there.

We'd driven past the huge Britannia Stadium which is where the Potters play their games, a huge steel structure on a hill that dominated your view as you drove past on the A50 to Nottingham. When Mike had last been to a game they were still playing at the Victoria Ground so when we stopped my Dad asked him excitedly: "What did you think of the Britannia Stadium then Mike?" Mike looked all confused when he answered, "What? You mean we went past it? I never saw it." On hearing this part of the tale Q started wetting himself laughing: "You can't bloody miss it, the thing is huge. You are going to have to take him to see it on the way home Holgs." So that's what we did, Mike followed us and on the way home we pulled into the stadium car park.

Mike was excited about going into the shop to get a shirt, and the rest of us decided to stretch our legs. Two of us limped very gingerly across the car park trailing behind the heavily pregnant lady and three 60-year-olds. All of a sudden I was aware of a black blur as Mike sped off across the car park like Usain Bolt. He'd spotted a car pulling into the players' car park, and in seconds was stood by it.

The transformation from cripple to sprinter was like something described in the Bible. Miracle Mike was reborn. He tapped on the driver's window and asked excitedly: "Are you Ryan Shawcross?" The poor footballer behind the wheel must have thought that he had a right weirdo on his hands as the 40-year-old shaven-headed Mike jumped up and down like a toddler at Disneyland. The Stoke City captain posed for a photo and then quickly ducked inside the stadium to safety.

"That was the highlight of the weekend. Much better than doing my first Ironman," said Mike and then started limping badly again as he went into the shop. Miracle Mike was no more.

On returning home I had the small matter of a bet I had to settle. In the months running up to the race I and a fellow Pirate by the name of Fat Buddha had been talking 'smack' on Twitter, light-hearted p**s-taking basically.

I had a huge amount of respect for the 50-something young-at-heart Ironman veteran who'd completed his first race while I was still welded to a couch eating pizza in a past life. We were both former rugby players and both of shall we say a "large frame" so it seemed only appropriate that we would name our little wager the "Donut Challenge".

Basically the bet stated that whoever was the last to cross the line would have to buy the other some donuts. On paper our best Ironman times were almost identical. The bet was just a laugh but we both took it seriously and on the day the better man won. Fat Buddha well and truly kicked my arse, storming home in 12.54:44, and in typical Pirate style he stopped metres from the line to down a freshly pulled pint of lager from the bar before finishing, arms aloft in celebration.

In all honesty he was so far ahead of me he could have downed the whole barrel and eaten a five-course meal but he was watching his figure. So the first thing I did on returning home was to log on to the computer and order him two dozen assorted donuts, and a couple of days later I had it on good authority that they tasted "bloody lovely"!

My body took quite a battering during the Outlaw, but I was mentally drained as the whole post-Ironman blues kicked in a little. I was a slightly disappointed with my finishing time and rather than have my usual attitude of "I'll come back stronger and get what I want", truth be told I felt a little disheartened with the sport of Ironman.

Maybe it was because I hadn't really had a break from it for four years, maybe it was because with the baby on its way I had new things to focus on in my life? Whatever the reason I just felt burnt out. I happened to mention this to my Mum and she urged me to go and see my doctor because she'd recognised a few tell-tale signs in my appearance before the Outlaw that set alarm bells ringing.

Back in April as I prepared for the London Marathon I happened to be whinging one day about how I was "doing all this running and not losing any weight, in fact I'm putting it on". My Mum heard and said that she'd noticed that my eyes were extremely sunken. I looked like an extra from *The Addams Family*, which in me is usually a sign that something is amiss with my thyroid.

I suffer from an underactive thyroid and after almost 20 years of messing with medication levels I was on a very high dose. Mum urged me to go and get my blood levels tested but I refused, placating her by saying I would once the Outlaw was done and dusted. I didn't want my medication messing with as it can take my body a while to adjust, and I was frightened that it might have an adverse effect on my race day preparation. So I promised her that as soon as I got back from our holiday in France I would go and get a blood test. I even booked it the day I arrived home from Nottingham.

I resumed running again when we went to Beziers in the south of France for two weeks just after the Outlaw. I'd taken my running gear "just in case" I got the urge to do something. It took me three days of lying by the pool to realise that I'm not that sort of person. Em was aware of me fidgeting, reading in short bursts and getting in and out of the pool more times than a penguin at a zoo.

"I think you need to go for a run, it'll help you relax," she said from behind the safety of the latest Pat Barker novel. I didn't need telling twice, I was back at the apartment and in my running gear before Em had even lain back down on her sun lounger. That first run was a simple one mile out and back along the deserted vineyard track that bordered the complex where we were staying. It was simple but oh so effective, and I ran every day of the holiday after that. I loved the feeling of the sun, I loved watching the ducks on the canal. I even loved shouting "bonjour" to the old men playing chess and smoking like chimneys outside the village café.

The first time I passed them in the afternoon heat I was greeted with looks of bemusement from under their berets, but as the days passed by we progressed from smiles to "bonjour" to berets being waved and something shouted that I didn't understand. I know it was positive though and friendly. I can't help thinking of that old man by the canal every time I watch the Disney movie *Up*. He's the spitting image of Carl, the old man with the balloon house. These are the sorts of memories and moments that running gives me. If I'd stayed anchored to my sun lounger I would have missed out on a memory that never fails to make me smile.

The heat in France was stifling. One day the needle was above 40 degrees. After that first day of running I progressed to following a five-mile loop along the Canal du Midi to the next village and back. On my return to the complex I'd remove my running shoes, and my shirt would already be off ready for me to jump into the swimming pool to cool down.

The cool water was rejuvenating but I swear that you could get lost in the steam as my overheated body sizzled as it entered the water. That particular day when the mercury soared, the dry Mediterranean heat actually burned my throat (it felt like one of my regular tonsillitis outbreaks) and on returning I drank a litre of water without coming up for air.

My Garmin was telling me that my heart rate was just shy of 200 bpm, but it felt like it had been much higher as I collapsed on a lounger knackered. It took my throat a couple of hours to properly lubricate and for me to stop talking like Darth Vader with a head cold. Despite the heat each run I did got quicker and by the end of the holiday, my five-mile time had dropped from 50 minutes to 42 minutes. I was back running but I still didn't feel particularly fit so rather than make any rash decisions about racing again, I sat down and talked about it with Em. I needed a goal to focus on but with our first baby due in December I had to be realistic in what I could aim for. Em said that she was more than happy for me to do the Outlaw again but I wasn't sure that I'd be able to get the level of training into my legs that I would need to do a long-distance race.

What I decided on was a two-year planned return to Ironman racing. Although I was proud to have finished the Outlaw I was really disappointed with my time. I was still determined to get that sub-12 hour time that so far had eluded me. I believed that it was well within my capabilities if I was race fit and had some luck on race day. So as I headed home from France for a date with the doc and a needle I'd decided in my head that in 2012 I would be returning to Ironman, most likely in Germany or Nottingham.

I saw 2011 as a transition year, building up my fitness, reducing my weight, getting faster at shorter distances, and adjusting to life as a Dad. I'd decided that my 'A' race the following year would be a half Ironman, most probably the Cleveland Steelman in July. That was a race that I had done twice before and thoroughly enjoyed.

The morning after I stepped foot back on British soil two little vials of blood were taken out of my left arm and sent for analysis. Ten days later I had the news that in the back of my mind I'd been suspecting. The results showed that my thyroid gland had gone haywire, explaining why I'd piled on weight despite intense training, been experiencing lethargic moods, and suffering with joint pain among other things.

My medication wasn't helping me at all, and in layman's terms it would have been like giving an asthmatic an empty inhaler. My dose was doubled and I was referred to the hospital for further tests and treatment. The endocrinologist at the hospital put me on a second hormone pill known as Levothyronine, or T3.

I'd already been taking Levothyroxine, or T2, for most of my adult life but my T3 levels had never been tested. The results showed that I desperately needed help with that hormone as well. Pesky things thyroid glands, it's amazing to think that such a tiny part of the human body can do so much internal damage when it goes wrong.

It took a couple of months but I started to feel like my old self again. I had energy, I was positive and I could run without too much pain. The weight was slow to come off but it was reducing so that also made me feel better. I was warned that I would need regular testing and that things could go wrong again, as keeping the thyroid gland stable is a long and sometimes tricky process. I'm no medical man but I think of it as two parts luck and one part science. All I could do was hope that it would be a long time before I was unlucky enough to have it go haywire again.

It drives me nuts that it's something that affects my athletic ability and performance massively but is something I can do absolutely nothing to prevent. But I mustn't moan. It's not cancer, it's not going to kill me, and people with far worse conditions than me have pushed their bodies to further extremes than me and done it with a smile. The late great Jane Tomlinson for one, who did amazing things despite being wracked with terminal cancer, and inspired millions with her running and cycling exploits.

People like Joe Townsend and the other brave ex-soldiers who compete for Team True Spirit who have completed Ironman UK despite losing limbs in battle are also inspiring. They don't let things stop them, they truly are inspirational and "just get on with it". These are the people I strive to be able to walk in the shadow of, to have just a fraction of their resolve and determination.

They're not athletic gods, they are normal people dealing with difficult issues that affect their everyday lives let alone their endurance sport ambitions and they succeed and prosper. If you haven't heard of Team True Spirit then I urge you to have a look at their website *www.truespirit.org.uk* and I challenge you not to be inspired by what you see there. Oh and I bet like me you won't moan as much about that blister or a stitch on your next run.

In September 2010 I began working with a coach, Richard Mason, of Inspired Personal Training. He's a veteran of multiple Ironman races, a BTA regional coach and a great motivator. He's also the captain of COLT. I must admit that I was a little nervous when I went to his gym to be assessed. Although Richard is very friendly I'd always been a bit scared of him, due to his ex-marine persona, and his straight-talking, ass-kicking attitude to triathlon.

I needn't have worried as Richard encouraged me as he pushed me to my physical limits. There was no drill sergeant shouting, I didn't feel like a recruit in *Full Metal Jacket*, just a bloke wanting to better himself.

We conducted a fitness test which involved working out my heart rate zones on the bike. My heart rate was recorded over a set time period as more and more resistance was added to the gel pad touching the back tyre. I never knew a turbo trainer could be such an instrument of torture, and by the time I'd finished the 20-minute session I thought my heart and lungs were going to come out of my chest.

It was death by friction. Sweat was dripping off me on to his nice polished wooden floor, but thankfully Richard resisted the urge to shout at me. If he had I probably would have dissolved in tears or lost control of my bowels as every nerve and fibre of my being seemed to be pulsing with fatigue. But I had survived and after running a few bits of data through his computer Richard e-mailed me my first weekly training plan.

My key weekly sessions were highlighted for me, and each week I could see what the aim was; endurance one week, climbing the next, interval running speed the week after. It all seemed so simple and all seemed manageable. In the past if I trained myself and looked at an endurance week, I'll be honest there were probably quite a few 'junk miles' done. Running without a purpose, just to say "I've done X miles this week" when really I should have been aiming for specific outcomes from each run. With Richard's help I was now training smart, every session was done for a reason, and that could only be a positive thing. If you've never worked with a coach I can recommend it. I know they cost money, and to be honest with you I wouldn't have been able to justify the cost if I was paying. In return for Richard's services I was building and maintaining his website, a mutual trade-off of desirable services I guess. I build him a website, he beasts me into an inch of my life all in the name of triathlon. It was a great deal.

Seriously though I found that when you have someone to answer to, it means you really put the effort in. If you don't have a coach, find a training partner, join a club, again gauging yourself against others will make you train harder.

As November arrived my training schedule started to focus on my desire to get quicker over the 10k distance. A five-week plan arrived in my inbox one Monday morning focusing on progressive interval sessions, done on a treadmill. They were tough.

Warm Up: 10 Minutes
Intervals: WK1 - 8 x 1 minute Interval @ 15kmh with 1 minute @ 10kmh

WK2 - 8 x 1.5 minute Interval @ 15kmh with 2 minutes @ 10.5kmh

WK3 - 8 x 2 minute Interval @ 15kmh with 2 minutes @ 11kmh

WK4 - 8 x 2.5 minute Interval @ 15kmh with 2 minutes @ 11.5kmh

WK5 - 8 x 3 minute Interval @ 15kmh with 2 minutes @ 12kmh
Warm Down: 10 minutes

I don't know about you but I'm really not a fan of treadmill running. It's a bit like turbo training, I know it does me good but so does cod liver oil. I guess what I'm trying to say is these sessions where I melted under the gym lights while mashing my feet into a glorified supermarket checkout belt were a necessary evil rather than a joy.

I also had to concentrate really hard on where I placed my feet. In the past my mind tended to wander on the treadmill and I had a few nervous moments where I've had to grasp for a handrail to stay upright as one of my feet had gone off the belt, resulting in an impromptu attempt at doing the splits. I'd just finished one of my sessions at the gym when my phone buzzed, and it was Em. She explained that she was in pain and that it really felt like the baby was on its way. It was 19th November and she wasn't due for another month. I've never dressed so quickly in all my life, and despite being knackered I sprinted to my car like Mike chasing a footballer.

By the time I made it home in less time than was legally possible, Em had spoken to the hospital and was advised to go straight there. She seemed remarkably calm, taking it all in her stride while I was trying to be a caring, calm husband whilst internally feeling like I was about to implode with nerves.

She was admitted straight away and within minutes nurses and midwives were attaching wires and belts, and hooking up monitors. It reminded me of a Formula One pit-stop as the crew worked seamlessly and were then gone in 30 seconds. I blinked and just the midwife was stood there now talking to Em. I'd not taken in anything of what she had said. Talking to Em moments later it was probably just as well as it was "women's matters", and those sorts of things were best left to the experts.

Mind you having worked with women closely all my working life I could probably talk you through most problems to occur from pregnancy to menopause. Over the years I've heard it all but given what I'm like with bike maintenance it's probably best that I leave the technical stuff to those that are trained to deal with it. The main thing was that the baby seemed to have a strong heartbeat and that although Em was getting contractions she wasn't dilated. Her cervix was tighter than an Orca wetsuit. She was however being very sick again and there had been protein and blood in her urine sample so it was decided to keep her in for a few days.

I didn't sleep at all that night after I said goodbye to Em. I was on tenterhooks, subconsciously expecting the phone to go at any moment. By 6am it hadn't rung and bleary-eyed I decided to crawl out of bed for a shot of much-needed coffee, and it was then that it dawned on me. It was my birthday. Would I be getting the ultimate present to celebrate my 38th year?

When I got to the hospital, poor Em was most apologetic that she hadn't even written my card. I reassured her that at my age it really didn't matter. Unfortunately I didn't get my birthday present, the contractions eased off and baby Holgate decided it was on to a good thing staying nice and warm as it was icy cold outside. "It's a smart baby, it must take after you pet," I joked with Em. Funnily enough she didn't disagree.

Winter seemed to have arrived both early and with a vengeance that year in the United Kingdom. The surprising thing however was that we seemed to have got away lightly in Lancashire. A few days later when I picked Em up from hospital there was a light dusting of snow on the ground. Watching the weather reports showing huge snow drifts just over the Pennines in Yorkshire I'd been concerned that I wouldn't be able to get in the car to pick Em up.

We lived on a steep hill and whenever it was snowing or icy using the car was a gamble. The previous winter a car had skidded on black ice and ended up in the living room of a house not 100 yards from ours. It was very icy but thankfully the snow stayed about ten miles away. It was like someone had sprinkled icing sugar here on top of the cake instead of encasing it in proper icing.

The weather though was a factor that weekend as Andy H and I opted to run instead of riding. Em's Mum was staying for the weekend so I felt that I could safely get out for a much-needed plod with my mate. As a precaution my mobile phone was strapped to my arm in my MP3 player holder.

It was the first time I'd run with Andy since the early summer as he had injured his knee. Several visits to the physio had resulted in him being fitted with orthotics, and this was only his second run since acquiring the hard plastic shoe inserts. It was good to catch up once again with the jovial Evertonian. It's all we seemed to do with work and family commitments meaning that we were no longer weekly training partners.

There had been a hard frost overnight and the air was breathtakingly cold. I actually wore tights for the first time that winter and was so glad of them as my legs were uncomfortably cold running along the iced up coastal path. I was also very glad of my new thermal top that I'd bought in the 90-degree heat of the south of France (probably why it was cheap) back in August. It came from the French retailer Decathlon and I'm very impressed with it – fleece-lined, windproof and all for the amazing price of 17 euros.

So often in the past I'd been caught out by the weather but on this occasion I was dressed for success. Have you got that Roxette song going round inside your head now? I bet you have. Sorry about that but you can't beat a bit of 1980s Swedish pop.

Anyway let's get back on track. The run was a success and we averaged just less than nine minutes a mile, which was great considering it had only been a week since Andy H was green lit to run again after his injury and I was knackered from hospital visiting and worry. I'd also made a change to my shoes that morning.

On one of the forums I frequent I'm teased – and that's being polite – for being a "comfy shoe-wearing librarian". I can't remember how it started but it's stuck. So that Sunday I lived up to my reputation by being comfortable, in the hope of solving a recent problem that was beginning to plague me.

After the Outlaw I retired my running shoes and reverted back to my old favourites, the Asics Nimbus, described by my ultra-running friend Gobi as "sofas for your feet". From that description I'm sure that you can ascertain that these are indeed "comfy shoes". However they'd been crippling me, as after every run both of my Achilles tendons would be really sore.

Being too tight to pay for a physio I self-diagnosed with the help of a few internet searches that with it being both legs it wasn't an actual injury but a shoe issue. The shoes just felt heavier and more constrictive around the heel than the previous model that I'd used. Don't you just hate it when your chosen shoe manufacturer messes with your favourite model? I find it so frustrating and over the years it's probably cost me a small fortune in shoes that were bought for running but were downgraded to "knocking about shoes" after a few painful runs.

These ones had cost more than a weeks' worth of food for the pair of us so I was determined to make them work. So before Sunday's run I inserted heel wedges into my shoes, thus raising my Achilles by approximately half an inch. It seemed to work because I felt no pain while running and have felt none since.

Of course there was another theory as to what was causing the pain, and I'd be interested to hear from any Dads out there on this one. My wife was due to give birth at any point and as such was feeling very heavy, so understandably she was literally walking at a snail's pace. In response I modified my usually brisk walking pace to match her ultra-slow shuffle, and my whole legs ached as a result. Could this change in walking have been the cause of my Achilles pain and not the running? Anyone else suffered with this?

After a couple more pain-free runs I decided to chance my luck but it was with some trepidation that I ventured out into the cold, frozen, wastelands of Lancaster, north of the River Lune.

"It's not that scary over there," I hear you cry.

The fear wasn't stemming from a duelling banjo-type scenario but from a "can I still cut it?" one.

I was making my return to COLT running training for the first time in six weeks, which is a long time and although I felt like I was ticking over nicely I knew that I would have lost some of that competitive edge that you get when you run with like-minded individuals.

Once the banter from Chris Lawson, Andy Ley and the IronHobbit had passed and this "newcomer" was welcomed back into the fold we set out for our run. I needn't have worried because once again the dangerous ice-encrusted footpaths made any sort of interval/speed work impossible. The four of us who had braved the freezing temperatures decided that we'd just have a sociable run instead, and it was great fun.

We weren't messing about though as I still managed to cover nine miles in an hour and 25 minutes. If I'd been running on my own I'd have probably called it a night after about four or five miles as I was so cold, but the beauty of having club-mates and training partners meant I couldn't "wuss out" and go home early.

It was minus four degrees and breathtaking (not in a WOW!!! sense, more a "where's the air to breathe" sense). Despite the thermal tights when I got home I had to stand in the shower thawing out my frozen thighs for ten minutes, each one looking like a frozen turkey. Now there's an image I bet you could have done without? The reason that I had been missing for those six weeks was because I was attending antenatal classes at the hospital in preparation for the whole birth thing. I really wasn't a happy bunny when Em told me that they'd clash with COLT running training as it was my one night out a week, sad I know, but even before fatherhood I didn't have a social life on account of being an unsociable sod.

The classes didn't get off to the best start when we missed the first one because Em was two floors above the classroom lying in a bed thinking she was actually in labour. So we were a week behind when we joined eight other expectant mothers and their various supporters. The class got off to a disastrous start when the midwife said in front of everyone: "Andy wasn't here last week and missed out on the fat experience, so I'll make him wear the suit tonight."

She approached with something that looked like an overly padded straitjacket, which was supposed to simulate what being pregnant was like. I'd spent so many years cocooned in my own natural fat suit that there was no way I was humiliating myself in front of a room full of strangers.

160

If most people saw one of these when open water swimming they'd take up duathlon. I saw this beauty in South Africa in 2009, it was the realisation of a lifelong ambition.

hree happy COLTs after finishing the Lancaster Half Marathon in 2009, Sarah 'atterson and Stu Foy had just completed their first race at that distance. I was ever ɔ proud after helping Stu train for the event.

With Charlie Spedding, the winner of the 1984 London Marathon. Twenty-six years later I wouldn't win but I would follow in his footsteps to complete the famous race. (Courtesy of *North West Evening Mail*)

The Donut King – Fellow Pirate Fat Buddha kicked my arse at the Outlaw, winning the 'donut challenge', he even had time to down a full pint before crossing the finish line. (Courtesy of Helen Kenneth)

The Hug – My favourite photo of Em and I. She was heavily pregnant and I was physically and emotionally drained. It captures the raw emotion of taking part and witnessing a loved one put themselves through hell. Seconds later I'd cross the line and become an Outlaw. (Courtesy of David Rowe)

The pain is forgotten, at least for a moment. Sharing the experience of becoming an Outlaw with my greatest supporters, Dad, Mam and Em. Seconds later the pain came back but the smile didn't fade.

'Miracle' Mike Cubin, my cousin with Stoke City player, Ryan Shawcross. That might actually be fear in Ryan's eye having been pounced on by a very excitable forty year old. For Stoke supporter Mike it was the highlight of the weekend, on a par with finishing his first iron distance race.

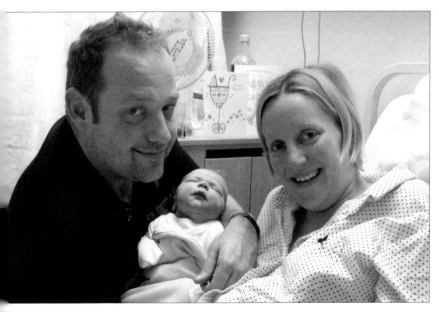

The happiest day of Em and I's life when Charlotte joined us. Nothing beats being a parent.

Pity it didn't come in carbon – having lost my saddle less than two miles into the half ironman race in Ely my dad rescued me some thirty odd miles later by wrapping a tartan travel rug around my seat post. It offered a little relief and got me to the run. Most sane people would have given up, luckily my shrink tells me I'm normal at our weekly meetings.

You really don't want to know where that screw has been. Once there was a saddle, then there was an instrument of pain. I rode for over thirty miles on that screw, it took my skin but not my resolve.

He's behind you – the 'tw*t in the pointy hat' is about to catch the 'crap swimmer'. The start of mine and Chris Lawson's personal race battle at the Fleetwood triathlon in 2011. We would resume the banter at Ironman Lanzarote and The Outlaw in 2012. (Courtesy of *www.martinholdenphotography.co.uk*)

One of the men that I respect the most in triathlon, the 'Grandmaster' John Knapp at the finish of the Norseman triathlon, without a doubt the toughest iron distance race in the world. John has taught me more than any training manual, and was influential in my decision to enter Ironman Lanzarote. (Courtesy of Valerie O'Donnell)

Chris 'The IronHippy' Wild and Richard Mason after completing the Ironman World Championship race in Kona in 2011. If it wasn't for the enthusiasm of Chris I would never have had the belief to even start Lanzarote, and the coaching of Richard got me across the line in one piece. (Courtesy of Fiona Wild)

Maybe I should have stayed in bed? 9am on a snowy Sunday morning, having ridden for an hour myself and Sarah Patterson stop to discuss our sanity. It was the sort of morning when a turbo session would have been more sensible. Sometimes I think it would be nice to live somewhere warm.

Sharing a well earned pint with Dave The Ex-Spartan at the Le Tour de Staveley sportive. I stuck to the blackcurrant whilst Dave had a beer, his drink obviously worked because moments later he left me for dead as we completed the last few miles of the gruelling course. (Courtesy of Sue Walsh)

How hot? It's just after 9 o' clock in the morning, within an hour it would reach 50 degrees. That morning the conditions in Lanzarote terrified me. (Courtesy of Fiona Wild)

He's the only gay in the village – Daffyd, err I mean Andy Ley in the women's tri top that he bought and wore ever so well. Thankfully Andy's fashion faux pas was just what the rest of us needed to take our minds of the task at hand. (Courtesy of Andy Ley)

GOOD LUCK

DADDY

Inspiration! – The photo I received on my phone the night before the Lanza race when I was feeling very nervous. I almost cried when I saw this photo of Charlotte, it was the mental image I relied on throughout the race.

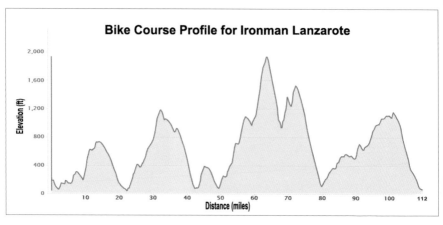

Bike Course Profile for Ironman Lanzarote

Like Sharks' teeth – the scary profile of the bike course at Lanzarote, it deserves its fabled reputation. It's as tough as they come with its oppressive heat, soul destroying wind and leg cramping monster hills. It is not a course for the faint hearted or under prepared.

I'm the one in the orange cap – the washing machine effect is there for all to see as 1,500 athletes churn the waters of Puerto del Carmen as they begin the long, tough journey to becoming a Lanzarote Ironman. (Courtesy of Fiona Wild)

Slap – actually although it looks like I'm about to slap Mandy Ley I'm actually about to 'high five' fellow COLT supporters Matt Hirst and Jack Billingham. Their support rescued me at times on the bike when my mind started to play tricks on me. (Courtesy of Andy Ley)

eauty & The Beast – The beautifully scenic view from the top of Mirador del Rio, he highest climb on the course. No photo could do it justice, it is simply stunning. very beauty needs a beast and Mirador is no exception as Richard Mason onquers the climb with iron determination. (Courtesy of *www.trilanzarote.com*)

Almost done – I love this photo of Jack Billingham and I in the last couple of miles of the race. It captures the last deserted part of the course, just around the corner was the biggest neon welcoming party I've ever seen. I'm feeling it but Jack's enthusiasm just kept me going, that and the thought that I was about to achieve all that I thought was beyond me. (Courtesy of Fiona Wild)

Proudly wearing their medals Chris Wild and John Knapp (right) join the immense COLT supporters. They had cheered themselves silly all day and would continue to do so for another five hours or so whilst they waited for me. (Courtesy of Andy Ley)

I'm so excited that I try to push down the finish gantry, well actually I'm high fiving Chris Wild in celebration of finishing and becoming a Lanzarote Ironman. I should point out for the sensitive amongst you that no finish gantries were harmed in this photo. (Courtesy of *www.trilanzarote.com*)

A man hug of mutual respect – Chris Wild and I embrace in a mixture of relief, pride and a sense that something magical had happened that day. I'm sure that it will be a day that will never leave either of us or anyone else that experienced it. Ironman Lanzarote gets under your skin, more than any other race I've ever done. (Courtesy of *www.trilanzarote.com*)

My own personal ambulance escort – I suffered so badly in the last half of the marathon at the Outlaw in 2012 that it would have actually made sense for the ambulance to follow me. On that run I fell apart, I hated triathlon at times but I managed to run through the darkness. I had good reason to keep pushing forwards.

Journey's End – The proudest moment in my triathlon journey, crossing the line with Charlotte in my arms at the 2012 Outlaw. The thought of that moment kept me going and the joy on my face is genuine. In that moment I fell in love with triathlon all over again. (Courtesy of *www.marathon-photos.com*)

She took two steps towards me and just stopped dead. I glared at her with intent. "Maybe we'll leave it," she blurted out, which resulted in a smile from me. Thankfully Em saw my point of view and I didn't get in too much trouble for it. I found the classes to be a complete waste of time, and come the actual birth none of what we'd learnt was applicable. I think as the weeks went on the midwife and I rubbed each other up the wrong way on more than one occasion. I found her tone and manner to be totally condescending in a room full of intelligent adults. I was annoyed as we weren't going into this thing blind, we'd read the books and learned the theories. And I'm sure that she found me to be a stubborn, awkward, and uncooperative so and so, and most Wednesday nights she would have been correct.

One night we were "role-playing" which is an awful concept much loved by management types in training, where we pretended to be in a situation that was given to us on a card. I looked down at the card in my hands and burst out laughing. It read: "Three days after giving birth you are in your local branch of Next wanting to buy wallpaper to decorate your lounge. The lift is out of order and the wallpaper is on the second floor. What do you do?" She asked me what was wrong.

"Seriously, who thought this up? Three days after giving birth who the hell in their right mind is going to be thinking about wallpapering a lounge and shopping in bloody Next! Surely you'll be knackered and trying to cope with an alien situation, and the last thing on your mind would be home furnishings," I snorted probably a little too bluntly. "I wrote the cards," she said as she turned with a click of her heels and a dismissive shrug and moved on to the next poor couple. After five weeks of suffering, we were all shown some rather graphic photos and given an uplifting pep-talk at the end of the session. The photos didn't bother me, as after all I'd spent many hours holding Em's hand while she watched the documentary series *One Born Every Minute*.

I never understood the attraction though of watching and scaring yourself s**tless as mother after mother screamed in pain on the TV, knowing that you were about to put yourself through that. But the pep-talk actually was going quite well and seemed to make a lot of sense. I hadn't done anything to warrant a 'look'. However that was about to change when the midwife came out with an interesting statement.

"Now remember ladies childbirth is harder than running a marathon." I couldn't help it, I snorted, and as everyone was silent she picked up on it straight away and out came the 'look'. "Oh I see, I take it you've given birth then and think it's easier," she finished with a chuckle. My back was up and I was on the defence. "No obviously I haven't but I've run several marathons, have you done one?" She wasn't expecting that and stammered "errr no, no I haven't but..." "So let's face it neither of us can back that statement up, so let's agree to disagree." I know I was being a git but at least I'd given her an out. I realise I was probably being immature, but I'd had enough and thought that she shouldn't make sweeping statements that were just plain wrong.

However I was about to find out that she was right. Women mostly are of course and being a happily married man I should have known that. Emma was about to take part in the hardest marathon I have ever witnessed. Never mind childbirth being harder than a marathon, it was a lot harder than any Ironman.

16

CHILDBIRTH

For those of you with a nervous disposition, those of you who are expecting or planning your first baby and pretty much all of the blokes, I suggest that you skip the majority of this chapter. The title kind of gives it away don't you think? Instead just find the paragraph in italics at the end of the chapter and you'll get the short and still realistic version of events. Aren't I good to you?

My world changed forever at '3.47am on Thursday 30th December 2010. Not ten minutes earlier I was walking briskly down the hospital corridor from the birthing suite, a glorified private room where Em lay exhausted in her bed surrounded by doctors and midwives. I turned into the waiting room and broke the news to my anxious parents and Emma's mum.

"Em is exhausted, the baby is getting stressed and the umbilical cord looks like it is wrapping around the neck. They are prepping her for theatre, as they might have to do an emergency caesarean if things stay like this. I've got to go, I'll let you know what's going on as soon as I can."

The last thing I saw as I turned and headed back to my wife was her Mum bursting into tears and being comforted by my Mum. It had been the longest and most stressful night of all our lives and it wasn't over yet.

It had all started two days before on the cold, crisp and bright morning of 28th December when Em and I had reported to the maternity ward. There was no mad rush, no panic trying to find her 'birth bag' of essentials, we even had time to feed the cat before we jumped in the car for the mile and a half drive to the hospital.

Em was scheduled to be induced that day as she was officially two weeks past her due date. Baby Holgate was a lazy little thing and was enjoying a nice warm lie-in, and given the fact that it was freezing outside we couldn't blame it. But it was time for junior to be coaxed out into the big wide world and let its poor Mum get back into normal-sized pants and to be able to see her own feet.

For the last couple of months I'd been putting Em's socks and shoes on for her because she couldn't see or indeed reach over her bump. I behaved myself and resisted the urge to put one brown shoe and one black shoe on her feet, but it had been tempting.

I guess like any new parents we both naively expected to be holding our baby in the December as we had been told that was when it was due. We should have known better. I don't think Em has ever been early for anything in her life so it was obvious to me that Baby Holgs was taking after its mother from an early age.

I've never been known for my patience and as every day passed the tension seemed to grow, every twinge, every kick brought an expectant enquiry from me only to be met with the same discouraging response: "Nope, it's just a kick."

One thing we were both glad of was that the baby wasn't born on Em's birthday, 21st December, or indeed Christmas Day. We were pleased that our child would have its own special day to celebrate each year and not have to share it with its Mum or a bearded carpenter from a best-selling book.

The day of 28th December was probably the longest one of both our lives. Emma was induced at 10am and we sat there and waited. Again naively we expected things to kick off straight away. After the midwife performed a procedure known as a sweep she reassured us that she thought we'd be parents before the day was through.

At 8pm I kissed my very calm and still very pregnant wife goodnight. We were both shattered, although nothing physically had happened other than the pair of us walking two grooves into the ward corridor. It was the mental anguish and anticipation that sapped the energy from us.

I got home, fed the cat and made a raft of calls to concerned family, updating them on nothing really and then fell into bed. I don't think I actually had the energy to eat that night. I didn't sleep a wink as I expected my phone to ring at any moment with the news that the baby was minutes away. Throughout the early hours my mind played tricks on me as I drifted just on the wrong side of unconsciousness. I imagined I'd heard a faint rendition of my rather appropriately chosen ring tone, Insomnia by Faithless. I was mistaken. "I can't get no sleep" didn't chime its ironic melody that night.

I returned bleary-eyed to the hospital the following morning, looking like a tramp who had been out on the lash with Oliver Reed, George Best and Charlie Sheen. Em on the other hand sat up in bed eating her toast and glowing radiantly like a Disney princess. Between mouthfuls of tea and toast she informed me that she'd been induced again and that she was dilated more than the day before. Things were indeed starting to happen.

Within a couple of hours we were on the move, transferring down from the maternity ward to the ground floor labour ward. The porter who moved us joked that it was kept two floors away from the expectant mothers and behind soundproofed doors so that the screams didn't scare the s**t out of those still ready to pop. I thought it was funny, I'm not sure that Em did though. Suddenly we were no longer on a shared ward but in our own private room, with the attention of our own midwife. She explained the procedures and what to expect while we were there, what each machine did and why Em would be put on each of them. It all seemed very sci-fi and the *Star Wars* geek in me wondered where they kept the Bacta tank.

Surprisingly she said that Em could have two people in the room at any one time and that others were welcome to visit also. On hearing this Em told me to go outside and ring both our parents and they were as surprised as us. "Procedures have changed since you were born Andrew, I wasn't even allowed at the hospital until after it was all over with," said my Dad with an air of nostalgia.

Within 90 minutes both sets of expectant grandparents had arrived, and a prospective uncle in Emma's brother Matt, to offer moral support. Throughout the day and into the night as things moved slowly they were all amazing. The two mothers who knew a thing or two about the process of childbirth kept Emma company, giving her some much needed female presence to counteract my nervous male fretting.

The three blokes kept whisking me off and plying me with coffee, and making sure that I ate. "You need to eat, you'll need all your strength over the next few days to help Em and the baby," said my father-in-law John as he passed a plate of sausage and chips under my nose. Although they were made up to be sharing in the experience all the blokes admitted that a labour ward was "no place for a man", so I think I was giving them an excuse to get away from the sharp end of things.

I was actually fascinated by it all and pretty much had to be ordered away from the bedside by Em to go for something to eat and drink, and give others a chance to come and chat. Her waters had been artificially broken hours earlier but nothing was happening. Then just after the clock ticked past midnight the midwife examined her and announced that she had reached the magical 10cm dilation mark where she could really start to push and hopefully deliver the baby.

Intense bouts of pushing followed. Em was breathing in short fast bursts, which for an asthmatic must have been hard. She reminded me of how I sound in the last kilometre of a fast 10k race. Sweat poured out of her and it was my job to mop her face and head with the ice cold flannel that I'd been given by the midwife. Em took huge gulps on the gas and air that she had resorted to as the pain intensified. She'd also been talked into having an epidural by the midwife and a surgeon as they looked at the worst case scenario of maybe having to deliver our baby unnaturally.

Em was devastated and told me through floods of tears that she felt like a failure, she had wanted to do it all naturally and without drugs. I held her close, kissing her forehead and reassuring her with words that felt so inadequate.

It broke my heart to see her like that. I had never witnessed another human being sacrifice so much of themselves for the life of another. I don't mind admitting that I shed a tear as I reassured her that she was a wonderful Mum and that she had done everything that she could have done. I loved her more in that moment than I ever had done, and I suspect than I ever will again. I felt humble and honoured that this amazing woman was bringing our child into the world.

Just after 3am and following several examinations and much talking the doctors and midwives decided that enough was enough. Em was a wreck, I had never witnessed exhaustion like it. I owed the antenatal class midwife an apology as she hadn't lied. Marathons are a piece of cake compared to childbirth. The heart rate monitor that had been pretty constant in its readings of the baby's heart started to have huge swings.

The graph now looked like the bike profile from Ironman Lanzarote with jagged steep teeth, as opposed to the flat Ironman Florida profile it had exhibited all day. This was an indication that the baby was getting stressed. They examined Em again and announced that they could see the baby's head emerging. This was great news or so I thought. One of the midwives asked me to step outside and she said: "We don't want to panic Emma as that's the last thing she needs right now but the cord is wrapped around the baby's neck and there is a real danger to both it and the mother. We need to get her into surgery right away. We'll try a forceps birth but we may have to do an emergency operation in order to have a successful outcome."

My world fell apart. It was never meant to be like this, it was supposed to be comfortable, I was supposed to cut the cord, and it had never crossed my mind that both Em and the baby would be in danger. "My colleague is in there telling Em that we are going to theatre as a precaution because she is so tired, we don't want to panic her OK," I was told. I nodded my agreement and followed her back into the room. I kissed Em and told her it would all be OK and that I'd see her in theatre, I was just going to get scrubbed up.

After delivering the news to our stunned parents I was led through the doors into the outer operating theatre and instructed to go into the locker room where I would find hospital-issue scrubs and a pair of static-free rubber Crocs for my feet. As I pulled on my starchy navy blue overalls I caught sight of myself in the mirror. I looked like I'd aged 40 years overnight. I pulled on the blue paper hat and took a moment to compose myself, my wife and child needed me. I had to be strong, I had to be calm and above all else I had to be conscious.

Into the bright operating theatre and I've never felt so helpless in my life. I was a spare part really as medical staff buzzed around a stirrup-prone Emma like wasps on a discarded apple. I was sat on a stool holding her hand, Em was shielded from what was going on by a curtain across her chest but I was sat just far enough away to see everything.

There was blood everywhere as the surgeon sat on another stool between Em's legs. Steel instruments that I couldn't even begin to describe without thinking of a horror film were laid on an equally cold and glistening tray next to her skilled gloved hands, hands that I was entrusting with the lives of my two loved ones. "We'll try the forceps but I don't think that will work, let's prepare for a section," she said, more to the room as a whole than to anyone in particular. "Emma – on the count of three you push as hard as you can, we'll give it one last try." The anaesthetist worked on getting a cannula into Em's hand that I wasn't gripping tightly, in preparation for the operation. Em pushed with all her might. I thought I saw something but was immediately distracted as Em howled in pain at the needle going into her hand.

"Congratulations, you have a baby daughter," said a grinning surgeon as she held up our baby above the curtain. The baby was covered in blood and didn't appear to be moving as it was quickly handed to a midwife and wrapped in a blanket.

Poor Em had missed seeing our daughter, as she had closed her eyes in pain, trying her hardest not to swear as her hand burned. I suppose it was a testament to the power of the epidural that she felt no pain 'down below' and at the point of birth was in agony at the introduction of a needle into the back of her hand.

Over in the corner of the room three midwives worked rapidly on the baby. She hadn't moved or made a sound. They were the most terrifying seconds of my life. Had the wrapped cord cut off her air? Would she ever make a noise? Where we about to experience the greatest heartache of all? The world had stopped, would it ever spin again?

"Waaaaaah."

It was music to our ears. We both cried as the tension visibly left our bodies and we realised that our daughter, our Charlotte Emma, was alive and had a good set of lungs on her. The midwife reassured Em that Charlotte was fine, and a very healthy if not dainty eight pounds and seven ounces. We were parents and life would never be the same again.

I have never felt so much instant love for another person as I did when I held my baby for the first time. It's something that you can never fully understand until it happens to you. I knew instantly that I would lay down my life to protect the one that was in my arms. I knew that no matter what I ever achieved in my life nothing would be greater than this achievement. I was a dad.

Here we go for those of you that skipped the long version above. Em went into hospital. She woke up to find that overnight a stork had visited and left a little bundle of joy at the bottom of the bed wrapped up in a Marks & Spencer baby blanket. Attached to her left big toe was her name tag. Charlotte Emma Holgate is the light of our lives. See, easy this childbirth lark, I've run harder marathons...

17

MY SECRET LIFE

The first few months of 2011 flew by at a lightning pace. Being new parents is hard work and no matter how much you read or listen to advice from friends and family that have been there, done that and changed the nappies nothing can prepare you for the total reversal of your life, routine and thought process.

The two weeks of paternity leave that I took went by quicker than Alistair Brownlee on a bike. One minute I was holding my newborn baby and the next I was back at my desk bleary-eyed and mainlining caffeine just to get me through my working day.

I'd always been a morning person and could quite happily have gone to bed at 9pm every day. That seemed perfectly acceptable to me. Unfortunately Charlotte had other ideas. Like most new babies she slept when she wanted to and it didn't conform to my usual sleep schedule.

Emma was managing to grab a little bit of sleep during the day when Charlotte slept but I didn't have the luxury of a pillow on my desk. We kind of got Charlotte into a routine, as all the books say, but realistically she got us into a routine. If we were lucky she'd go to sleep about 1am and sleep through until after I'd left for work at 8am.

As the months progressed she started going to sleep earlier, mostly before the witching hour but as a consequence she'd be up before the dawn chorus. There was little consistency in those months and it just meant that Em and I walked round with that constant 'new parent' look – not caring about dribble down the back of your shirt, opening your mouth to speak but only ever having a yawn escape your lips, unkempt hair and bags under your eyes that could hold the contents of a shopping mall.

Despite the lack of sleep, nothing picked me up more than a cuddle from my baby. I could hold her against my chest and watch her sleep for hours, it's therapeutic – although in reality as soon as she closed her eyes I'd be snoring as I tried to find some much-needed shut-eye.

Coupled with the constant lack of energy was a realisation that days were suddenly shorter. OK, so they were longer in the time I was spending awake, but the amount of time when nothing needed my immediate attention had disappeared. There was no me time anymore. When the baby slept, things still needed doing. Housework didn't do itself, nappies didn't buy themselves, the cat still hadn't figured out how to use the computer and order tuna (actually that was a good thing), and most of all Em needed some space, even just to go and have a bath or a shower.

I was knackered but at least I had some downtime from dirty nappies, crying and sick when I was at work. Em had all of that and was breast-feeding too, so I'd come in from work and try to take over as much as I could, just so I felt like I was at least pulling my weight as a husband and father. There wasn't much time for training, and on the occasions when I did get out I found myself mostly on autopilot. I managed to run to work and back a few times, but more often than not I fell into a downward cycle of get up, fall into the car, drive to work, drink coffee and wake up.

I had intentions of running in my lunch hour but again the lure of the staff room, where it was warm and they had comfy seats, seemed a much better prospect than the wet and cold roads around campus. I was conserving my energy, I'd need it when I got home. I'd not been swimming at all, and finding the time to get to the gym didn't happen. When I did get out running a few times, I was averaging about eight-and-a-half-minute miles, so the excess weight and lack of energy didn't seem to actually be destroying me too much, despite how I perceived things.

Eventually my body and mind started to adjust somewhat to the circumstances. One icy February morning I just woke up feeling not entirely alive but not my usual undead self that materialised most mornings. Suddenly five hours of sleep seemed like it was more than enough.

I started leaving the car at home and headed out on my bike managing a luxurious hour or so a couple of times a week, deliberately targeting the hills in an attempt to burn more blubber and increase my leg strength.

I was going to need that strength as while waiting for Charlotte to appear back in December I'd entered the Cleveland Steelman in July. I'd done the half Ironman a couple of times before and I loved the race as it offered great value, a fun course and best of all a start that didn't involve getting up at 4am (little did I know that would no longer be difficult for me come race day!).

I had no aspirations to a time yet because my thyroid issues were still not resolved and I had no idea how the training would mix with fatherhood. Doing a half Ironman as a bleary-eyed new dad could be as dangerous as jiggling a baby too much just after it's been fed. Note to any prospective dads, sometimes burping and barfing go hand in hand. All I'll say is it's a good job we have laminate floors, and that I no longer cared about the state of the clothes that I wore.

I adapted to life as a parent and started fitting in training around family life, using my commute and lunch hours to get some activity done. I spent most lunchtimes running around campus, working on getting my speed sorted out. I'd run two laps, approximately 2.6 miles, really working hard at trying to beat my time for the first lap. It's a very small thing, but I find it quite motivating.

My motivation for those runs was helped by the fact that I was joined by my mate Simon Vaukins. We'd met when he worked in the library and struck up a friendship over running. He'd been an avid footballer but found that as he got closer to the "ripe old age of 30" as he put it (no hope for me then) that he was picking up more injuries. He had recently turned his attention to running and had literally jumped in with both feet, entering the Chester Marathon at the back end of the year.

Simon started coming out running with me and it made me work that much harder trying to keep up with the younger and fitter bloke. It also meant that I'd go out in my lunch hour on days when I may have just nipped into the staff room for a sandwich and a quiet catch-up nap.

I also managed to get out running a couple of times with Andy H and his youngest son David as they prepared for the Skipton Triathlon in April. This mostly consisted of us all donning our head torches and getting pretty mudded-up as we ran off-road. David, being a lot younger and fitter, was generally a good 50 to 100 metres in front of us, acting like a rabbit to mine and Andy's greyhounds – not that either of us would ever be as quick as a greyhound you understand. It was on one of these head torch runs that I turned my ankle when placing it down on a rock. It hurt like hell but after hobbling for a while I managed to run through the discomfort. Not thinking much more about it I ran the following lunchtime with Simon and experienced quite a bit of pain in my left Achilles, and on examination later there was a pea-sized lump about 3cm above my heel. Unfortunately it began to trouble me and cause me pained concern, especially first thing in the morning as my legs tried to wake up as I took my first steps from the bed to the bathroom.

I'd also find that if I'd been still for a while, at my desk or driving the car, that I'd have pain and stiffness when I rose to my feet. The actual motion of running or cycling didn't seem to affect it, which seemed weird. I started taking anti-inflammatory drugs and icing the area in the hope that it wouldn't develop into full-blown Achilles tendonitis – the internet is both a scary and helpful place for self-diagnosing a running injury.

One Sunday when I was back home on Walney Island I went for a run and recorded my fastest splits since 2009, averaging eight minutes per mile for the five miles with several at 7:30 pace. That was a massive motivator and I hoped to build on it in the following weeks. It didn't quite go to plan. The following Saturday morning after only five hours of sleep the previous night I met my mate Stu Foy for a run at 7am. The last time we had met up for a run had been just after Christmas when I was full of cold and had to abandon after a couple of miles. As I was no longer bunged up I hoped that this run wouldn't be such a short disaster.

It was a drizzly, nondescript sort of morning, one of those when you really want to spend it in bed. We headed out along the cycle path to Morecambe where we proceeded to run along the seafront. The wind was howling and I couldn't see the Cumbrian hills through the raincloud curtain that was drawn in the middle of the bay.

I was feeling fine, we were chatting away and the run was going good. Things started to change as we headed past the Town Hall, the halfway point of our planned run. I was frustratingly aware of a growing burning sensation in my left leg. My Achilles, which had been playing up in recent weeks, was soon throbbing like Christian Grey and Ana Steel in a lustful entanglement. As we reached the Trimpell cricket club, which seemed much quieter without several hundred runners setting out on a 20-mile race, I had to walk and stretch. My Achilles was on fire and the flames had spread up my leg to my dodgy left knee. I started running again after a few minutes, gritting my teeth through the pain. Each step was uncomfortable but it was manageable.

It was unfortunate because Stu was running really strongly and I was just hanging on for dear life for those last few miles. He'd been very patient and understanding, curtailing his own efforts to make sure that I made it home in one piece. I managed to run 10.24 miles in one hour and 27 minutes, which in reality given the pain I was in wasn't bad. I got home and applied ice. It seemed to alleviate the immediate problem but I spent the rest of the day limping around. I rested on Sunday, and stupidly felt guilty about missing training but knew that I had to be sensible. I also needed a lie-in as the lack of sleep was catching up with me, and actually overtaking me and heading off into the distance with a two-fingered salute. I was still awake before 7am, but it was blissfully relaxing just lying there for a couple of hours with Em, Charlotte and her cuddly bunny. If I wasn't a triathlete it could have been the perfect Sunday morning.

So this all brings us to the Tuesday when I finally ventured out running again. I'd walked the three and a half miles to work and my leg felt fine, so I thought I'd chance a run after work. If I'm being honest I fully expected to have to stop and walk home but I felt really good and ended up doing a steady eight miles in one hour, 14 minutes and a single second. There was no pain, and I could walk fine all night without limping which was something of a rarity at the time.

The only thing that I did differently was tape my knee, placing a strip of Elastoplast under the knee cap to help my patella track better with each step. That simple method I'd used for years to good effect, and it didn't let me down, so maybe my Achilles pain had been caused by my dodgy knee not tracking properly again when I ran. The lump remained on the tendon, and my leg ached first thing in the morning, but I wasn't troubled again and thankfully continued running relatively pain-free.

Buoyed by my renewed enthusiasm for training and the real fear that my cycling mileage wouldn't be enough to get me through the Steelman, I entered the Jodrell Bank Sportive. I had about six weeks to train for the race and then I'd be joining Andy H for this 80-mile pedal-fest around the Cheshire countryside.

Having done it the previous year he assured me that it wasn't too hilly but that there was one cobbled climb. "That could be fun if it's p*****g it down," he joked. I gave him a mock concerned look and said: "We're doomed then because that seems to be the norm when I race."

Of course the other significant thing that happened in those early months of 2011 was that after much stress, hard work and the odd tear I finally became a published author. My book, *Can't Swim, Can't Ride, Can't Run*, hit the shelves on 1st January, although I didn't actually see a copy for ten days. People were reporting that they'd received copies from Amazon and my copy from the publisher still hadn't turned up.

When it finally did and I held it in my hands I can't tell you how proud I felt, although it was very surreal to go home and place it on my shelf next to Dean Karnazes, Paula Radcliffe, Bradley Wiggins and many others in my "triathlon" collection. Come on, I'm a librarian, you didn't expect my books just to be randomly placed now did you?

Suddenly as an author I was in demand. People wanted to talk to me. My first interview was for Talk Radio Europe based in Spain. There was no training for this kind of thing. I'd receive an e-mail from the publisher saying this station wants to talk to you about the book. The radio presenter or production manager would ring you up about 30 seconds before you went live on air just to check the quality of the line and then bang, you are live to several hundred thousand people on the breakfast show.

It sounds daft but although I was nervous I just pretended I was having a chat with a mate in the pub and it seemed to settle me down. I listened later online and I didn't sound as nervous as I felt and some people have actually said that I sounded posh. Surely they must have been listening to a different programme? I don't do posh.

A few days later I had a whirlwind morning doing two interviews for the British Forces Broadcasting Service, a great radio station that broadcasts to our hard-working armed forces around the world. I feel quite honoured to have been given the chance to talk to them.

My first interview was with Lynne Duffus on the breakfast show. Lynne was lovely and a great interviewer, and she made me feel really relaxed off air as we chatted briefly about the format of the interview. Then after I listened to 30 seconds of Take That I was on the air live around the world talking about my blog, the book and racing triathlon, and how the armed forces take part in Ironman and usually pass me on the bike and run. I really thought about my words and I didn't swear. Lynne had warned me about that – our soldiers obviously have sensitive ears.

I talked about how the book came about, what the Ironman involved, how I got into it, my medical history and what inspires me to do such a tough event. I got off the phone and was grinning like a kid who's just been told they are going to Disneyland, I just really enjoyed talking to Lynne.

No sooner had I put the phone down and it rang again, this time I was talking to Simon Marlow, BFBS Radio 2's breakfast show host. Simon again chatted to me off air and with seconds to go cut back live to introduce me as the last bars of a song I didn't recognise played.

Simon was a great interviewer, asking good questions and again made me feel relaxed. We pretty much discussed the same things, and before I knew it was time to say goodbye. It did feel strange knowing that while I was sat at home in relative comfort and safety those listening to me that morning were in places like Iraq and Afghanistan putting their lives on the line in the name of freedom. I couldn't do it, I'm not that brave. I'm not religious but after I put the phone down I said to the empty room: "Look after them."

Not to be outdone by the radio, several newspapers got in touch for interviews as the media circus seemed to roll on. *The Lancaster Guardian* from my adopted hometown interviewed me over the phone and after looking at some photos I'd e-mailed them decided that they needed their own 'action' shots. How the hell they got the daft idea that I did action after looking at photos of me competing was a mystery that still to this day eludes most great minds, and Viking.

They sent a photographer to take shots of me riding my bike one lunchtime. I was frozen in the hail and rain wearing shorts and my COLT cycling jersey, shivering while lenses were attached and a tripod was set up at the side of the almost deserted campus perimeter road. It all went well until I was just saying goodbye. I went to push off the icy tarmac with my leg to ride away, and my cleated foot slipped and I fell over. The photographer, who happened to be a keen cyclist, picked me up and said: "We've all done that." I think he was just being kind, and thankfully he'd put his camera away.

It must have been a slow news day the following Friday as one of my colleagues came in to the staff room and put the paper on the table. There staring from the front page was my ugly mug. It was good publicity for my first public engagement the following day, and one that I was quite nervous about.

I don't recall that I was given lines often at school, on the odd occasion perhaps. I guess I was a bit of a swot? It was probably no great surprise then to my classmates that I grew up (allegedly!) to be a librarian. In the same vein I know it's a bloody shock to my English teacher that I grew up to be an author as I think she must have worn out more red pens correcting my grammar and spelling than I've worn out running shoes over the years.

Writing the same thing again and again (what lines are if you didn't know) would have been good practice for my first book signing. It took place at the Waterstones book store in Lancaster and was part of the celebrations for the inaugural World Book Night, a celebration of reading.

To say that I was nervous would be a severe understatement. I couldn't sleep the night before and my poor wife Em said that I was worse than any pre-race state I usually get myself in. It was fear of embarrassment I guess. This is probably hard to believe as I'm naturally very shy with people I don't know. I was always the one stood in the kitchen or sat on the stairs at a party. I guess years of not being comfortable in my own skin made me that way, and although I'm more confident these days it still lingers. So the fear of talking to strangers and the embarrassment of being sat there on my own not selling one book was gripping me.

I turned up at the bookshop ready for a two-hour signing stint, having remembered to pick up a pen on the way out of the house. It turned out they were going to provide me with a few pens, and the manager looked a bit bemused that I'd brought my own. "I'm new to this," I shrugged and smiled as if by way of an apology for breaking some unwritten book signing code. I was shown to a table right by the front door set up with a pile of my books on it and a sign explaining who I was and what the book was about. Also sat there was Pauline Turner, the other author signed to the event.

Pauline was a very nice lady, and one of the world's leading experts on the craft of crochet. She was the first person to ever crochet ice cream after a TV producer bet her she couldn't do it. She was there promoting her latest book, a self-help/make you think read entitled *Why Do You Think You Are?*

Pauline had done loads of signings all over the world, and to be honest I was a bit star-struck by the grey-haired black belt in crochet. It seemed that she was to yarn what that Rowling lady was to wizards. She reassured me that I'd be fine when I told her that this was my first signing and that I was feeling very nervous.

My worries were soon quashed, I hadn't even got comfy in my chair when I signed and sold my first book. And from there it didn't really stop for the next 90 minutes. There weren't queues out of the door but I wasn't sat twiddling my thumbs either. It was great to see many friends such as Andy H and family and Richard G popping in to say hello and lend moral support. They knew that I'd been bricking it in the days beforehand. Em and Charlotte also popped in to see how it was going. My daughter took it all in her stride and slept through the whole thing.

The highlight of the signing was meeting people. I loved having the opportunity to chat about triathlon and champion the sport, although mostly it was to triathletes so it wasn't a hard sell. The highlight of the night was Dennis. Dennis must have been in his late 70s and very slowly limped up to the desk with the use of a cane. I initially thought he wanted to talk to Pauline but no, he'd come to see me. Isn't it funny how initial appearances control our thought processes?

I'm embarrassed to say that I saw the limp, the cloth cap, beige mac and walking stick and instantly and wrongly thought: "He's not here about triathlon."

Dennis had been a cyclist in his youth and had seen my interview in the paper the day before. He had travelled for an hour on the bus to get to the signing because he thought that my story sounded like a good one. He had a massive grin on his face when I wrote: "Dennis, hope you enjoy my book, best wishes Andy Holgate".

That grin made my day. Simple words and scrawl making a man like Dennis who's seen more in a lifetime (he was a Barrow shipbuilder and then travelled the world on oil tankers before retiring to Heysham) than I have yet to experience was priceless. It was the first moment of magic that I experienced as an author.

My signing finished about 40 minutes early as I unbelievably sold out all of the shop's stock. The manager actually took me to one side at the end and apologised for not getting more books in and promoting me being in store more. I was quite happy to have just had the opportunity to meet some fascinating people and to have a gentle introduction to feeling like a proper author signing books.

I shook Pauline's hand, wished her well with her books and went off to join Em and Charlotte for a well-earned latte, perfectly anonymously among the early evening crowds. My secret life as an author was put back in the closet. It was time to just be me again.

18

A DIGITALLY SHORTENED VIKING

March started with a really good training week, probably the best for almost a year. I guess not in terms of numbers like time or distance, but just in how I felt. I was a happy little bunny and things were going well. Granted I still wasn't sleeping or training as much as I would have liked in the build-up to a half Ironman, but it wasn't stopping me from smiling. Or maybe it was just wind?

I seemed to have a positive glow about me whenever I laced up my running shoes or buckled on my bike helmet. It seemed a long way down the line but for the first time since the previous year's Outlaw I felt like I was back on the road to Ironman. This year was part of that journey, almost like a 'gap' year that I was taking out in order to better myself. It was going to be a long and hard journey until the summer of 2012 but it was one that I was determined to enjoy.

I certainly enjoyed getting out with Team Thurnham Cycles for a bike ride. Team Thurnham Cycles is the name for Andy Holme and sons, on that particular occasion Andrew and Gareth. I'm an honorary member of the team. Andy H even had custom cycling tops made for us all featuring the family crest, and 'sponsor names'. The shirts are naturally in royal blue and yellow, reflecting the riders' support for their beloved Everton Football Club. I had thought about asking for one in the black and white of my team, Newcastle United. However I kept quiet and decided that it's best not to upset a Scouser, and particularly one that looks after my bikes for me. We ended up battling the wind through the flatlands of the Fylde coast. I tucked in at the back for most of the ride, trying without success to find a little shelter behind the wiry figures of my fellow riders. I completed 35 miles in just over two hours but I was hanging on for dear life as we sped through the last few miles. The brothers hit the front letting their competitive juices flow like a flooded mountain stream as the mph rocketed well above the 25 mark.

On returning home I was totally spent. Those last miles of intense riding had stiffened my quads and calves, muscles that of late had belonged more to a runner than a cyclist. Despite my fatigue I was pleased to have got a decent distance into my legs as it was my first time out on the bike all year that took me beyond the hour mark.

The Jodrell Bank Sportive was only a week away. Andy H and I had entered the 80-mile ride but given my lack of bike miles I began to think that the 50-mile option might see my odds of survival increasing.

In the days that followed I found my way back to the pool for the first time that year. Now I've never been a big lover of swimming but I really enjoyed that session. I ended up doing a mile in 40 minutes, nothing fast, nothing clever, just swimming. No pressure. I was just pleased I could remember what to do. I'd had to ask my coach Richard to adjust my training schedules in those first few months after Charlotte arrived as it just wasn't possible for me to get to the pool, the logistics just didn't add up.

Running-wise it went well with distances of eight and a half and nine miles that week. Both sessions were on my plan so at least I was doing something right. I sat one night with Em and told her how I felt guilty for missing key training sessions, how it pained me that Richard was putting the effort into coaching me and I was failing as an athlete. I could have given more, I could have cycled more, but something had to give in my work-training-life balance and unfortunately I needed to pay my mortgage and provide for my family in terms of time and money so I had no choice but to let training slip.

I still feel extremely guilty typing that now. I was caught between a rock and the proverbial hard place. I couldn't sleep, I couldn't train but most of all I couldn't stop. Being a triathlete was part of my evolved DNA now and I was entrenched in the mindset that any time not spent training, or any key sessions missed made me a failure.

It didn't help seeing my COLT club-mates getting stronger and faster, or my online buddies posting their training volumes and "willy waving" at their huge measurements. It was a testosterone-fuelled nightmare and I was in severe need of hormone replacement therapy. I was the ugly sister being left on the shelf whilst all the beautiful people went to the ball, but unfortunately my fairy godmother was on an all-inclusive holiday with Saga in Bournemouth.

My own beautiful person in the form of Em cheered me up somewhat when she reminded me of the circumstances. "You have to remember you aren't a pro, it's not your job and I think you do wonderfully well. I guess most new dads wouldn't even consider going for a run or racing a bike. You need not to be so hard on yourself or you'll crack up." It was the sort of pep-talk that I needed heading into Jodrell, knowing that I was about to cycle further than I had in seven months.

The alarm went off at 5.30am. It took me a few minutes to adjust. "This isn't my bedroom, where am I?" Don't worry Em hadn't kicked me out. I was sleeping on the sofa bed so that I wouldn't wake her and baby Charlotte up when I arose at that unsociable hour. I had less than an hour until Andy H would be picking me up and we'd be making our way down to Cheshire for the Jodrell Bank Sportive.

The time passed by quickly as I went from task to task: put the sofa bed away, eat porridge, fill drinks bottle, take cold tablets (as feeling like crap), feed the cat his breakfast (very important for keeping the peace) and pump the tyres up on the bike having got it out of the cellar. Thankfully I managed to do all of that and sneak out of the house without rousing my girls. Phew.

Before I knew it we arrived in Cheshire. It was only 8am but it felt like the middle of the day. As Andy H pulled his car into the school car park he surveyed the colourful scene that was unfolding before us. "If this many middle-aged men in revealing lycra were seen in a school playground during the week, the place would be on lockdown and the armed response unit from Manchester Police would be called," he quipped. Thankfully however the only thing under threat that morning was good taste, which took another blow as we pulled on our bib shorts and the rest of the lycra uniform and joined the love parade.

I bumped straight into fellow Pirate Silent Assassin who greeted me with a big hug. He never ceases to crush me and one of these days I'm sure he'll crack one of my ribs with his enthusiastic welcome. It was great to briefly catch up with each other as we hadn't met since that well-earned fry-up the morning after the Outlaw back in August 2010.

Minutes later he and his wife Jo, who didn't quite look awake but still managed a huge smile, headed off to do battle with the 80-mile loop while I headed off to put my number on my bike. It was a phased start with small groups of riders setting off at various time intervals. That way the organisers hoped that the roads wouldn't get too congested with cyclists.

We had decided to downgrade from the 80-mile loop to the 50-mile route. There was no shame in doing so, we'd still face a tough challenge and would come away fit enough to ride again another day. Sometimes you have to put your pride aside and keep your focus on the bigger picture. This wasn't my 'A' race, it was part of the journey and not the destination.

One last check of the bikes and Andy H and I headed out onto the highways and byways of Cheshire. The weather stayed kind to us and despite the earlier forecasts we remained dry and not buried in snow, which was most unusual for any ride that I was involved in.

The course itself was a very pleasant one, a few long uphill drags but nothing major. It was certainly no Le Terrier, the hilly event that we'd done a few years back that caused pain and visions of Elvis. It was probably a good indication of my fitness and lack of bike miles that I struggled on the climbs. I was carrying a bit of extra weight, a self-inflicted handicap that certainly wouldn't have helped my performance.

As I puffed my way up a slight incline coming out of Middlewich I joked that I was climbing like a hippo on a unicycle. Although he didn't disagree with my candid assessment thankfully Andy H waited for me at the top of that rise and every other one on the course.

The route took in some of the Macclesfield Triathlon bike course and I was riding along thinking I've seen this before without actually knowing where I was. There was just a vague feeling of déjà vu. The other landmark of course was the promotional Sky TV dish that happened to be stuck out in the middle of nowhere known as Jodrell Bank.

OK, so it's not really a TV dish, but an observatory that was originally built for looking at cosmic rays. It is home to the world's third largest moveable radio telescope, the Lovell Telescope. It's so powerful that on a clear day you can see the whites of Victoria Beckham's perfect teeth when she smiles in California. I made that last bit up. We all know that Posh Spice never smiles.

We certainly made the correct decision to change from the 80-mile to the 50-mile route, as when we finished Andy H could feel his back starting to twinge. It didn't however stop him from showboating over the line 'ahead of me no-handed, arms aloft in a Mark Cavendish-style salute, only without the two fingers. Rather boringly in comparison I rolled to a stop with my hands firmly on my bars, knowing if I'd just attempted to copy my mate we'd have been visiting Stockport's accident and emergency department. I had a bad track record with two hands on the bike, none would be suicidal. I was really chuffed that I had completed my longest ride since the Outlaw. I was particularly glad of the cup of coffee that awaited me once I had unclipped. I had a hell of a head cold and the hot liquid helped ease it somewhat. My nose was also running "like a glass blower's arse" as my riding partner is so fond of saying. I was very glad to get a tissue and relieve some of the pressure from my head.

We finished in three hours and 23 minutes, not fast, not spectacular and certainly not flat out. It was a sensible ride, mostly comfortable and just what I needed to ease me back into riding my bike for a few hours at a time. I had predicted that we'd finish in three and a half to four hours, so it was better than I thought. My only gripe of the day, and this probably comes from being a triathlete, was the "wheel-huggers". At a few points every time I turned around I rubbed noses with a guy behind me, he was that close. More alarmingly he was riding with his front wheel overlapping my back wheel, a very dangerous action and one that can lead to crashes. He and his mates just sat there for miles.

I was on the verge of saying something when they got delayed at a road junction and Andy and I hit the gas to get away. In triathlon drafting isn't allowed unless you are racing in the elite category, and I'd ban it from there as well to make it all more of a race rather than a ten-kilometre flat-out run, and I was used to that. Sportives such as this one don't conform to the same rules. Huge pelotons form and wheel-hugging is the norm.

When I ride with Andy H or the COLT crew we all know each other really well, we can anticipate the way the other will ride, the way they will react, and we use hand signals to warn each other of road obstacles. I found safety in the familiarity, when I was surrounded by strangers that familiarity was gone and with it a sense of safety. But I should stop being a big girl's blouse as nothing happened, my limbs are intact and my bike is in one piece, and you can't ask for more than that from a 50-mile adventure.

But that day was very special for a different reason. Those of you who have read my blog and my first book will notice something missing from this account. There were no punctures, no falls, no crashes, no mechanicals or any incidents that delayed either me or Andy H. This was the first time that we had completed a sportive together in five years without incident. A first time for everything!

My insufferably heavy cold seemed to get worse over the next week or so, and it caused me to abandon my COLT running session on Wednesday night. It was probably a good thing that Em and Charlotte were away in Liverpool because I was a grumpy so and so, even Crosby the cat avoided me that night. He slept on the sofa rather than our bed. Maybe animals do have a sixth sense after all? My mood was daft really because I still managed to plod for six miles, so it wasn't a complete waste of time.

Things got worse and I had to take the rest of the week off work as the virus moved to my tonsils, causing my throat to feel like someone had poured acid down it. I was no longer p****d off that I was running badly, I was quite happy to wrap myself in my duvet and try and survive until the virus was done. My next run was combined with a swim and a cycle. Sound familiar? Well actually it was about as far removed from my usual triathlon outing as you could imagine and much like a Michael Johnson race it was all over with in under 50 seconds.

Now that 50 seconds took two and a half hours to create. The BBC had got wind of my story and sent a local news crew to film me for the *North West Tonight* show, a news and current affairs programme. It didn't take that long because I was crap in front of the camera, actually we didn't have to shoot anything more than once. The BBC have loads of footage of me that they never used because the piece was cut short because the main news was extended, and rightly so, showing the devastation of the tsunami in Japan.

The filming started with me being a librarian. What do librarians do? Yes that's right they shelve books. Well actually I don't, and haven't for years but apparently the BBC's viewers would expect to see me shelving books, so that's what I did. I didn't however wear a cardigan and I drew the line at having my hair in a bun. Next it was off to the university swimming pool. The press office had arranged it all with the pool manager. They'd obviously heard about my swimming prowess and reputation because they'd roped off two lanes for me. It was actually more to stop anyone else getting accidentally filmed (there are strict rules about filming people without their permission, especially in a swimming pool).

So we did close-up shots of me putting on my swim cap, my goggles, and looking out over the pool in wistful anticipation. Instead I probably gave them: "I hope he'd focusing on my face and not my swimming shorts because it's bloody cold in here." Yes things come in small packages, but I didn't want mine on primetime television.

This was followed by me diving in, despite me explaining that I'd never actually done that in a race, and then swimming lots. All of this took the best part of an hour and was condensed into about two seconds. Probably just as well because any longer and my swim technique would have had people calling into *Points Of View* to complain.

I quickly got dried off and changed and then it was back to my office to get the ROO before heading off to the new campus woodland trail to film me running and biking. Now we were outside so we had to recalibrate the microphone that was attached to my cycle jersey, as the frequency needed adjusting to eliminate noise pollution from the nearby M6. Earlier inside I had been counting to ten (I struggled a bit) to help get the right sound level, unfortunately that was too short, and this led to perhaps one of the most surreal moments of my life.

Picture the scene:

Me in the woods, dressed from head to toe in figure-hugging lycra, holding a carbon bike, wearing a bright yellow helmet and staring into a BBC television camera being directed by another man to recite the popular nursery rhyme *Baa Baa Black Sheep*. I kid you not. I did make him promise me that the footage would never see the light of day. And people think it is glamorous appearing on TV.

Once we'd established that Baa Baa did indeed have some wool it was more shots of me running: towards the camera, away from the camera, planting my foot as close as I could to the camera without kicking it, putting one shoe on, putting two shoes on, holding my shoes, stretching against a tree and finally pretending to run out of transition (bike leaning on a tree to demonstrate the transition area) with the ROO.

Finally we got to the biking part of the filming. The one important thing to say is that I never fell off...phew. I did however look very wobbly on the bike. This wasn't really my fault. I use quite small LOOK clip-in pedals, designed to be used with my bike shoes. On camera and on the ROO I was wearing very chunky running shoes. The two are not a match made in heaven.

My bike shoes were stuck in transition, keeping the tree company. "You don't need to get changed, your trainers will look OK," said the director. I didn't feel experienced enough to argue, and yes I suppose they did look OK, even if my bike wobble did not. Thankfully we wrapped (get me with the lingo) just as the heavens opened and it started to pour down.

OK, so it took two and a half hours of filming, and only 50 seconds got shown, and they didn't mention the title of the book but it was a great experience and one that I'd love to repeat. I never ever dreamt that I'd be the subject of a TV interview, no matter how short. It's something that I can show Charlotte when she grows up, and one day my grandkids.

Maybe the cold water on the day of filming caused a malfunction in my brain but I began to make a concerted effort to start swimming again. I spent several lunch hours in the pool. I didn't do any technique work or drills, I knew I wasn't the most efficient swimmer but I also knew that I had enough stroke knowledge to get through my upcoming races. Instead I concentrated my aquatic efforts working on endurance and reminding my lungs what it was like to work hard in an alien environment.

I tended to swim a mile while really thinking about the breakdown of my stroke, particularly the catch to pull which I knew I was lazy with. I also found it much easier and more enjoyable to swim because I had learnt how to bubble breathe. Until late the previous year I had never realised that you exhale underwater and therefore get more air into your lungs when you turn your head to inhale. I'd completed countless triathlons and three Ironman races while exhaling and inhaling all at the same time. No wonder it always took me an age in T1, I was getting my breath back.

Suddenly it was April, and I was faced with the prospect of a Saturday afternoon book signing in the Trafford Centre in Manchester, the second largest shopping mall in the United Kingdom, attracting over 35 million visitors a year. So no pressure then.

I don't mind telling you that this was one of the most terrifying and exciting days of my life. I was a complete stress-head from the moment I woke up. We arrived at the Trafford Centre in plenty of time, and located the bookshop only to discover that they weren't advertising me being there at all; no posters, no signs. Instead they were advertising a signing by another author, with banners and posters. She also had the prime spot at the front of the store while I was tucked away at the back.

Again with being so nervous my mood wasn't made any better, thinking she'd have huge queues and I'd be a "Billy no mates". Poor Emma could see that I felt so deflated. "Go and ask the manager to move you and to put the posters up that your publisher designed," she told me, but in typical English style I didn't want to create a scene. Besides who the hell was I to make a fuss, I didn't want the manager of one of the busiest bookstores in the country thinking I had Mariah Carey tendencies.

After lunch with my family the time of reckoning had arrived. I left them to shop and I went and reported to the store manager and was shown to my table, piled high with books, it looked pretty cool. I was swiftly joined by Viking who had come along to support me. He really calmed my nerves by chatting away about what good form he was in ahead of the upcoming London Marathon. I was so glad that he was there and I no longer felt out of my depth.

A few seconds later I had my first customer of the day, an amazing bloke called Alan, a paramedic who had read my book whilst recovering in hospital having donated one of his kidneys to his sick wife. Now that is truly inspirational in my eyes. He was looking forward to doing his first triathlon after reading my book, and the three of us chatted briefly. He came out with the quote of the day when I introduced him to Viking: "You looked much shorter in the book."

I collapsed in laughter and said: "Yeah, I had him digitally shortened."

And from there it just got better and better. Several Pirates turned up to lend support and have their books signed. It was great to catch up with some old friends and meet some new ones. I had great fun signing a copy for my mate Laura. The pretty Liverpudlian had a naughty sense of humour, she'd had great fun telling everyone online that she'd "been going to bed with IronHolgs every night and that she couldn't put him down". So I signed her book: "I've loved going to bed with you." It amused her, although I don't know what her husband Mark thought of our flirty banter, but he must have a good sense of humour because he married her.

Pretty soon the bookshop looked like a triathlon conference as lots of people stood around discussing the sport, marathon and ultra-running. People had travelled from as far away as Sussex, Rotherham and Liverpool. I even signed a copy for a Danish woman whose daughter is a pro-Ironman based out in Singapore.

I also ended up signing several autographs, a birthday card and posed for several photos. It was very strange when the first person, an ultra-runner, asked: "Would you mind posing for a photo with me?" I just looked bemused and said: "Really? OK then." I smiled for all I was worth, and by the end of the day I'd signed lots of books, met some wonderful people, arranged a couple of bike rides, and had a thoroughly good time. You've got to love triathlon and the people who take part.

Oh and just for the record, in real life Viking is only four foot tall and he carries a step stool around with him to stand on whenever a camera comes out.

By the end of April my racing year was thrown into turmoil. My 'A' race for 2011 was meant to be the brilliant Cleveland

Steelman, a half Ironman that I've done twice before. I'd entered last year and had been gearing up for it mentally and physically. Then I got an e-mail from my publisher telling me that they'd signed me up to a major book signing deal in Bristol.

The signing was scheduled for 2nd July, at about the exact time I would have been pedalling my way through the 56 miles of the Steelman several hundred miles away in the North East. There was nothing I could do as I was contractually obliged to appear. It wouldn't be third time lucky for me at my favourite half Ironman.

In the days following my withdrawal from the Steelman I entered a few races. I needed something to focus on before I foolishly entered an Ironman on the spur of the moment. I entered two sprint triathlons, St Anne's on 22nd May and Fleetwood on 25th September.

Both were pretty much on my doorstep, and both took place on closed roads, an unusual bonus mostly found at big races. I'd only ever had the experience of two closed road races and both of them were abroad, so to be practically racing that way in my own back yard was a really exciting prospect.

And at £25 each to enter they didn't break the bank either. I hoped that St Anne's would get me back into racing and that Fleetwood would finish off the season. I just needed to fill in the gaps in between.

19

MOUNTAINS, LAKES AND SANDSTORMS

Whoever it was that decided that willingly jumping into a lake in the north of England was a good idea on the early May bank holiday must have either been a masochist or a non-swimmer. While most normal people were enjoying the traditional Great British moved indoors because of the rain barbecue and beer I rather foolishly subjected myself to an outdoor ice bath, or as we triathletes like to call it open water swimming.

As I drove the ten miles to the lake I thought that as it was pouring down, blowing a gale and generally the sort of weather that you'd think twice about cycling or running in that it would be quiet. Boy was I wrong as 60-odd neoprene nutters turned up and for the first time in five years I was actually parked in an overflow car park.

The facilities are basic, after all it is a private lake attached to a restaurant. There is no indoor changing and no showers, the overhanging lip of the roof provides a shadow of shelter, and that's it really. However the restaurant had left the gazebo up on the patio from a weekend wedding for us to shelter under. "Let's do the safety briefing under the gazebo to stop everyone getting wet," Andrew McCracken, the organiser, announced without a hint of sarcasm.

That was the only part of the briefing that I could hear. I already had my ear plugs in and was wearing two swim hats in a futile attempt to keep the heat in. I looked to my right and Chris Lawson and Andy Ley were both shivering away, Chris's arms folded sternly across his rubber-clad chest like he was trying to stop the heat from escaping. "We must be bloody nuts, it's going to be a lot colder in there," grumbled Andy as he pulled his wetsuit up over his toned torso, turning to reveal his "Disney Thumper" tattoo on his shoulder as he gestured for me to zip him in to his wetsuit.

He hoped that his drunken tattoo from his military days would soon be joined by a rather less ahem pretty and more manly M. as he was aiming for his first Ironman at the upcoming Bolton race.

Within seconds of hitting the water I couldn't feel my hands and feet. I dived under the water to get my face wet and after the initial shock it didn't feel too bad. I'd agreed to swim with my mate Chris, like Andy Ley he was also aiming for his first Ironman at Bolton. Chris has an even greater fear of open water than me, although he'd been taking measures since the previous year to improve. He was making a hundred-mile round trip each week to get an extra session done outside. Strangely he had completed swims in places like Liverpool's Albert Dock and Derwentwater without panicking, yet at our own familiar lake his fear returned each time he stepped onto the sandy man-made shore.

We let Thumper and the rest of the main bunch swim away, and then we followed suit. We weren't the last ones into the gloomy looking soup, which I took as a positive. Gently we swam out to the start buoy, about 50 metres from the shore. Stopping briefly, we verbally checked that we were both 'good to go' and then I just shadowed Chris for a couple of laps.

Staying on his left at all times, I was there just to help if he panicked. I wasn't needed and Chris swam confidently. I struggled a bit with my breathing, a combination of the cold breath-stealing water and the remnants of a virus I'd picked up.

I especially floundered when swimming the longest part of the course into a headwind. The wind whipped the water into a frenzy, making each stroke a war of attrition. I'd never seen waves like that on a lake before, and I came out a few pounds heavier than when I entered due to the amount of water I'd swallowed.

Funnily enough standing on the side of the lake, peeling off the wetsuit, I suddenly didn't feel the cold anymore yet I was shivering. Chris was standing there just grinning like a Cheshire cat. Andy Ley soon joined us and smirked, "Told you it would be bloody cold," as he pulled down his wetsuit to let poor Thumper grab some air, after all bunnies don't breathe well underwater.

I was just relieved to be there enjoying the banter and company of my mates. I very nearly wasn't. My right shoulder although very stiff had behaved itself as I battled my way through the water. I was a little worried as it still felt sore after being hit by a car four days earlier. Yes, you read that right, let me regale you with a tale that still to this day makes my blood boil.

It was a glorious early summer evening. Clear blue skies perfectly complemented the lush green fields containing the late-arriving lambs that seemed to be everywhere. I'd told Em that I would be a bit late home as I was going to try and get an hour of cycling into my legs.

I left work and made my way into the village of Galgate, taking the deserted back road to avoid the bustling A6 that was full of my fellow university workers escaping for the evening. From Galgate I continued almost alone except for the odd cow that would raise its inquisitive head as the colourful creature with two wheels whizzed past.

Through the village of Dolphinholme I climbed up the leg testing ten per cent gradient hill into the Trough of Bowland, an area of immense natural beauty and home to some of the best cycling this Fair Isle has to offer. With the climb behind me, I threw the Giant into the big ring as the next section was all about speed. Rolling hills made the descent into the hamlet of Abbeystead, with its chocolate box cottages and humpbacked bridge, an absolute delight. The wind whistled past my head, making my speed seem more intense. It only lasted for a mile or two but it was pure unadulterated cycling bliss. It was the sort of ride that makes you glad that you bought a bike.

But what goes down must come up right? The road out of Abbeystead can only be described as a shock. Not entirely the north face of the Eiger, but the short sharp 20 per cent wall of tarmac makes you use every nerve and fibre in your legs as your lungs and heart struggle to pump enough oxygen to the pained limbs.

The Giant was a triple and I needed every gear that was available to me on the 28-tooth chain ring as I mashed the pedals, standing and grinding away with as much grace as a tightrope-walking heffalump. I couldn't help grinning when I reached the flat road just over the summit. I took a perverse satisfaction from the pain I'd just suffered.

As much as I know I'm a crap climber I really get a buzz out of dragging myself to the top of a climb, no matter how short. If I ever made it over to the Alps I'm sure that the French would have me committed, I'd be the mad Englishman who just wouldn't stop grinning like the Joker from *Batman*. That particular flat and very straight section of road is wide enough for two cars to pass each other comfortably so I wasn't concerned when I heard a car approaching from behind. As usual I was hugging the grass verge giving them plenty of room in which to pass me. I was on a deserted country road with plenty of space, I was wearing a bright red jacket and it was a clear evening, dusk was some time away over the horizon. Trust me, I didn't blend in and I knew I had nothing to worry about.

BANG.

I'm not even aware that I'm falling, there's no sensation, no moment of panic as the ground hurtles towards me, no screeching of brakes as I react trying to remedy the situation. It's like I just simply lost a few seconds of my life, gone, no memory, nothing. I could have been dead and I never would have known.

And then just as suddenly as it had been stolen away from me, reality floods back into my senses and I realise that my immediate perspective of the world around me has changed. I'm no longer staring at the grey tarmac of a country road with green fields and hillsides. Wheels are no longer turning beneath me. I'm static.

I'm now lying in a crumpled heap on the grass with my bike next to me, my left leg still clipped into the pedal.

It took me a few seconds to register where I was. As those precious seconds lapse my memory comes back and I instinctively reach for my shoulder which is stinging. Those few seconds probably saved the bastard that had done this to me. Turning around I could make out a black people carrier speeding away. Unfortunately given their generic shape I couldn't make out the make and model, and I had no chance with the registration. Who knows, if I'd turned a few seconds earlier I may have glanced a sliver of detail that may have helped the police catch the nasty piece of work that assaulted me. Slowly I picked myself up, waiting for a jolt of pain from an unseen injury. Thankfully none materialised and although my shoulder felt stiff it was mobile, I could manipulate the joint without pain, meaning there was no break. Gingerly I picked up my bike and examined it. The chain was off but there was no other visible damage. I quickly repositioned the chain and wiped my oil caked fingers on the grass verge that now displayed an IronHolgs impression on its surface. To this day I really don't know what happened. Having examined a few similar cars since, and having visualised my bike position that day in relation to the car I'm guessing that the wing mirror hit me as the vehicle sped past, I was lucky that it didn't hit me in the back of the head. Given the force of the impact and the quickness of it all I'm also guessing that the driver was beyond the national speed limit. What got to me the most was that the bastard didn't stop, they just left me there on a deserted road in a heap. I could have been seriously injured or worse. Thankfully I wasn't. The person behind the wheel obviously had no regard for human life, and it scares me somewhat they are still out there and driving on the same roads that I regularly cycle on.

When I arrived home half an hour later I think I was still in shock because I just swept Em and Charlotte into my arms and hugged them so tightly. I was suddenly aware of how life can suddenly change forever on the slightest twist of fate. In my arms I held my world, and some cold hearted sod had almost denied us that moment and all future moments. I mumbled what had happened to Em and she immediately rang the police. A traffic officer came and took all the details but we all knew that without any concrete identification from me that it would go no further. They'd got away with it.

Please don't let this put any of you off cycling. Think of how many miles we all ride each year, and how rare these accidents are. Each time we get on a bike on the road we are at risk, but statistics show you are at greater risk in a car. People said how unlucky I was to be hit, but I prefer to think how lucky I was that it wasn't worse.

Just be careful out there. As cyclists we are vulnerable. It's not rocket science that a collision between a vehicle and a bike isn't going to go well for the two-wheeled user, so be extra vigilant but at the same time still have fun. Being hit by a car is rare, being hit from behind and left for dead on a deserted road is as rare as rocking horse s**t, and could probably only happen to me.

A couple of weeks after my accident I had one of the busiest and most fun weekends in recent memory that didn't involve an Ironman, a birth or a wedding. Instead it was all about geography, well sort of.

The Keswick Mountain Festival took place from Wednesday to Sunday and featured a whole host of events from a sportive taking in several Lakeland passes, a tough triathlon, and a Derwentwater swim. Besides the physical there was also the entertaining as informative speakers from the world of adventure such as Mark Beaumont, Ray Mears and Sir Chris Bonnington MBE waxed lyrical to their respective audiences. And then there was little old me. I had been invited to give an hour-long talk in the Fell Theatre about my Ironman experiences. I was extremely nervous in the days beforehand, and I apologise to Em for that, she puts up with a lot you know. I wasn't a grumpy git, just kind of withdrawn a little, as I tried to formulate what I'd say, and what I'd do if no one turned up.

Thankfully I needn't have worried as two of my Pirate mates, Dave the ex-Spartan and Cake, turned up to support me. Cake, never one to do things by halves, had cycled over from Sheffield, just for the craic but unfortunately he got lost, only realising when he passed through Penrith for the third time that something was amiss. After getting Dave on the phone he managed to follow the directions given and set off pedalling on the road to Keswick rather than the road to nowhere.

When he arrived about half an hour before I was due on stage he headed straight for the rehydration tent, where he was joined by Dave for a pint of Jennings' best Cumbrian bitter. I settled for a coffee to try and warm myself up. I'd been frozen watching Dave take part in the Derwentwater swim that morning in horrendous conditions. Poor Dave was still shivering as he clung to his beer, and it made a change for him not to be drinking Guinness.

Both were a great help as we sat in the bar next to the theatre. They managed to calm my nerves as the world-famous opera singer Lesley Garrett warmed up the audience for me with a few songs. OK, that's a slight embellishment of the truth. Yes, she was on directly before me, but I guess most of her fans left the theatre before I took to the stage.

People actually queued and paid money to hear me speak (all for charidee mate) and they laughed, and asked so many questions that I overran my time slot, much to the annoyance of the production manager who was stood there dragging his hand across his throat in a classic 'cut' gesture, and eventually when I finished they applauded. It was a nice feeling.

I loved being able to talk to people about triathlon and Ironman. Hopefully I sparked some interest in some that were there, hopefully they will have gone on to race in their first triathlon, or been inspired enough to make the step up to an Ironman.

I thanked Dave and Cake, they had been brilliant, and we all headed back down the M6 to prepare to race the next day. They were both doing the sprint tri at Nantwich and I was off to St Anne's to sprint there. Luckily for Cake, he was getting a lift off

Dave, if not who knows where he would have ended up.

Now on a good day the course at St Anne's has PB written all over it, almost like the road builders used a spirit level to keep it perfectly flat. Unfortunately it was far from a good day. Listening to the local radio on the way to the race I was a little concerned to hear that the Met Office had issued an amber warning for high winds. "There will be gusts of up to 50mph," warned the presenter. "That'll be great if it's a tailwind on the bike," I replied to the voice as I pulled into the car park.

The event takes place right on the exposed seafront with the only shelter coming from the sand dunes that separated the million pound houses from the harsh eroding Irish Sea winds. I imagined that it would be a wonderful seaside setting on a bright summer's day, and I would be able to appreciate the splendour of the houses with their Malibu-style balconies. However Malibu had morphed into a bleak, grey apocalyptic wasteland on this particular day.

Transition looked like a battlefield as helmets blew all over the place, so in response I clipped my strap through my front wheel spokes to secure it for when I came out of the swim. The wind was so strong that several bikes were lifted off the racking or blown into others. My own bike fell victim to the elements for when I came into T1 after the swim the ROO was actually entangled with the one next to it, a crocheted mess of handlebars and pedals, a result of the wind.

The swim went well. As you'll all be aware I'm never going to set any records in the pool. I was feeling quite relaxed because I had put no pressure on myself, I had no time in mind and given the elements I knew that any sort of fast time was out of the question anyway. As I queued to get into the pool I was recognised for the first time, I guess the fat lad in a Pirate tri top kind of gave me away.

"I really enjoyed your book Holgs," said one of the other competitors. I really didn't know how to react, I'd never expected anyone to recognise me, I'd never even thought about it. I mumbled a few words of thanks, smiled and blushed, it was obviously hot on poolside. Into the water and I had fun waving and pulling faces at the diver who was lying on the bottom taking photos. As a qualified diver myself I'd have been quite happy to have that job.

I emerged from the pool into the disaster zone that was T2 and was almost blown off my feet. It was very tempting to just go back inside and keep warm. All around me in transition people were putting on rain jackets, extra tops, gloves and other protective clothing. I'm sure that if I waited around long enough one of the many beginners that were taking part would have carefully placed Wellington boots on their feet and attached an umbrella to their handlebars.

I didn't wait though. Sopping wet in just my tri top and shorts I unclipped my helmet from the safety of my wheel and placed it on my head, swiftly followed by my cycling shoes and finally my glasses. I set off running for the mount line, struggling to keep upright in my cleated shoes, my feet sliding on the wet surface as the strong side wind pummelled me. I moved like a few of the lasses I'd seen in skyscraper heels in Liverpool, only they were drunk and it was 3am. I didn't have that good an excuse. This was going to be one hell of a ride.

Immediately I was very thankful for the sunglasses protecting my eyes as the sheltering dunes failed and instead became objects of torture as I was sandblasted for the next 15 miles of cycling and running. I'm sure that people pay good money for that sort of derma-abrasion treatment at a spa.

I tried to keep tucked and aero as best I could but a lot of the time it just wasn't possible as I needed all my power just to keep the bike upright. Going flat out on the bike, overtaking people and still not reaching 12mph is a different experience I can tell you. Only one other cyclist passed me, and I managed to pick off a few poor souls that were struggling as we made our way back towards the sports centre for the run.

On returning to transition the longish run from the dismount line in cleats was not fun. The wind was still determined to take me off my feet. Off came the helmet, this time I didn't care if it blew away, I quickly changed my shoes and headed for the run course. Turning on to the coastal path on the sea-side of the dunes made anything I'd already experienced seem trivial. I'm no lightweight but I was running as much sideways as I was forward. I felt sorry for the kids who raced later on, they did the same course, and many were in tears. All I could taste was sand. It was lining my gums, it was even in my ears. It must have been hell for the marshals policing the route so I made sure that I thanked them as I passed, even the one who sent me about 100 metres in the wrong direction. The poor guy obviously realised his mistake and came sprinting after me, but because of the howling wind I couldn't hear him. It was only when he tapped me on the shoulder, which made me jump about six feet in the air, that I got back on the correct course.

The good thing for me about the run was how strong I felt. There must be something in my genetic make-up that makes me thrive in harsh conditions. I'll take wind and rain any day over excessive heat and sunshine. Surprisingly no one caught me or passed me on the five-kilometre course, which was very satisfying.

I don't mind telling you that I was very relieved to have finished the race in one piece. I crossed the line, knackered, cold and with red raw skin in a time of one hour, 20 minutes and 23 seconds. On crossing the line I was met by fellow *Triathlete's World Forum* member Razor, who looked as fresh as a daisy.

He had just finished only his second triathlon in just over an hour and a half. He'd been inspired to get into the sport in part by reading my book. He was keen for me to also meet his son-in-law Des who was taking part in his first triathlon. It was great seeing the enthusiasm that the pair radiated for their new found sport and it took me back to the moments just after my first triathlon when I felt like I could conquer the world.

The three of us were like drowned rats but as we chatted we all forgot the weather for the first time that day, caught up in our own little private bubble of sunshine. I would become quite pally with both of them over the coming year, offering advice and tips as they joined the Pirate ship of fools and prepared to take on their first Iron-distance race at the Outlaw.

I'd had a cracking weekend, two days of very different fun. I just hoped as I drove home with the car heater on full blast and my windscreen wipers wagging quicker than a labrador's tail that the next time I went to the seaside I'd get a bit of sunshine.

Just over a week later I learned a lesson, one that I already knew and should have been mindful of over the previous few months. But it was one that I'd neglected, and as a result I paid the price for it. Let me explain.

I took part in the midweek Capenwray Sprint Triathlon. It's less than ten miles from my house, and so I figured I'd give it a shot. Em and Charlotte were out, so I had a free night. It would have been rude not to race. I was being spontaneous, which is something of a rarity for me. The race kicked off at 7pm, which meant it was a bit of a mad dash to get home from work, get my stuff together and get through rush hour traffic in the car park that is Lancaster's awful one way system. I made it to the race venue with half an hour to spare, and quickly said hello to fellow COLTs Ian and Danny as I joined the big queue at registration.

Ten minutes before the start and I was still not ready. I quickly racked the ROO and hurriedly set up transition before putting my wetsuit on. It was only then on checking my gear in transition that I realised that my number belt was empty and that the race number I'd been issued with was still on the front seat of my car.

I looked at my watch, I had five minutes, so I bolted barefoot across the coarse gravel car park. It was only when I started to think about what I was actually doing that my brain registered that my exposed feet were grumbling about what I was subjecting them to. I returned to my transition patch, breathless and flustered that I couldn't get my bloody number to attach to my number belt as the press studs holding the number just wouldn't close.

Standing next to me Danny Rogerson, who always seemed so calm, wise and mature saw how frustrated and panicky I was getting, and took over. In seconds my helpful club-mate had succeed in attaching the number. He made it look so easy that I felt such a muppet. A word of advice: NEVER enter a race on the spur of the moment unless you know you are organised enough to get there and set up in plenty of time.

Still it could have been worse. Our other club-mate Ian Bailey had turned up to race without his running shoes and he owned a bloody running shop. I wasn't the only COLT muppet there that night and it made me feel a bit better.

We all got into the drink for the deep water start in the crystal clear depths of the disused quarry that now serves as a dive centre. I don't think I've EVER experienced cold like that, not even in our club lake in the middle of a storm. But it was wonderful and the most enjoyable swim I've ever had in a race. I quite simply loved the fact that I could see underwater for miles (well not literally but you know what I mean!), and that I was surrounded by fish.

I could see the scuba divers below us as they explored their underwater playground. I watched on fascinated as several emerged from a sunken plane. Before I knew it the 500-metre swim was over and I emerged from the water, stride for stride with Danny. The stony run to transition hurt like hell, my feet still hadn't recovered from the earlier abuse I guess, but I was soon on my bike and that was where my night took a nosedive.

Within seconds of leaving transition Danny powered past me. He's a really strong cyclist and there can't be that many more 60-year-olds that could compete with the veteran of several Fred Whitton finishes. In a flash he was gone. I tried to respond, I tried to focus on his back wheel but I had no chance. I felt like I was pedalling in squares. I just didn't get into any rhythm the whole way round the 18-kilometre route.

People passed me, and then even more people passed me, I had no response. My frustration just grew and grew, "AARGHH" I screamed out to the cows as I rode past. I was so angry with myself that I think I took my emotions through a full 360-degree flip. I wasn't 'over tired' as us parents are so fond of describing our kids, I was 'over angry'. I was so angry that I became calm again in a 'meh' sort of way.

In my head I figured "just enjoy the rest of the race, it's not an important one". And you know what, I probably cycled better after that. It was a hilly course, and that was my downfall. I'd just not done enough time on the bike that year, or enough hills, and I was found severely wanting.

Surprisingly I flew out of transition on to the run. Maybe it was just sheer relief at being off the bike. My legs felt fresh as I focused on the person in front, about 80 metres away. I would eventually catch and pass them as I ran along the canal towpath.

Shouts of encouragement from club-mates as they passed me coming back spurred me on. Ian stormed past and just beamed "found my shoes". I would later learn that he'd found an old battered pair under the driver's seat in his van, and hadn't even known they were there.

As I approached the turnaround point all I could hear was "come on Holgsy" as John "IronFarmer" Carr was bouncing up and down waving his arms excitedly. He still remains the most animated marshal I've ever encountered in a race. I couldn't help but complete the rest of the race with a huge grin on my face after that. The five kilometres flew by and pretty soon I crossed the finish line in one hour 22 minutes and 37 seconds.

I was knackered, frustrated, relieved and happy. The race had been a useful one in keeping me in a racing mindset, it had been fun, especially the swim – did I really just type that!? But most of all it had been a learning experience, in that it reminded me that it's all about the bike.

Quite simply if I had been bike-fit I would have been a lot higher up the results table, several minutes faster, and probably would have enjoyed it more. It also made me think a hell of a lot more about a decision I had been contemplating.

I had been caught up in the excitement of discussions with my COLT club-mates about my return to Ironman in 2012 but my confidence was now dented slightly. I had a dream: a battle with my demons in a desolate land was what I craved. Would I be biting off more than I could chew? I needed to talk to the man in the know. I needed to talk to Chris Wild.

20

I BLAME THE IRONHIPPY

Gasping for breath, bent double, I angled my right wrist so that I could see the screen of my Garmin 310xt, a great gadget that usually taunted me with how slow I'd run or cycled. As I stood between the rows of vines alongside the canal, the hard Mediterranean sun-scorched earth beneath my feet, the screen offered me hope. We were enjoying two relaxing weeks at Em's Mum's place in Beziers again, and I of course couldn't resist getting out and running along my 'usual' routes.

As I panted in the mid-afternoon heat I was pleased with my effort and indeed my progress. Over the five-mile route I had just made an improvement of almost two minutes since last August, recording a time of just less than 40 minutes. OK, maybe it wasn't as hot as it was then, and it was still a few minutes off where I wanted to be but progress is progress. Most of my running that holiday was done in the high heat to try to improve my tolerance to running in higher temperatures, something I knew had been my downfall in the past. And there was a good reason for this.

Before leaving for France I finished my last blog post with the following: "All this week I have been contemplating entering Ironman Lanzarote in 2012 but if I can't cope with the hills of Capenwray how the hell would I cope with Lanza? One dream too far maybe?"

Those of you that were paying attention at the beginning

of this book will recall me saying that after my self-destructive marathon in the oppressive heat of Frankfurt I promised Em that I'd never enter Lanzarote. She was genuinely concerned for my safety. It wasn't that she doubted my ability, far from it, she just couldn't stand to see me suffer.

We had talked briefly about it before we left England, and one night over a couple of bottles of local cider the subject came up again. Em told me her concerns, she knew my strengths and weaknesses and I agreed with her on all her points. The heat and the hills were my enemy, nothing about Lanzarote played to my strengths. But that was the attraction, the challenge was what I craved, I wanted to test myself to my physical limits and it was an added bonus that I'd be joining plenty of club-mates in the sun.

I explained to my wife that I had been blown away reading the race reports of Chris Wild and John Knapp, COLTs that she knew and liked. She also knew that I regarded them more highly than anyone else I'd met in triathlon, along with my coach Richard Mason. I ducked back inside to make a brew, the cider had gone down a little too well and when I returned I handed Em a couple of sheets of A4 paper.

On unfolding them she looked up at me in disbelief: "You brought copies of the race reports with you on holiday? How sad are you!?" She sat there gripped as she read the reports, drinking her tea, occasionally lifting her head quizzically and giving me a look that I knew ever so well. I could sense the tide turning, she was realising just how inspired I was by the endeavours of John and Chris. I sat silently drinking my coffee as she inhaled the following:

Ironman Lanzarote by John Knapp.

Ironman really is a family. I'm not elitist but it is different to other forms of triathlon, there's a bond between those who have gone through it together whether it's sub 10 or 16hrs+. No one finishes without huge commitment to get it done. I'm the old lag at this. Lanza was number 16 so I should know what I've let myself in for.

Getting to Lanza was a relief, ash clouds and also that there were no more hard or long sessions to do before race day. I had to fight the urge to use all the extra time for eating and drinking. Fight the doubt that comes from the way the legs ache when you do less, the visual illusions that your legs are shrinking and there's lard appearing around your stomach. The way everyone else looks fitter, leaner, and hungrier for it.

"What do you hope to do?" I was asked at dinner one night. I couldn't think in times, too dependent on weather, but more it seems to tempt fate to name the real ambition. "To get round", "get under 11 hours", "race him (Richard Mason)" is what I said. In my head it's "top ten", "top five", "Kona"...

What you never know when you line up on the start is how the day will go. You do the training, peak and taper, set up your gear, and then it's a conveyor belt that delivers you on to a crowded beach as the sun rises with 1,500 others who all feel as keyed up and adrenalin fuelled as yourself.

You never know if you'll get a sh**t fight or good feet in the swim. I went wide, added some distance but stayed out of trouble, set off hard and eventually at about 800m some reasonable feet I could stay with went by. I latched on and swapped when they slowed. When I emerged I was five minutes up on my time from 2004.

T1, loads of swimmers stripping in the shower. "Keep moving forward" is my mantra. Why stop if you can make progress towards the finish? HR in the first 5k out on the bike was 90%+. Struggled to get my effort under control but the legs felt fresh and with my slow swim there's loads of cyclists to overtake.

Biggest surprise was seeing Richard up the road after 20k, as I passed he told me he'd been sick in the swim. He's not had much good fortune this year.

First half of the bike my HR kept nudging up, too fresh, too enthusiastic, felt fantastic, tried to reel it back in with partial success. On reflection I need to reduce my HR target for the first 90k. At halfway you are also halfway through the longest bit of climbing on the course and it was the first chance to ask the Wild support crew (they set out their support plan with a huge commitment to get out on the road side as many times as possible, so cheers right round the course for the COLT. Very appreciated) "how's Chris doing?". "He's not far in front..."

What can I say, he was having an epic day, the kind that in cycling would start all kinds of gossip and allegations, I was gobsmacked. My own early enthusiasm is beginning to hurt, legs heavy, can't keep the HR up, by the end of the bike even 70% is difficult to achieve and I'm thinking I've blown it. Seeing Cat Morrison come past me on the last descent and beating her out of T2 was the only consolation.

The biggest thing I've learnt that you cannot tell when you are on the start line is whether you've brought your run legs with you. Sometimes you think you remembered the legs then at 20k they fall off and it all goes into meltdown.

In my first five Ironman races it all went pear-shaped, it was only the sixth in Frankfurt when I finally nailed running the whole marathon and it still doesn't always go right. Kona last year I was walking at just one mile. But in Lanza it appears I had them.

Genuine doubt crept in at 18k when I finally caught our own Ironhippy and the quads were going. Time for the second mantra, "repair yourself". When it's getting real tough slow down and do what you have to do to get your body together. Usually its fluid and nutrition that have crept off the radar when you were feeling too good or too bad to concentrate.

And that was it. I spent all day ignoring the possibilities of success, my watch hadn't started so I didn't know the time, just concentrated on doing the bit I was in, or the next small chunk of the race, take no notice of the big picture just focus on what you need to do now. Sat in the finishing pen hoping, but not daring to get the result, very happy when it came. I was Kona bound once more. My time exactly an hour quicker than my 2004 attempt on the same course.

But we've done races before in other places but this now ranks as the best. The COLT away team was immense, competitors and supporters alike. There's a great camaraderie in shared suffering, it builds the wish to support your competitors rather than destroy them.

Ironman Lanzarote by Chris Wild

Following the fantastic reports from my comrades in team COLT Lanza 2010 squad, I guess it's time I put fingers to keyboard too – as usual, this will be somewhat on the lengthy side – get a brew and prepare to be sent to sleep!

This was always going to be my most important Ironman race since the first, for so many reasons; I guess the initial motivator was that it was going to be number five. I can still remember the moment when race director Kenneth (a lovely guy I've known for 26 years now!) announced at the 2007 awards ceremony, that in future, they would be giving special achievement medals to anyone who completed five Ironmans in Lanzarote. "I've got to have one of those." Priority races 2008-2010 sorted! Foolish boy.

Last summer, it looked like things may not go to plan, with the cartilage tear in my knee, but making it round Ironman UK gave me the courage to enter, and after deciding not to have an operation, there was nothing to do but start training, and praying. This Ironman would decide my triathlon future – if it was going to be another Bolton, just getting round, then it would probably be my last. Five would be a good place to leave it.

As has been pointed out many times, Lanzarote is my spiritual home; it's my home race – I know the course, and I know so many of the competitors, organisers and athletes competing. Being able to share it with so many of my club-mates this year made it even more of an exciting prospect.

Race week came, but something was different this year – I was nervous. I couldn't settle until I'd counted all the COLTs in. Meeting up with everyone for the swim sessions, and visiting team HQ overlooking the swim start, made it a very special time. The wind was high, it was cloudy in the north; it was perfect conditions for the COLTs. But there was talk of the wind dropping. While many were celebrating, I knew this would mean HOT, and harder work for the last 60k of the bike. Fi had brought a thermometer, and our patio was cooking at 31°C (88°F) in the shade, and a disturbing 50.6°C (123°F!!) in the afternoon sun. The run course has NO shade.

Race morning finally arrived, and I got myself sorted calmly and confidently. Or so I thought! Fi was snapping photos and remarked "you look nervous". Ten minutes later I was chatting to a friend who also commented: "I've never seen you looking nervous before." I guess all the factors above were lodged somewhere in the subconscious.

The swim is always a lottery; you can get caught in the melee or end up with no one to draft. After a slight worry of thinking I'd broken three fingers on my left hand before the first turn, I soon realised I'd got a lucky ticket today. I managed to find space, but on the edge of the vortex, for the majority of the first lap. As I ran up the beach, I glanced at my watch, and read 31 minutes. What? Lap two went in a blur, as I spent the whole time grinning, again enjoying reasonable space. Out of the swim in 1:05, a spot of wrestling in T1 as I rounded the corner into a guy coming the wrong way, then off on the bike.

The bike started beautifully, climbing out of Calero into a breeze rather than a full on gale, was a joy; likewise Fire Mountain, where it had been blowing 25mph the previous weekend. I was already 15 minutes ahead of schedule. The small climb after Fire Mountain made my legs hurt – have I over-cooked it in the first 45k?

Stay calm, there's a good downhill section to recover. Up to Teguise at halfway – still way ahead. Onto the big climbs, and I don't seem to be going backwards like normal, but I'm still ticking them off on the descents.

No sign of Richard Mason by the side of the road, so he hasn't punctured yet, but the "Grand Master" John Knapp should be coming past at any moment. Spent too much time propping my bike against a bin at the special feed station and 'comfort break', so presumed John had flown past. I could see cloud still clinging to the top of Mirador, and prayed it would still be there by the time I arrived.

Slight hair-raising moments on the descent into Haria, as firstly a car pulled over right in front of me (luckily on a slow section), then testing my new tubs to the full as I whacked into a pot-hole at around 30mph, and expected both wheel and tub to disintegrate instantly. They did their job, and the cloud just about hung around on the summit of Mirador. A guy with a disc flew past on the descent, but I caught him on the long time trial back along the island – it's not all about the kit.

211

At the summit of the beastly new climb back into Teguise, someone shouted "your position 191". Top 200 – sweet. 25K from the finish Fi shouted "John and Richard are still behind you". "What do you mean, STILL?" I knew if I could crest the next hill, I could probably make it home, and as I came in towards transition and saw the remainder of the COLT crew, the look on Sarah's face was priceless, and unmistakably "what are you doing here?"

I'd been thinking the same since the first lap of the swim! My knee was sore, but as soon as I started running with the bike through transition, I knew it was going to be OK for a few miles. My Garmin read 5:36 – way beyond my wildest dreams of 5:56! More grinning!

I didn't see John come in on the bike, and was probably just over 1k when I saw Richard coming in. I had no pretensions of holding either of them off, but had hopefully given them a surprise to bring out great marathons.

I was running well, and hoped I could make them run 3:30 to beat me. Hold it together, and you've achieved the ultimate coup. Clocked John shortly after the turn, followed swiftly by the captain. Slowly, slowly, catchy Hippy! The timescale of the remainder is a bit of a blur. The heat was oppressive, and I was hitting the smart gels and cola hard, so no wonder really!

I was also wasting time sourcing ice at the aid stations, but a cube in each hand, replaced at each station, kept me cool, and feeling relatively good. I was running OK, and walking the stations was helping my knee.

At the next sighting, John complained of bad legs as he cruised by (oh for bad legs running that pace!), I knew he'd got this one in the bag. Richard came by late on lap two, no way was he going to get beaten by a vegetarian! Job done. I usually have something left for the last 5k, but not today. I guess there was nothing driving that extra effort out of me; I'd already given that, and was going to go sub-11 with time to spare. If someone had told me I'd do under 5:40 on the bike and 10:40 overall, I'd have laughed at them.

So that's it for another year; days like that probably happen once in a blue moon, and I feel very lucky to have had a near-perfect race. I managed to frighten the old boys, but class won out. JK showed why *he's the Grand Master, and all six COLTs, and our fantastic supporters did the club proud.*

Roll on next year – I'm in already, although I'm on a hiding to nothing as I can't possibly go quicker on a 'normal' weather day. Anyone fancy a trip to the toughest and best Ironman?

Em looked up, smiled and said "There are conditions..." She didn't get the chance to finish. I bolted out of my chair and ran round the table to kiss her. I was going to Lanzarote. Thanks GrandMaster and IronHippy.

Oh s**t, I was going to Lanzarote.

The race has a mystical following among Ironman triathletes, known throughout the world for being the toughest official Ironman race on the planet. A combination of unforgiving sun, zero shade, hills, hills and more hills amongst a desolate volcanic landscape means it requires every ounce of an athlete's respect to make it to the finish line.

And then there is the wind. Lanzarote is basically a volcanic rock stuck in the Atlantic Ocean and the winds swirl around it with tremendous force, just another limiting factor naturally designed to make the race interesting. I'm crap at riding uphill and I wilt in the heat.

Everything about Lanza screamed "Holgs, this is one race too far", and quite frankly that is why it appealed to me. I owed it to myself to see if I had what it takes to face my demons and triumph. If I didn't at least try this would have been one of life's regrets, and I don't do regrets.

I e-mailed IronHippy and jokingly told him I was blaming him for my loss of sanity, and his reply was brilliant:

"Whoo hoo! I thought you may be wavering when I read your blog this morning! I'll start with the honest truth – it is a tough race. Hot and windy, it is probably still the hardest of the M-dot races. Go for it. People told me it was stupid to do Lanza as a first IM, but I knew if I got through, there would be no race I would be scared to enter (maybe the Norseman!). You're an experienced IM athlete yourself, and are far better equipped to get round

Lanza in good shape and in a good time, than many who sign up. But then again, my opinion may be slightly biased. It's a bit like asking a car salesman for advice!"

On returning home the first thing I did was enter the race, and 400 euros poorer there was no turning back. I had ahead of me 11 months of hard training, a lot of mistakes to correct from previous races, new things to try, and a hell of a lot of hills to conquer. I was following my twisted dream. Would this be a triathlon too far?

Well after the revelation that I'd be sunning myself in Lanzarote in May 2012 I thought that I'd better get some hills into my legs that weekend, so I decided to visit an old friend – the Jubilee Tower climb just outside Lancaster as you head into the Trough of Bowland.

I'd had a very busy day on Saturday in Liverpool signing books for a varied audience from an Olympic medallist to a guy who'd had his ankle fused and was getting into triathlon. It was a rewarding but a very tiring day but by Sunday I felt energised and ready to test myself.

The testing Tower climb is a long one, peaking at over 900 feet above sea level, and is perhaps at its steepest at the bottom with a gradient of 14 per cent. There is no way I would contemplate taking the ROO tri bike over this climb, so I was on my trusty Giant road bike with the triple gearing.

I did keep one gear in reserve but at times it felt like I was pedalling in squares as I battled into the constant headwind. The heat also made the climb tough but I was rewarded by the stunning views across Morecambe Bay at the top as I sipped on my energy drink before descending down into the Trough. By the time I made it home, beating the thunderstorms by a matter of minutes, I was feeling it, having completed almost 22 miles with 1,829 feet of climbing. This had to become the norm over the coming months.

The second old friend that I revisited that week was a 2.4 mile open water swim. I'd not done one since the Outlaw the previous year, and COLT were putting one on for those racing Ironman

UK the following month. I had no aim other than seeing if I could still do it off little swim training.

The water was unusually warm as 30-odd people entered the lake, but by the time I emerged from the depths I was feeling the cold on my face. Hitting the occasional warm current didn't make me comfy, it just made me close my mouth and wonder "who's been p*****g in their wetsuit?" I swam steady and mostly controlled, and I wasn't the last out of the water. I finished in one hour 25 minutes and 50 seconds, which I was encouraged with. I'd forgotten just how far 2.4 miles is in a lake, it's a long way.

Throughout the year when promoting my book I'd been constantly saying that distance to people/interviewers, rolling it off the tongue like it's a casual dip. It isn't, and that night I renewed my respect for that particular challenge. Could I have jumped on my bike and cycled 112 miles, and then ran a marathon still? Well yes I think I could but it might not have been pretty. Again I had lots of work to do.

So these two old friends had reminded me that if Ironman was easy they'd call it football. Hard work, consistency and quality are the key to success, something that I've been guilty of neglecting. Changes would be made in the long run but first of all I had a couple of races to get through, including that season's 'A' race.

My hip throbbed which to be honest with you I took as an improvement because the evening before I had been walking like John Wayne, bow-legged and slowly. Although I hadn't been near a horse I'd spent just over four hours in the saddle of my trusty Giant bike. It was probably a good advert for the quality and comfort of my specialised saddle and my Decathlon bib shorts that the only thing that didn't hurt was my arse.

My quads were on fire, my feet ached, my left knee, well, was being my left knee, and my hands were sore from pulling on brake levers. Not what I was expecting from an event my training partner Andy H had described to me as "a nice gentle ride round the Lakes".

Le Tour de Staveley is a 48-mile sportive organised by a Cumbrian cycle store. It has 4,029 feet of climbing, and features a two-mile "Bianchi Strada" climb over Gummers Howe, but more about that later. I was doing the event with Dave the ex-Spartan, who was fresh off a trip to the other Tour that was going on across the Channel at that time. It was great hearing tales of his trip and about the training he'd been doing as we waited for the start. Suzie and Annie of Team Spartan were also present to offer support and to tell us about their arduous afternoon following the course and stopping for afternoon tea – sandwiches and cream cakes or hill after hill, I think they had the more sensible approach to a nice afternoon in the Lake District.

The fast riders started at 3pm, while the more sedate competitors such as Dave and I started ten minutes later. The first ten miles or so were a bit twitchy as 300 riders streamed down narrow lanes, heading away from Staveley into the flatlands of Levens Valley.

This was Cumbria, my home county where sometimes life just has its own pace, especially in the country. The peloton was halted by a slow-moving herd of cows on the road, hooves and wellies shuffling along to their own rural rhythm as agriculture trumped sporting endeavour. Riders jovially passed the time with conversation and jokes, patiently waiting for the road to clear. This was in complete contrast to the atmosphere that was about to descend over the riders as we approached 14 miles and the climb of Tow Top.

The climb was a 20 per cent monster. I can safely say that I've never experienced anything like it. At the foot of the climb Dave rode away from me, his strength and his recent loss of weight paying off. Switch back after switch back snaked out from between the dense forest, each one getting progressively steeper, each one sapping both my legs and my spirit.

Through bloodshot eyes I could see a pile-up as I forced myself around another hairpin. Dave was there standing by his bike. Thankfully he was fine, he hadn't crashed but had been forced to a halt by the mass of fallen bodies and machines. I weaved through somehow and kept pedalling squares, my lungs were on fire and I sounded like a nuisance phone caller but I was upright.

It didn't last. I was about three-quarters of the way up the climb when two riders fell in front of me. They just couldn't pedal anymore, the steepness causing their wheels to lose traction on the near-vertical tarmac, and they started to roll backwards before crashing hard to the floor in slow motion. It sounds funny, but it's heart-stopping. I had experienced it when I did Le Terrier and it was a feeling of helplessness that I didn't want to repeat in a hurry.

In a split second I unclipped, as without that I would have crashed over them. It took all of my strength to keep the bike upright as my feet touched the ground. Getting back on was not an option, gravity was against me. I wouldn't have been able to generate enough power to turn the pedals on such an incline. I started to walk pushing the bike, joining the now long procession of riders on foot, a lycra-clad millipede clip-clopping through the tree line.

My cleated shoes slipped on the steep road like brogues on an ice rink. "Sod this for a game of soldiers," I thought and 30 seconds later I was walking up the harsh surface in just my socks, my shoes hanging off my brake hoods. My feet hurt but at least I could walk. Dave overtook me walking and we both kind of grunted at each other. Those grunts spoke volumes.

Finally nearing the top it levelled out enough to jump back on the bike and pedal very slowly up the rest of the hill. I caught Dave at the top where he was engaged in conversation with Team Spartan, I couldn't repeat what I said when I pulled over to talk and have a gel. Thankfully Suzie and Annie later forgave me as I apologised for my ungentlemanly behaviour. The climb had gone from 62 feet to 514 feet in less than a mile. Now that is brutal, no wonder it hurt and no wonder I swore.

There was a little time to recover as we headed through High Newton and over Bigland Fell before dropping down into the village of Backbarrow. At this point we were spurred on by my parents, who'd come out to offer encouragement. It was turning into a much tougher day than I'd expected and their familiar faces were a welcome shot of motivation to push on.

We then hit the Furness Fells and more climbing. As my Garmin showed 25 miles I remarked to Dave: "That's the hardest 25 miles I've ever ridden." Little did I know the rest of the course wasn't going to get any easier.

Descending down towards Newby Bridge we both blinked in disbelief, what the hell had they put in the bottles at the last aid station? We weren't seeing things, it was just our brains slowly processing something neither of us had ever seen before.

We were treated to the unusual spectacle of a huge wild boar running towards us up the road. It was a magnificent creature. We feathered our brakes, ready to stop so it could pass. We needn't have bothered as when it got to within 20 metres of us the amazingly powerful and surprisingly agile pig easily jumped a wall and headed into the forest as we prepared for the next challenge of the day.

The "Bianchi Strada" or "white road" was a forest track that went off-road over Gummer Howe. There was the option to stay on the road which was a hard enough climb, but we decided we might as well give the harder climb a go. Two miles uphill, covering 587 feet on slate and loose gravel on a mountain bike would be hard, on a road bike it was bloody tough.

Dave had obviously been on the Spanish beef as he shot off away from me, riding like a man possessed, making Alberto Contador look ordinary. I found an easy gear, sat back and methodically worked my way up the climb, passing plenty of fellow riders. It was tough on the legs and the arms keeping the bike level on such an uneven surface but the sense of achievement at the top and the stunning views of Lake Windermere were worth all the pain and effort. This for me was the highlight of the day. What goes up must come down, right? Knackered and sore I started the two-mile descent down 662 feet of steep gravel track. I'd have been nervous driving down that track in my car let alone riding my bike, and my 23mm slick road tyres were sliding all over the place. It was squeaky bum time.

I got cramp in my wrists as my brakes were squeezed for all they were worth, and even with my overcautious riding it still felt like I was going to have every one of my fillings vibrated out of my teeth. That feeling wasn't quashed by the fact that the uneven ground caused my chain to come off.

Soon after though relief came in the form of a proper tarmac road that led to a pub checkpoint where free drinks were on offer. Dave had a beer as we caught up again with Team Spartan. I feared the alcohol would not help the cramp I'd been getting sporadically in my quads and groin since about 22 miles so opted for a blackcurrant and lemonade. That soft drink was pure bliss. Despite consuming three bottles on the bike I was parched, so it went down quicker than Cristiano Ronaldo in an opposition penalty area.

Suitably refreshed, we hit the road hoping that the final eight miles would be easy, but we should have known better. Almost 400 feet of climbing awaited us. With about three miles to go Dave went away over a slight climb. I couldn't react, I couldn't get on his wheel, I was done.

After a minute or so he must have realised I wasn't there and looked around. I waved him on. "Get the drinks in," I shouted but I don't think he heard me. Pulling in at the finish I was both relieved and pleased that the ride was over and I'd completed it. I'd turned myself inside out to get through it in four hours and five minutes, and Dave was ahead of me by about 12 minutes.

We flopped, sorry I mean we basked, in the early evening sunshine, a well-earned free beer from the Hawkshead Brewery accompanied the cassoulet and French bread from the wonderfully good Wilf's Cafe. It was a perfectly civilised end to a tough day, great food, great beer and the company of one of my best friends.

It was a tough day out but a thoroughly enjoyable one. I really must thank Team Spartan for their support and Dave for dragging me round when he could have easily ridden away from me early on and got a much quicker time. He was in the form of his life. I thought it was a pity that he wasn't racing an Ironman that year because his PB would have been smashed.

Would I do it again? I would actually, I'd love to get climbing fit and attack this course. My lack of bike miles really showed but I think I can improve on this time quite a lot. If I dropped the weight, trained the lungs and worked the legs I'd improve massively. Le Tour de Staveley – I'll be back, see you again.

A week after my cycling endeavours I was feeling suitably chilled out and relaxed following a week off work with the family. We went up to stay with my parents in Cumbria and it was great just to get away from everything and enjoy life. I think sometimes we all need to do that, if we didn't we'd probably end up insane from the nine to five rat race.

I suppose it's all about getting the work/life balance right (go have a look in the self-help section in your local library for a suitable read) and as triathletes I guess it's all about getting the training/life balance right. I'd be surprised if your library has that book!

It was great to get away, to spend time playing peekaboo with Charlotte, playing on the swings on Walney beach and generally being a dad. Of course with the presence of grandparents to take over I also got a bit more training time. I managed to get some decent running done but the bike was left at home.

I'd had grand plans to cycle there (approximately 56 miles) and then back the week after, but it was like a monsoon on the morning we were due to set off. And before you start thinking "harden up Holgs, you're supposed to be an Ironman" – the reason I went in the car is that Em was a newly qualified driver and wasn't confident to drive in those conditions on her own.

So my planned training took a different path. I didn't lose sleep over it, I simply adjusted, as family is more important than training. Yes I had a week of no biking but I had a happy wife. You do the maths!?

I ended up doing more running and this resulted in two levels of progress which pleased me no end. The first was that I ran my fastest five-mile training run for three years and I wasn't on my last legs when I finished. I guess the speed work that I'd been doing with COLT on a Wednesday night was paying off.

Granted the time for five miles is where I would love to be for six miles, but progress is progress. One thing I'm learning as a new dad watching Charlotte develop every day is that "baby steps", although seemingly small, lead to much greater things. So be pleased with any progress you make, however small, it's better than going backwards.

The second was that I recorded my longest run of the year with a steady 15 miles in the heat. I didn't actually plan on going that far, I just felt good so kept plodding. It was hot and I didn't have any money on me, or drink, or gel. So when I hit 11 miles I was daydreaming about a pint of orange and water (I'm not very adventurous) and Jelly Babies. Spurred on by thoughts of little jelly men I fell through the door in two hours and eight minutes. More baby steps completed.

Another amazing thing that happened while I was home was that I was asked by my old English teacher to go into my old school and talk to pupils. 2012 is the year of reading in schools, so I was asked to launch it, to get the kids thinking about what to read over the summer. Although I teach and have given talks to various people it was quite nerve-wracking stood in front of my whole school talking. I then gave presentations to four different classes about writing and triathlon.

The kids were great and asked loads of questions. Who says teenagers don't communicate? My favourite was: "Do you live in a mansion?" Not quite. It was a wonderful morning, one of the best I've had as an author, being able to give something back to my school: a place I enjoyed going to, although this time my English teacher wasn't picking me up on my grammer and spelin! I had hopefully inspired some impressionable young minds to think about their future ambitions and it was now my turn for my old mind to be inspired about my own long-distance future. It was time to pay a visit to Ironman UK.

21

A PAIN IN THE ARSE

Just before 6.45am on an overcast August Sunday I pulled the car into the deserted motorway services a little south of Lancaster and waited for my friends. As I was stood in shorts and t-shirt, passing motorists glanced for a second and went back to their thoughts and their journeys. Little did they know that I was about to experience a day of epic proportions.

Standing there in the light drizzle, goosebumps forming on my forearms, I spared a thought for the 1,300 men and women who just down the road were already swimming like their lives depended on it. It wouldn't be the last time that I had goosebumps that day.

Ironman UK takes place just outside Manchester in an old mill town called Bolton, and being only an hour's drive away it is essentially a local race for me. I was excited because COLT had 17 athletes competing, 12 of whom, including my mates Chris Lawson, Andy Ley and big Kev Lindeque, were experiencing the pain and elation of Ironman for the first time.

I felt particularly cool about Kev racing because I was directly responsible for a lot of his journey to his date with destiny. He had been reading my blog for years and actually joined COLT and took up triathlon after being inspired by my misguided adventures.

The gentle softly-spoken giant who hailed originally from

222

Africa was a really strong cyclist, probably on account of the fact that his muscle laden thighs were as wide as my waist. He had also been running with the COLT mob on a Wednesday night and had made great progress, unfortunately he'd picked up a back injury in the weeks before the race and it was still troubling him. I knew though that he'd be all right, he had the right mental attitude to match his physical prowess. Add into the mix the old guard of Wild and Mason and you had the makings of a perfect Ironman smackdown for a small Lancashire club. For the previous three years the club had supported in Addlington, a small village on the bike course. And that was where I was headed, my friends following in convoy behind me down the deserted motorway. "COLT Alley" as the patch of tarmac was now known was a sea of black and white supporters waving flags and banners while making enough noise to earn an ASBO. It didn't matter where the competitors were from, they all got screamed at.

I stood there from 7.40am until 4.30pm, my club-mates and I never stopped clapping or screaming at people. My hands were red raw and my voice had gone when I arrived home that evening. I was also sporting nuclear sunburn after I made the rookie mistake of only applying sunscreen at 8am, and not redoing it because it was overcast.

Each time a COLT shot past we went ballistic, goosebumps every time. These were my friends, these were people I felt that I belonged with, people I trained with. It was an amazing feeling seeing them put their bodies on the line and watching the smiles on their faces as they passed through the wall of noise on each lap. Not one of them once failed to crack a smile or give a thumbs-up. Not even the sub-ten-hour guys.

One of the biggest cheers of the day came early on when Chris Lawson rode into view. He was the last COLT to get onto his bike but given the torrid time he had with his swimming demons it was such a relief to see him. Nothing could now stop him. I'd never seen him look so happy. "I did it!" he screamed as he went past.

As the hours sped by and the riders passing thinned out it made the interaction seem that much more personal. Coming up the road was a rider displaying characteristics that I recognised only too well. His shoulders were slumped forward in defeat, his hands gripped the bars too tightly, his front wheel weaved instead of rolling true and his head hung limply on his chest.

"Come on mate dig in," I shouted. From beneath the helmet came an anguished voice: "I'm done, I'm stopping, I've had enough." I wasn't having that, no way, this guy was only ten minutes from finishing the bike. Granted he had a marathon to run but he'd come so far, he couldn't quit now. I ran out into the middle of the road and jogged alongside him.

"You aren't quitting, and you are almost done with the bike. Get to T2, sit down, have something to eat and things will seem a lot better. If you quit now you'll forever regret it," I warned him. The helmet lifted and questioning eyes hidden behind smokey lenses glared at me: "Holgs?" Oh bugger, this couldn't be good. "Err, yeah that's me." "All right mate, it's because of you that I entered this f*****g race. I read your book and jumped in." His tone thankfully was one of appreciation and not one of aggression. My arse cheeks unclenched. "Well you'd better bloody finish then, I don't want that on my conscience. Come on, you can do it." He smiled and held his fist out, I bumped it with mine and then gave him a running push to get him moving. I later found out when he contacted me on Facebook that I saved his race and that after taking my advice, he had a blinding run to finish his first Ironman. I never expected that I would ever motivate anyone, and certainly not get the chance to do it to one of my readers in the biggest race of their life. What a buzz that was.

I didn't make it to the run course as after nine hours of clapping and screaming I was knackered. I needed to see my family. I saw the last COLT safely past on the bike; it was Ian, who this time unlike at Capenwray had remembered his running shoes. I headed home and kept in touch by phone and the online athlete tracker.

What a day though, what an atmosphere, the banter with the riders, just amazing. If you've never experienced an Ironman race as either a competitor or a supporter, go and do so, you won't regret it. Go and shout at strangers from all parts of the globe. I guarantee you'll get a smile, and it will make you smile.

It was a huge success for COLT with a range of personal bests, newbie Ironmen and for the third year on the run we would be sending people to the big show in Kona. My coach Richard Mason and the IronHippy Chris Wild both qualified. It couldn't have happened to two nicer blokes. It had been their dream for years and both really deserved it. It was just the icing on the cake for Team COLT.

A special mention MUST go to Team True Spirit, a team of British armed forces men and women who had been injured, and we are taking horrendous injuries. They became Ironmen and raised a hell of a lot of money at the same time.

I have never – and I mean NEVER – been so inspired as I was watching double leg amputee Joe Townsend come past on a handbike. That guy should be the definition of brave, inspirational and tough. He and his team-mates got the biggest cheer of the day. As the French would say: "Chapeau".

I was buzzing after witnessing the courage of those competing at Bolton and I was really keen to go and emulate them. My 'A' race was only a few weeks away. I had entered the Monster Middle in Ely, Cambridgeshire, after I'd had to withdraw from my original race, the Cleveland Steelman. It was a new half Ironman that had PB written all over it. Flat and fast didn't need much selling to me. Unfortunately the week after Bolton I was struck down with a nasty virus, and couldn't act on my enthusiasm. The illness was pretty unavoidable really. Charlotte had started nursery and as such was being exposed to a whole new world of germs. The poor little lamb was actually quite sick and we ended up at hospital with her after she vomited more than her body weight all over me. I was dripping from head to toe in what looked like rancid rice pudding. But you know what, I didn't actually care. I was more in shock that my baby could produce that much puke.

Thankfully after a few hours and some medication we were allowed to bring her home. It was three in the morning and I had to be up at seven for work. In the end I didn't sleep, I just held Charlotte in my arms on the sofa watching the soothing lullabies on baby TV. They didn't work, well not for her at least. In those four hours Charlotte went through three changes of babygrows and I had to abandon two shirts.

At seven I handed my red hot, pink bundle of germs to her Mum, and headed on autopilot to work. By the time I got home Em was in a worse state than Charlotte, and by the next day I felt like my insides would make a bid for freedom with every movement. If we had been living in medieval England they'd have nailed our front door shut and painted a big red cross on it or burnt us at the stake. Either way we would have been toast. Thankfully the virus was short-lived and I was feeling fighting fit and raring to go as I packed up the car ready to drive to the flatlands of East Anglia. I had a really good feeling about the race. I felt strong, fast and most of all confident. I knew it was going to be a race that I would never forget.

The beauty of the race taking place in Ely was that it gave us the opportunity to visit my brother Craig and his family as they lived in the picturesque cathedral town. My parents were also making the trip so it was one big Holgate get-together. My nieces, three-year-old Georgia and five-year-old Eloise had great fun pushing "Baby Charlotte" through the streets in her buggy, and teaching her all about *Star Wars*. My brother was obviously bringing his girls up well. How much my six-month-old daughter took in about Anakin Skywalker, R2D2 and the others is questionable but she sat there smiling contently. Her mother was obviously bringing her up well. I left the family watching *Mickey Mouse Clubhouse*, which was more Charlotte's scene than the Clone Wars, and walked the half-mile or so from Craig's house to go and register on the Saturday evening. I was looking forward to meeting several online friends for the first time. I'd shared daily banter with them over the last 18 months but never actually met because of geographical boundaries.

Deenzy, TRO, AJPAR, Battlecat and the Cockney wide-boy

HOD – although they sounded liked they belonged in the Mos Eisley Cantina they were all thoroughly nice people in real life. It's great when that happens because sometimes you meet people and they are the complete polar opposite of how they come across online.

Deenzy laughed at me when I said I couldn't stay long because my sister-in-law, Abbie, was cooking tea, apparently a very northern thing to say. As the only one there from climes further north than Watford Gap I was severely outgunned. Banter was given and taken and we went our separate ways with handshakes of luck, just in case we didn't meet up the next day. And just for the record I made it to Craig's just in time for tea and not dinner.

I was awake before my 5am alarm, creeping around the hotel room trying not to wake Em and Charlotte. I wolfed down a bowl of porridge, grabbed the ROO and headed out the door for the Ely smackdown, nervous and excited at the prospect of racing long.

I methodically racked the ROO, positioning my gear around it so as to get away quickly. My helmet rested on the tri-bars, and on the floor in order from the front was my number belt, my cycling shoes and my running shoes. I wasn't leaving anything to chance as I wanted to be in and out of transition later in a flash. I pulled on my wetsuit, taking extra care to apply lashings of lubricant to the back of my neck which usually suffered from friction burns on longer swims. Suited and booted it was time to catch the bus up to the start which lay downriver. The swim was a straight 1.9km upstream back to transition. The start was delayed by about 30 minutes as athletes were channelled down the single path through the protected reeds into the river. We then had a 200-metre swim to the start line through the murky silty water. "Oh well," I thought. "It's a bit longer than my usual warm-up." I don't think I've ever done a swim warm-up, other than shivering while treading water.

Then as the sun started to move higher in the sky and the cathedral clock struck 7.30am, 250 athletes were unleashed upstream by the mayor, and the smackdown was on in a whirlpool of white water, arms and legs.

To be honest I had a fairly uneventful swim, naturally avoiding the faster swimmers and much of the brutality. I came out of the water in a rather pedestrian 51 minutes, and I was disappointed with that but swimming isn't my strong point and I'd found battling the current to be hard work. Little did I know at that point that the best part of my race was now behind me.

On exiting the river there was a one-minute "dead zone" where time would be deducted as we had to walk from the river bank down a very steep banking, a restriction imposed to protect the wildlife at the riverside. I was quite glad to get the blood circulating in my legs before I faced the 300-metre run to transition.

My methodical planning served me well as I stepped sopping wet through my number belt, pulling it up to my waist, making sure the number was on my back as instructed. Next the helmet went on along with the shades and finally my cycling shoes. I'd shaved time that I knew would take me one step closer to my PB of five hours and 35 minutes.

Out of transition and on to the bike I was feeling good, looking forward to the flattest and potentially the fastest 56 miles I'd ever ridden. The bike was in the big ring and my legs were turning quickly, 23mph, 89 revs cadence, heart rate sitting below 140 beats per minute. Perfect.

The route took me past our hotel at 1.7 miles and there as expected were my parents and Em and Charlotte shouting encouragement. I shouted back a cheery "morning" and gave a thumbs-up to show that I felt great.

Less than a minute later I was thrown forward with a jolt onto my tri-bars. My chest smashed into the arm rests with such force that I thought I was going over the handlebars, but thankfully I didn't. What the hell just happened? Did something hit me? Did I hit something?

No, the road is smooth and clear I thought. I was confused and something just didn't feel right with me or the ROO. It was then that I looked behind me, and to my horror my saddle had gone.

It was no longer attached to my expensive carbon bike, instead I saw it lying at the side of the road. I stopped the bike, laid it on the grass and walked back to retrieve the missing part. I was annoyed but I wasn't panicking, s**t happens, it is how you deal with it that determines what the outcome will be.

I reached for my tool kit, thinking I could reattach it and get going. On examining the damage the nightmare became a reality. The connecting bolt had sheared off and the top saddle clamp was nowhere to be seen. Presumably it had gone into the long grass next to the road. I searched for a minute or three but it was to no avail, the grass was too dense and the clamp too small. It was like looking for Viking in a Wembley rugby crowd. It very quickly dawned on me that there was no way to fix this.

I was faced with two choices: a) Turn round and quit or b) Try and ride without a saddle and hope for the best.

I somehow formulated the desperate idea that I could lean the saddle on the seat post and just grip it tightly with my thighs keeping it in place. Of course I soon learnt that it was physically impossible to do so while having to move your thighs to pedal. It was also way too dangerous as I had no stability and found myself wobbling further and further into the road. Thankfully as it was so early on a Sunday morning the roads were deserted.

I had no choice. The saddle was stuffed in disgrace into the back pocket of my tri top and I set forth switching constantly between riding stood up, or impaled on a carbon seat post with an exposed metal screw that unfortunately was positioned well enough to perform a prostate exam.

I couldn't get any power, I couldn't use my tri-bars, I couldn't even change gear as the gear levers were at the end of the tri-bars. Every time I reached forward to attempt a gear change it threw the whole dynamic of the ROO out of sync, I felt like I was going to crash and had to shift my weight back onto that intrusive screw. After a few failed attempts I gave up trying, it just wasn't worth it.

Another consequence was that I couldn't corner properly. All of those simple, basic, cycling movements rely on you being seated. Eating and drinking was also a nightmare. Again it just couldn't be done on the move because of the balance issues. If wanted to drink I had to stop. If I wanted to eat I had to stop. My nutrition plan for the race went the way of the dodo.

Several times I screamed out loud in frustration on the deserted Fen roads, and only my laboured breathing replied. I was mentally retiring from triathlon as the literal pain in my arse got too much. Then two things occurred to me. Firstly, I was determined that I wasn't going to let this freak incident get the better of me, no way was I recording my first DNF. Secondly I thought of my mates and the banter I'd face if I quit, I'd never live it down. They already had enough ammo for taking the p**s out of me and I wasn't giving them a full arsenal. I turned my legs and ploughed on.

At about 36 miles my family came past in the car. I desperately flagged them down, gesturing to Em in the back seat like a loon. They pulled into the side of the road and looked in astonishment at what was missing from between my legs. I asked my Dad if he had any cable ties in the car, he didn't. He tried lashing the saddle to the castrated ROO with his shoelaces but that didn't work. While my Dad scrabbled in his car boot looking for a miracle Em and my Mam offered comforting words. Charlotte was fast asleep, looking cute in her car seat.

Em told me she couldn't believe how well I was taking things. "I've been through every emotion over the last 30-odd miles but now I feel quite chilled about it, there's nothing I can do so there is no point getting stressed. I'm in pain but it can't get any worse. I'm not letting a little thing like a missing saddle beat me," was my nonchalant reply.

However I was conscious of how much time I was losing and how little progress we were making. I was restless and my Dad was out of ideas. "Get going Andrew and I'll have a think about it, we'll pull in down the road," he said, giving me a running push as I set off again for more torture. Not a mile later he was stood at the side of the road signalling for me to pull over. He beamed: "I've got an idea. It's not a solution but it might make things a little comfier."

He wrapped a tartan travel rug around the seat post offering me a little respite. Trust me, it felt like a big comfy leather armchair after what I'd just been through. For the remaining 20 or so miles, I could get some relief. It still hurt, I was bleeding, and I'd lost skin and feeling in places that no man should ever have to experience.

As I prepared to get off the bike for the run I just kept thinking: "This is going to be a world of hurt!" My legs were shot after 54 miles of riding out of the saddle. My left knee and Achilles were in agony having been forced to pedal at unnatural angles. I got off the bike in three hours 42 minutes and 22 seconds, averaging about 16.8mph which is remarkable if you think about it. It was a bloody good job it was a flat course. I racked the bike as one of the marshals stared at the carbon dream machine with its new Edinburgh Woollen Mill accessory. I shrugged: "Long story." I couldn't bend down to take off my cycling shoes in transition.

I'd seized up. Eventually I managed to get going out on the run. Heading for the river path I was passed by a fast-finishing Deenzy motoring in the other direction, looking every bit the quintessential triathlete with shades and an Ironman branded cap. "Go on Holgs," he screamed as I shuffled past.

I started to run/shuffle but it was just a futile attempt. I was in agony and my legs were spent. Pride kept me moving for the first couple of miles while I passed spectators and the bulk of the field heading back to the finish. HOD passed me and shouted much-needed encouragement as he whizzed along heading for a PB.

As soon as I got on the deserted roads I crumbled into a shuffle/walk strategy. The mind was willing, the legs weren't. I kept thinking of one of my favourite quotes from Confucius: "It does not matter how slowly you go so long as you don't stop." It was a wonderful piece of wisdom that never failed to inspire me onwards but I couldn't help cheekily thinking "yeah, I bet you never had a carbon post shoved up your arse".

Heading back I was convinced that all my friends and family would have gone home as I'd taken so long. At the turnaround point I'd worked it out that there were only two people behind me. Soon it was to be only one. With a couple of miles to go I was caught by a tall, athletic-looking 54-year-old. I know how old he was because we would become friends after this race.

Brian Kinsella was taking part in his first half Ironman. He was a fellow Cumbrian, racing for Carlisle Tri. We both couldn't believe that we were racing at the other end of the country and running along together. I told him what had happened to me and he was amazed that I'd even made it to the run, let alone that I was still moving forwards towards the finish. After a few moments he pushed on, moving gracefully in stark contrast to my efforts.

I'd timed the gaps at the turnaround so I also knew that I had a good 20-minute lead on the last person, so I wasn't going to be last. Again pride forced me to muster a run, or what I thought was a run in the final mile. I was amazed that everyone had waited to see me finish. It must have been the nice weather and the hog roast. My five-year-old niece, Eloise, waited patiently for me and held out her hand, I grabbed it tightly and she escorted her uncle home safely, making sure he got in no more trouble in the last 100 metres. RELIEF.

I was met by the race referee, who asked about my bike. It had caused quite a stir in transition while I was out running and word had got round about what had happened. I declared the outside interference, the help that I'd received from my Dad, and expected to be disqualified. At that point I told him "I really didn't give a..." with a grin on my face. He just laughed and said it didn't matter, adding with a hint of respect: "Congratulations on finishing, I wouldn't have done." My mates all came over and offered all sorts of accolades, I'd certainly earned their respect and we all had something else to laugh about on Monday when we returned to cyberspace. Trust me, the banter about this one still hasn't stopped!

Beaming at my efforts I limped back across the meadow towards my family. My other niece Georgia, my three-year-old bundle of blonde dynamite, skipped over and took my hand. With beautifully large eyes she looked up at me and chirped with the innocence and factuality that only a child could: "Uncle Andrew you were rubbish, you came last." Bless her.

I got a personal worst time by two hours, and my run was a shockingly slow 2.49:14. It's no wonder I finished second to last some three and a half hours behind the winner. But I reached new levels of toughness or stupidity depending on how you look at it.

Personally reflecting on events I think it was a bit of both. Yes it was tough, but probably also stupid. I had little control over the bike, and if I'd crashed I probably risked being impaled by carbon fibre, something I did think about but dismissed. I couldn't be that unlucky in one day.

Always looking for the positive I proved to myself that I could dig deep when things go really bad, and that I can shift my mentality from hunting down a PB to just surviving, something again that can be a difficult skill to master, but a skill that could save you in an Ironman race.

But the biggest positive to take away from 'Saddlegate'? Well the way I looked at this, it was best to get these things out of the way, folded up and put in the hurt locker before my next 'A' race. I wouldn't fancy riding 110 miles in Lanza without a saddle.

22

NEVER GIVE UP

I had two weeks of enforced rest after Ely, interspersed with a bit of open water swimming. The cool fresh water really helped my legs and undercarriage recover. There was no way that I could run or cycle though as my missing skin reformed, so I was pleased that I could swim without disrupting the repairs.

Now I don't know about you but out of the three disciplines that make up our sport, I'm more likely to shy away from a swimming session than I am from a run in the rain or an icy bike ride. Even the warm water of a heated pool doesn't entice me. I'd rather be outside getting battered by the elements than inside like a goldfish swimming up and down in an enclosed tank. Sometimes I think I'm not right in the head.

It's not that I don't enjoy the actual swimming when I drag myself to the pool, I do. It's just the actual thought of dragging myself there. I can come up with an excuse in a heartbeat: I'm too busy, It's too cold, It's Friday, It's Monday, It's (insert any other day of the week here). You get the picture? I just don't get that adrenaline rush, that buzz that comes from a really good run, or hitting 30mph on the bike.

It might be because swimming is my weakest discipline, I struggle with it. And how many of us really enjoy something we struggle with? I know I can get through an Ironman swim in less than 85 minutes as I've done it three times already. I'm not going to make massive improvements. I feel that my time is better spent out on the bike building my strength in THE key Ironman discipline.

While unable to run or cycle I realised that I had come to like open water swimming, which is a real full 360 switch. It used to terrify me. The cold, dark waters of the deep, the feeling of not knowing what was lurking underneath combined to make donning a wetsuit a necessary evil rather than a delight. It was an unreal feeling considering I'm a qualified scuba diver, learning in water where visibility was so bad we had to use lights in a disused quarry. Hell I've dived up close and personal with two of the planet's apex predators, the Nile crocodile and the great white shark – yet I was scared of what was beneath my feet.

It's hard to put my finger on what changed to make me prefer open water swimming to pool-based swimming. It's still dark, it's still cold and I've no idea what lurks beneath. But in 2011 when the open water season finished because of the cold temperatures, I found that I really missed it.

In the past I could quite easily have gone from September to May only swimming a dozen times. I was determined that would no longer be the case, and as I put my wetsuit away for its winter nap I was stone-cold focused. I wanted to be in the shape of my life the following season, I wanted 2012 to be the year of success, and for that to happen I resolved to change my attitude to a lot of things including swimming.

I signed up to the Club Masters swim sessions on a Thursday night. I'd not attended before, the main excuse being Charlotte wasn't in a routine. Once she was in bed earlier than the 8.30pm start time I no longer had that excuse.

I was extremely nervous stood with my club-mates, including Kona qualifiers, on the side of the pool. I'd only ever swam in a lake with them before and it's easy to hide in a lake. There I was, about to be exposed. I felt like the new kid that's just transferred schools, walking into a classroom for the first time to be met by silence. Mad really, because I've known them all for years and consider them friends. That first night I really struggled, my breathing was all over the place, my stroke was embarrassing and yet I worked harder than I ever have before.

I felt light-headed but as the session went on something strange started to happen. I could feel myself starting to smile. I must admit I came away feeling I was further behind than I probably was but it gave me a determination that I would improve, I would overcome my inner swimming sloth.

As the weeks passed I was a man possessed and everything went right. I felt long and slippery as I cut through the water. Even the kick drills felt easier, and my swim kick is non-existent usually. It was hard work, drills and then 100, 200, 300, 200, 100-metre pyramids, more drills, another pyramid and a gentle warm-down to finish. I was surprised when the coach, Mark Smith of Carnforth Otters swimming club, said we'd reached the warm down. They say that time flies when you are having fun. Me? Having fun swimming? Oh hell yeah! I actually couldn't wait for my weekly session, this really was the start of a new romance, one that I hope ends in marriage.

At work our annual leave entitlement runs from October to October and I knew that I had a week's leave to use up as I'd worked some weekends. Feeling renewed after a great swimming session I decided that I would use the time to get a big training week in. This would be two weeks before my final triathlon of the season, and for once the weather forecast was good. I was really excited at the prospect of getting out on the bike every day, seeing a bit of the countryside and just generally chilling out. The best laid plans of mice and men eh?

I was definitely a man that week, but not one made of iron. I ended up with just one 40-mile ride and an hour on the turbo. This was all due to Charlotte being ill and absent from nursery. Nursery was bringing her along wonderfully both educationally and socially but she seemed to catch everything that was going.

I was reassured by the doctor and various grandparents that this would be good for her long-term immunity. It was best to get things out of the way while she didn't really know what was going on, and she would get stronger as a result. So my days were spent playing, reading stories, watching Disney TV, clearing up various substances (you don't want to know) and feeding a grizzly baby.

My evenings were spent collapsing in a heap as I was totally knackered. I had learned that it is hard work being a full-time parent. I gained so much respect for those that are, hats off to Em who did it for nine months before returning to work.

After Ely I couldn't ride the ROO, well I could but I didn't fancy putting my arse through that sort of pain again. I took the post and the saddle to two local bike shops and explained what had happened. To my disappointment they didn't want to know, they hadn't sold me the bike and didn't like the look of the aero-shaped seat post.

A national chain tried to help and they contacted the supplier but the design specification of the new model had changed, so basically they didn't make a seat post to fit my frame anymore.

I bought a replacement from eBay but it was millimetres too tight and I didn't fancy cutting or sanding it down to fit given my technical numptiness with bike parts. The whole sorry episode left me with a headache. Here was my very expensive bike that was basically rendered useless. I was feeling sorry for myself on the phone to my Dad, there was no way I could afford a new bike and who would buy a second hand one that couldn't be ridden? I was screwed.

As always he came to the rescue: "Bring the post, the bits and your saddle through at the weekend and I'll have a look at it." We arrived on Friday night and first thing on Saturday he disappeared into his workshop and emerged a little while later with it fixed. He'd managed to use a combination of a screw cut to size and washer locking nuts. The saddle was never coming off again. Good job he's an engineer and knows what he's doing.

When I got back home on Sunday night I couldn't wait to test the new saddle. After getting Charlotte safely tucked up in bed I headed for the garage, leaving Em to catch up on *Coronation Street* in peace without me commenting on the quality of acting.

I eagerly attached the ROO to the turbo trainer, not something that I usually do so quickly or keenly. I must admit that although I trusted my Dad's skills I did hold my breath as I put my considerable weight on the saddle and started to pedal. However I soon couldn't hold my breath as I managed an hour of intervals, working on increasing heart rates. I was amazed at how much it hurt and how much I sweated. I looked like I'd just stepped out of the shower. But I remained on the ROO, and more importantly so did my saddle. I had my baby back, just in time to race again at Fleetwood.

I'd had a somewhat disappointing personal triathlon season. It hadn't been a disaster, I'd learnt a lot but I knew I hadn't done myself justice. I wanted to go out with a bang, something positive to build on over a long hard winter of preparing for my 2012 season. Thankfully Fleetwood gave me something to smile about.

I recorded a new personal best for that particular variation of the sprint distance, by just over seven minutes, which when you think about it, in a sprint race is quite a big chunk of time. The best thing was I know that I could have gone faster as well. I actually held a lot back on the run to protect my sore hamstring.

I hadn't run for a month as a precaution, and I had no idea if it would flare up once I got off the bike. But I felt strong on the run and had to tell myself to slow down as I didn't want my leg to go pop and set me back months, missing vital winter Ironman training. I finished the five-kilometre run in 25 minutes 30 seconds, with no ill effects, which realistically in the longterm was even better news than my seven-minute PB.

The day had started out brilliantly and I just seemed to go from strength to strength. I'm never going to be a strong swimmer so my time of ten minutes 46 seconds (including T1) for 400m won't exactly scare Michael Phelps. However it was good for me, and I actually managed to lap one of the swimmers in my lane, which was a unique experience and one I guess I'm never likely to repeat.

But let's face it this is me, the guy that loses a saddle in a race so something had to go wrong didn't it? Well yes, but thankfully it was corrected by a scuba diver. My timing chip band slid off my ankle as I kicked off the pool wall after the first 25m lap was completed. When I returned to the deep end of the pool I scanned the bottom of the pool for the errant band but couldn't see it anywhere. As I swam I resigned myself to the fact that with no chip I wouldn't record an official finisher's time. That would be disappointing but it wouldn't be the end of the world.

Approaching the wall at the shallow end I could see the red board placed under the surface by the race official to signal that I only had two more 25m laps to do. Next time I reached the shallow end I'd be on my way to getting dry. In a flash I was out of the pool, pausing briefly to tell the official I'd lost my chip. "Here it is," she said and handed it to me, adding: "The scuba diver taking underwater photos saw it come off and retrieved it for you, have a good race." I thanked her and asked her to thank the diver as I ran out of the pool and into the car park that doubled as T1.

It didn't take me long to throw my helmet, sunglasses and cycling shoes on. I was soon into my stride on the bike, the ROO seemed to be a part of me (and in a good way this time, not the impaled way of my last race) as my legs spun the pedals in a cadence of 90rpm. The hours practising one-legged cadence pedalling on the turbo in an attempt to improve my technique suddenly seemed worth it.

I lost count of the amount of cyclists that I powered past. That makes me sound good doesn't it but this was an event for all-comers. Mountain bikes and hybrids were commonplace, though they were no match for my tri bike cutting through the Lancashire sea air like a hot knife through butter.

I soon had my COLT club-mate Chris Lawson in my sights so I shouted cockily, "Come on, try and keep up" as I sped past. I knew very well that my verbal challenge would appeal to his competitive nature and that my mate would react and chase me down. He'd set off 15 minutes before me and was actually on his second lap of the bike course while I was on my first. For the whole of that lap we switched positions more times than Paris Hilton in one of her "home movies", and each time the banter just got funnier. It's a wonder neither of us fell off our bikes.

"Don't you just hate these flash pointy hatted t**ts?" he said in a direct jibe at my new time trial helmet. It was angular, designed to make me quicker and I loved it. It really was a case of "all the gear and no idea" because I wasn't exactly quick enough to justify the purchase but I'd just wanted to indulge my inner "gear geek", and besides it looked good.

Chris, fresh from his Ironman training, pulled away from me at the end of the lap and finished the race in a new PB also of one hour eight minutes, a cracking performance. He was the only competitor that physically passed me on the bike, even though in race terms he was never behind me being one lap ahead. I was so pleased about that.

I felt that I could have pushed harder on the bike but again I didn't want to destroy myself – something I need to learn to become a successful Ironman. Although the bike is the key, burying yourself to gain 15 minutes is a false economy if it costs you an extra 90 minutes in the marathon. I had three Ironman finishes to my name but I was still a toddler really taking my first tentative steps, I had a lot to learn to stop myself from falling down with each step.

So there you have it, my triathlon season finished on a high. My performance gave me the confidence to face my winter of Ironman training head on. I also knew as soon as I finished that my short race goal for 2012 would be to go under 70 minutes at Fleetwood. I hoped that my increased speed and strength from a return to Ironman training would help me achieve it.

Back in 2009 when I was training hard for my attempt at completing Ironman Germany I took myself out of my comfort zone by tagging along with COLT's 'A' ride.

The club has two weekend rides, the Sunday ride or 'B' ride which is at a pace that most people could easily keep up with and lasts two to three hours normally. It also splits after an hour into a 'C' ride to allow the different paces to be catered for. This works really well and means that no one should get left behind. Normally you would find me safely entrenched towards the back of the 'B' ride.

The 'A' ride goes out at 7am on a Saturday and usually

lasts anywhere from three to six hours. The difference between the standard of rides is not only time and distance but also the speed. This is inevitable when you look at who is usually on the ride: four Kona qualifiers, three sub-11 Ironmen, Norseman and Embrunman finishers. If you also take into account that these guys race two to four Ironman races a year, the training is pretty much always in top gear.

Back in 2009 I would go out and try to hang on for an hour before getting dropped before riding on my own to my own plan. Eventually I got so I could stay in touch for the whole ride, a couple of times reaching 100 miles. This was a successful strategy for me as my cycling improved immensely.

So with that in mind, two years on I bit the bullet and dragged myself out of bed at 6am to see if I could hang on to the 'A' team. The weather was awful, driving rain and buffeting winds. I was geared up with thermals as the sun didn't rise until about 30 minutes into the ride.

Four of us were there, all Ironmen, all preparing for races: John Knapp, who was peaking for an Ironman Arizona race the following month which would see him finish on the podium in his age group and again book a slot in Kona, took the lead and set the pace out along the valley into the Cumbrian hills: John Towse tucked in, spinning the legs in preparation for Ironman St George; and finally you had me and Andy Ley, who fresh off his debut success at Bolton was stepping up his game. Both Andy and I were a little apprehensive of how we would fare on the 'A' ride as we started our long-range assault on Ironman Lanzarote.

The two Johns showed their class, setting a brisk pace as the fields whizzed by and the spray from their wheels splattered my glasses. Surprisingly I managed to stay with the pace, as did Andy Ley, who was a much stronger cyclist than he realised. He moved ahead of me and I just concentrated on holding his wheel as at the pace we were travelling a two-metre gap would very quickly grow into one of 200 metres.

After an hour we reached Kirkby Lonsdale and I informed my mates that when they turned right to head further out towards

Sedburgh, I would swing left and head home along the other side of the river. This had always been my intention as unfortunately I had to get back to go to work, and also I didn't want to destroy myself on my first ride back.

By the time I got home I'd done 32 miles in two hours. I slowed down when I was on my own which I think was a sign that I'd reached my limit for the day. I was quite chuffed that I hadn't been left for dead in the first 500 metres of the ride. That had happened to me once back in 2009.

The other lads ended up doing just over 70 miles, and Andy Ley managed to hold his own with the two Johns. He was pleased as punch when he texted me later that afternoon. Looking at my phone I hoped to be able to build up to that sort of effort. I hoped that a hard winter of long rides with riders stronger and faster than me would bring my cycling ability back up to speed. It was time to forget about comfort and focus on advancement.

Back in 2010 my 'A' race for the year was the Outlaw, a new Ironman distance event in Nottingham. I was excited about the prospect of racing a fairly flat and fast course in an attempt to get under 12 hours and achieve my fastest ever Ironman time. Unfortunately several factors saw the reverse happen, and I actually posted my worst Ironman result ever, limping home in 14.17:48.

Although very disappointed at the time, I was pleased with the fortitude I displayed as it would have been so easy to not have actually started, and even easier to have stopped within the first mile of the marathon when my back was causing me grief. One thing I'm not though is a quitter, and I ground it out, vowing to return one day and do myself justice with a performance I knew that I was capable of.

So one fateful October night while Em was out at the cinema, and I was left alone with a laptop and a credit card (always a dangerous combination), I entered the Outlaw for 2012. It was actually Viking's fault to be honest with you, he had posted on Facebook that he'd just entered and that places were going fast. Knowing that Dave the ex-Spartan and Min had already entered, I figured it would be rude not to.

The race would mark the first occasion that the four of us had raced together since that fateful day at the Big Woody back in 2007. It would be five years on, and I couldn't think of a more appropriate way of celebrating our anniversary. Plus it would give my parents, Em and Charlotte the chance to see me race, as we'd already decided on reasons of cost and the nightmare of travelling with an 18-month-old that I'd be heading to Lanzarote on my own.

Now OK, let's just pause for a minute there. I had never ever done two Ironman races in a year before, let alone two that were only six weeks apart. I was completely zoned in on Ironman Lanzarote, which was going to be the sole focus of my training and my efforts. There was no choice. If I wasn't prepared properly, that race would tear me apart and my day at the Outlaw would suffer also.

I hoped that as I got stronger, fitter and faster ahead of Lanza that I would be able to actively recover in the time before the Outlaw and use my top form to get the PB that I desired on a much quicker and flatter course. It was going to be one hell of a gamble, and at stake was my body but I had the confidence that I had the skills to win the bet.

This was a strange thing for me to feel as I firmly believe there is no skill in betting, it's just luck and sometimes even if you make your own luck it can go against you. I just needed to train smart, stay healthy and not lose the desire to attain my goal. I wanted it so badly that I was willing to risk my body. I firmly believe the mantra of "anything is possible" and this was my opportunity to prove to myself that it was.

The path to Puerto del Carmen and the starting line of Ironman Lanzarote started 23 weeks earlier on Monday 12th December 2011 in the less glamorous and certainly colder climes of Lancaster University. The previous night had been rough, my little girl Charlotte was teething badly, crying herself awake with pain as her gums burned. Aren't teeth a nightmare? They hurt like hell when they are coming through, they cause you nothing but problems when you have them and they hurt even more when you either lose one or have it taken out. They must be the worst design fault in the evolution of man, well apart from not giving us webbed feet for swimming. I would happily swap my teeth for webbed feet.

So needless to say Em and I saw pretty much every hour during the night. Thankfully however both my girls (and the cat) were flat-out asleep when I left at 6.30am to get to the university pool. Though heavy with sleep there was a certain sparkle in my eyes as I prepared to begin quite possibly the most important and toughest 23 weeks of my triathlon life. I was on day one of my Lanzarote Ironman plan, designed to get me round the hot, hilly and windy 140.2 miles of volcanic rock. Each week my coach Richard Mason would send me my training timetable, including details of what each session should be, why I was doing it and what the goal for that week was. It all kicked off at 7am when I was the first to break the water in the university pool. I love that moment when you are the first person to disturb the tranquillity, it feels so personal as you send the first ripples of the day across the water to all four corners of the pool.

It was an hour workout and after warming up I swam 1,000 metres, making sure my 100 metre splits were within ten seconds of each other. This session was all about feeling my swim pace, knowing what I was comfortable with. It certainly wasn't the fastest I've swum but I was bang on target; six of my splits were within five seconds of each other and all of them were within the allotted ten second target. On that initial day I followed the swim up with a 30-minute tempo run and my first week finished with nine hours' training banked – not a bad start really.

Unfortunately my good start didn't continue and a week later the last thing on my mind was triathlon. I would lose ten full weeks of training, but to be honest with you there were moments in those weeks where I would gladly have never swam, cycled or run again if it made things better. I'm not a religious man, far from it, but in those weeks I closed my eyes several times and spoke silently to whomever was listening. I shed more tears than I ever thought was possible and developed more respect for my loved ones, especially Dad and Craig. Together we made decisions I'm not sure I would have been strong enough to make on my own.

My Mum was taken seriously ill with breathing problems. She was rushed by ambulance to Furness General Hospital in Barrow-in-Furness where the doctors and nurses worked for hours to save her life. I will forever be thankful that those skilled and selfless people managed to bring her back. She spent weeks fighting in intensive care.

Sitting at her bedside I could see where I got my stubbornness and determination from. My Mum, who I always thought to be gentle and kind, was also a fighter. Her will to succeed was immense, and even though the odds against her were huge she fought them. Her courage and strength inspired me. I vowed to always follow her example and never give up. She battled on and defied the doctors to slowly recover and eventually to everyone's relief she was allowed home.

While my Mam lay in intensive care, Em had an asthma attack and was admitted to hospital in Lancaster. The two women in my life lay in hospital beds 50 miles apart with similar breathing problems. I felt awful leaving my Dad to deal with things but I had a wife and baby to take care of, I had responsibilities. I tried to keep it together for Charlotte's sake, she was too young to understand, but kids no matter how young pick up on these things.

In those few days I didn't know if I was coming or going with hospital visits, endless phone calls, dealing with a teething baby and more stress than I've ever experienced in my life. We were also supposed to be moving house but that fell apart the day after Em was admitted to hospital, and at that point I would have sold my soul to the devil for any sort of respite.

Em was discharged on Christmas Eve, and the three of us headed through to Barrow to spend it with my Dad. For the second year on the bounce we'd spent Christmas in and around hospital wards, although granted Charlotte's arrival had been a much more joyous occasion. As I write this now in September

2012 I really hope that this Christmas we all have our health and we don't have to go near a bloody hospital.

It had been an awful end to the year. My 2012 season was already in tatters but I had my Mum back, I had Em back and quite frankly the last thing on my mind was triathlon. I had plenty of time to worry about that in the year to come. It's probably not the best marketing quote in a book selling the joy, fun and challenge of triathlon but I'll write it anyway: Family was and always will be more important to me than triathlon.

23

CHASING SHADOWS

Throughout January and February I snatched at opportunities to train, and much like a lion on the hunt I didn't always get to feed. My weekends were mostly spent through at Barrow, visiting my Mum in hospital. During the week I had lost the ability to train on my commute to and from work as I was driving Em to work and Charlotte to nursery. Although Em was home, she wasn't strong enough to push the buggy up our steep hill. She had to take it easy or she'd end up back in hospital.

This also limited my training opportunities because when she was having a bad day she couldn't be left alone with Charlotte as she didn't have the energy to change her or even just pick her up and cuddle her. I guess a sensible person would have cashed his chips in and got a refund on his entry fees, but one thing I've never been known for is being sensible when it comes to triathlon.

I was in it for the long haul, if I didn't get the hours in I'd suffer but I still had the opportunity to do what I loved. Seeing my loved ones suffering to either sit up or cuddle their pride and joy gave me a serious reality check. So what if I wasn't training? I could still walk round the block, I could still go upstairs whenever I needed to, I could still play with Charlotte and when time and health allowed I could enjoy life outside, however briefly. I had a lot to be thankful for.

One Monday night after Charlotte was safely tucked up in bed, our friend Sarah came round to watch a DVD with Em. It was some chick flick featuring an Efron or a Clooney so I made my excuses and used the opportunity to get out for a brief run. It was the first time I'd been out in weeks, and it was bliss. I felt reborn with every step. I had missed the feeling of bouncing along in my own little world.

One thing I often do when I'm out running or cycling on my own is sing in my head. It helps the time to pass and if it's a good song I'm convinced that it helps my performance. I have eclectic taste, so it could be anything from Martin Solveig to Metallica. I defy anyone not to raise their heartbeat when running along with Enter Sandman echoing in your head. The iconic 90s rock anthem with its hard guitar backbone and the growling aggressive vocals of James Hetfield is worth a few seconds every mile.

This run was different though. I was confused, what the hell was the song in my head? I had the tune and some of the lyrics: "It's a brand new day, whatcha waiting for? Get up, stretch out, stomp on the floor..." but I just couldn't get it, and then it dawned on me and I just started laughing like the village idiot. It's a good job it was dark and the icy streets were deserted. I was singing The Hot Dog Song from the *Mickey Mouse Clubhouse*, Charlotte's favourite TV show. I'm sure at that moment James Hetfield would have been turning in his virtual internet grave. Oh how my life had changed. Despite the gatecrashing mouse I had a great run, just three miles as called for in my revised training plan but what made it great was that each mile was run in under eight minutes. This was a huge confidence booster as I'd managed to almost convince myself that I was seriously out of shape and unfit. OK, I still was, but not seriously.

I felt comfortable while running and suffered no ill effects afterwards. I had recently started running in Nike Lunarglides, which were a much lighter shoe than the ones I usually ran in. I had been keen to take my coach's advice and start working slowly towards a lighter shoe. He had done so and as a result had suffered with fewer injuries. I also discarded my orthotics as they didn't feel comfortable anymore and it seemed to work. I seemed to be experiencing less aches and pains after a run. I certainly wasn't going down the minimalist/barefoot running route that seemed to be sweeping the world but I was certainly getting closer to the ground in my choice of footwear.

So that Tuesday morning I woke up full of the joys of...er... winter. So it was with this confidence, and the fact that Em once more had company, that I decided to drag myself along to the COLT chain gang cycling session. It would be my first time on the bike in six weeks.

Now for those of you that never heard of a chain gang here's how it works: The rider on the front rides at speed for however long they can, then when they've had enough they swing out, and the rest come past, the new rider on the front now puts in the effort and the original front rider joins the back and drafts for some "free speed" until it's their turn on the front. The more riders there are the more rest you get. Simple eh?

Kev Lindeque, with his thighs of steel, led us out as we started along the deserted bypass heading towards the port of Heysham. I sucked his wheel and "Crazy" Ian Richardson (apt name) and "Tornado" Tom Phillips followed behind. After a few minutes Kev swung out and I was on the front. No longer sheltered by the six-foot plus windbreak I was almost blown backwards as the headwind slammed into me.

"Bloody hell he must have been strong to ride so easily against that," I reasoned as I sucked in a vital breath of cold air. Head down, arse up and pedal Holgate. I managed to get up to 21mph, my legs were on fire, my lungs were coming out of my chest – a few minutes later I swung out, knackered. I'd turned myself inside out.

The others came through, and Crazy Ian hit the front. Ian is one of the best cyclists in the club, his internal engine is phenomenal, and his appetite for suffering makes him one tough cookie. I realise now that it was a huge mistake of mine to be one place in front of him. He hit the front like a steam train, his muscular legs firing like pistons.

When Ian swung out and Tornado Tom hit the front I was doomed. Tom is a great fell runner, and in 2010 he became only the 25th person to complete the Bob Graham Round in winter. The race that covers approximately 74 miles, a daunting 42 peaks and a leg-crippling 28,500 feet of climbing in the English Lake District. Not only is Tom an amazing runner, he's also a machine on the bike, and a few months on from this night he finished 15th in the hardest sportive in Great Britain, the Fred Whitton.

Tom drove the train forward at speed. In direct contrast I went off the back like a wagon in sidings. I had no response and in the space of 30 seconds they had 100 metres on me. Alone and in a headwind, the gap just got longer and longer. I cursed as I tried to get my legs to respond but they just couldn't. I quite simply imploded with a whimper rather than a bang.

My lack of bike training had never been so telling. I spent the next 40 minutes trying to catch three other cyclists working together as a team. It was never going to happen.

In a sadistic sort of way I enjoyed it. I worked harder than I probably would have done if I'd been out on my own. And although it firmly put me in my place in terms of my fitness it kick-started me into wanting to work harder. Where I was and where I wanted to be were still poles apart – but that's probably the same for most people right?

There is only one way to solve that, work harder and work smarter. Over the following weeks I would turn up for my weekly beasting and on each occasion I would manage a little bit more time on the front of the gang. I was still dropped very quickly but I knew that it was doing me good so I stuck at it.

You know you are immersed in your ambitions when you spend cold, wet, miserable Tuesday nights on a dark Lancashire bypass chasing shadows. It was great for building mental strength, a strength that would serve me well in the future.

I was managing to fit training into my lunch hour at work, running and swimming, trying to hit the targets on my training plan. I was building up my running with these lunchtime sessions and I was also starting to sneak out for longer runs just after 5am, so that I could be home to help get Charlotte and Em out the door. I'd always been a morning person so it didn't really bother me, and there is something magical about running through a deserted city before sunrise. The lack of sounds, smells, and movement really hones your senses to the environment around you even if it is rain-soaked urban architecture.

My swimming continued to improve. Several two-kilometre swims and the coached interval sessions with COLT saw me gain more confidence in the water. I felt like my swim endurance was starting to appear again. My swim speed? Well, that probably never existed in the first place. I had been working hard on the turbo trainer, substituting long rides missed at weekends for several weekday trips to the "pain cave", that mystical nirvana much talked about by triathletes, as I pedalled myself into oblivion following sessions entitled "Pyramid 4" and the tough "Hard Intervals 2" which comprised the following:

10 minutes Zone 1-2 Warm up
2 minutes middle of Zone 4
2 minutes easy spinning
2 minutes middle of Zone 4
2 minutes easy spinning
2 minutes middle of Zone 4
2 minutes easy spinning
2 minutes middle of Zone 4
2 minutes easy spinning
2 minutes middle of Zone 4
2 minutes easy spinning
10 minutes Zone 1-2 Warm down

Zone 4 was an indicator of my heart rate working at 85 per cent of its maximum. Now if you don't understand that I'll put it in simple terms. If you didn't want to puke your guts up by the end of the session, you'd not done it properly. These sessions and the similar ones that I was doing each week hurt like hell, and kept my bike legs working. Each time I felt like dying and slumping heavily over the bars of the ROO I dug deep and thought of the inspiring and very true words from the ancient Chinese proverb: "The more you sweat in training the less you bleed in battle."

It was still very telling though that as March rolled around my longest bike ride of the year had been with the chain gang covering 30 miles. In a little over two months I would be facing the toughest bike course in the Ironman world, in Lanzarote. I really hoped I wouldn't die from the loss of blood.

On 10th February we finally moved house after a couple of months of stress. We have both decided since that we are never moving again, which I think says it all. The actual day of the move went well, and despite the removals guys joking about cracking my ROO, it arrived safely. I had lost the training cellar but I gained a turbo garage, so karma was restored to the world.

Actually when house-hunting my only stipulation was that I had somewhere for my bikes to be kept, and a turbo set up. This led to months of Em looking at the amount of light in lounges, if our wardrobes would fit in the bedroom, and if the garden would be safe enough for Charlotte to play in while I explored garages and cellars with a tape measure.

Several wonderful houses were excluded because when I measured them I found that I'd be sat on the turbo with my head through the garage roof. In the end we did find the perfect place, our "forever home" as they are so fond of saying on those housey-type programmes that I try not to pay too much attention to when they are on.

Life began to settle down a bit at home so I felt like I could spend more time training without feeling neglectful of my girls. Em was feeling much stronger, which was a huge relief. She now had the energy to chase around after the toddling terror, although in reality Charlotte was more of a shuffling sweetie.

On the second Sunday in March I managed to really shift my cycling up a gear, making a significant breakthrough in time and distance. I left the house at 7.30am, and the temperature was three below zero, the sun wasn't quite up, and the morning air left a low-lying fine mist hovering over the fields. I had the full winter gear on and I needed it.

Heading out across the hills towards the Trough of Bowland it was very tricky with black ice, the consequence of hard rain the day before and a cloudless freezing night. The frozen run-off from the fields was making cycling near the verge dangerous. Descending towards the village of Caton my back wheel lost traction and I felt the bike starting to fishtail, so without thinking I shifted my considerable weight in the opposite direction and somehow kept the bike upright. For a second I considered going home to the comfort of the turbo in the pain cave, but only for a second. I needed real miles in my legs.

After 90 minutes of solo riding I met up with the COLT Sunday ride. There was a good turnout of 12 people, which wasn't bad for a winter outing. We decided to head north-west through Silverdale, Arnside and then back through Holme and the Kellets – for those who don't know the area this is a great ride, some nasty short climbs followed by rewarding views of Morecambe Bay and the Lake District Mountains.

I felt OK as we headed out on the flat but as soon as we started to climb I got dropped. It wasn't surprising really, these guys were fresh and if I'm honest all stronger cyclists than me, and I'd got two hours in my legs by the time we hit the first climb of the morning. Thankfully at various points – usually on the steep climbs – Andy Ley and Kev Lindeque dropped back and kept me company. They waved away my breathless apologies and I felt so guilty that I was messing up their training ambitions.

I was particularly grateful to Kev who paced me up a tough but gradual 20 per cent climb out of Warton that I'd never seen before. The pain cave was no longer in a Lancaster garage, it was on this bloody hill. I could hardly breathe and he was chatting away to me like the hill wasn't even there. I'm telling you, when I grow up I want to have the cycling ability of Kev.

The guilt won me over as we caught up the 'C' ride just north of Milnthorpe. I thanked Kev and swung off left to take the easier route home. If I thought I was in for an easy ride though I was mistaken. The supposed slower ride that morning consisted solely of 'The Outlaw Ladies'.

No, they weren't a mystical bunch of female gunslingers wearing leather boots, hip-hugging jeans and silver spurs. Sarah Patterson, Christine Gardner and Mandy Ley were lycra-clad female warriors, the kind that made that Xena lass look like Penelope Pitstop. Feminine, tough and determined, they cycled like they owned the road as they trained hard for their iron distance debut at the Outlaw.

Christine and Mandy were relatively new to triathlon, in fact Mandy had done her first ever one at Fleetwood. Amazingly it would be her only triathlon until her date with iron destiny in Nottingham. They had seen their husbands become Ironmen the year before and decided that they quite fancied some of that.

Sarah had methodically moved through the distances, testing herself in a calculated manner at Olympic and then half distances. She had Ironman blood coursing through her 50-year-old veins, being the older sister of Richard Mason. It took all of my energy to tuck in at the back.

Mandy had obviously been taking tips from her husband Andy Ley as she powered up the road like a woman possessed, her long blonde hair streaming in her wake. I remember thinking "if Rapunzel rode a bike..."

It had been a few months since I'd cycled with the three of them and they had made serious progress. If I wasn't on top form in a few months in Nottingham they'd all be putting nails in my coffin. In total I was out on the bike for four hours and 40 minutes and those last 40 minutes were hell.

I had run out of steam, my fingernails hurt from gripping the bars on the climbs, and my feet were frozen. The Outlaw Ladies almost had to physically drag me home. I had done just over 58 miles when I got back which shows you that it was a tough ride and I wasn't on top form.

My training programme called for a 20-minute transition run, so, despite feeling like a zombie that's what I did and I actually shocked myself about how strong I felt. I was dead on the bike but my legs suddenly woke up and the 20 minutes whizzed by.

A big bowl of Shredded Wheat and a hot bath in which to defrost rounded off a hard session, but the recovery was even better as we took Charlotte out on her bike in the sunshine. Thankfully she was still at an age where she wasn't embarrassed to be seen out in public with her old man wearing his compression socks. Still at least it was too cold for my sandals.

Following on from that bike breakthrough I really stepped things up over the next couple of weeks, and as a result the challenges that lay ahead only seemed daunting and not impossible. It probably doesn't sound a lot given some of my training volumes in previous years, but I managed to put in two weeks each of 12 hours of training. Within those two weeks I completed my longest swim, longest bike ride and longest run since 2010 at the Outlaw.

Those sessions were complemented by shorter, focused training such as coached swim intervals, pyramid sessions on the turbo trainer and some fast interval running. I was taking a focused approach to training, complementing speed with distance, trying to reach a perfect balance to make myself as strong and as fast as possible in the short time that I had left before Lanzarote.

I was conscious that I was constantly playing catch-up, chasing a shadow of my former self as I pushed myself towards my greatest challenge and trying to squeeze as much into my day without risking injury. I was walking a fine line but I was driven by the fear of failure, and fear is a great motivator.

My longest swim kind of happened by accident. My coach had set me a 3,000-metre swim but I was having one of those mornings where it felt easy so I just kept going until I reached the Ironman distance of 3.8km. I could only hope that I would get out of the sea at Puerto del Carmen feeling that relaxed. I would be over the moon, but I guessed that adrenaline, sea water and 1,500 other people knocking hell out of me would be a lot less relaxing.

My longest run saw me out the door before sunrise, and again, much like my swim, I didn't intend to go far but it was a stunning morning so after the planned 30 minutes at eight and a half minutes per mile I decided to keep going for two hours. I relaxed the pace slightly and averaged just over nine minutes per mile for the two hours. I was supposed to run home from work later that day but my legs were trashed, so I ducked out and got a lift. That would have been pushing my luck.

The bike ride however was planned. I met up with Andy H for the first time in months, as with work and family commitments we just hadn't got together at all. I wished him happy New Year before we headed out for 65 miles on the bike in the drizzle. It was a solid, steady ride, just what I needed.

Again I think I could have kept going, which was a good thing as we'd both signed up for the Jodrell Bank 80-mile sportive that coming Sunday. I couldn't wait to have another crack at it, and I felt confident that this year I'd be sure to complete the longer distance after relegating myself to the shorter one in 2011.

The queues at registration seemed to be twice as long as they were the previous year, a testament to the rise of cycling in the collective psyche of the British public. We joined the long queue for the start and we were away just after 8.15am. I felt quite strong through the first ten miles but poor Andy H was suffering badly with a sick feeling, he couldn't take any drink in without wanting to throw it back up. It looked like he might have to call it a day, but then a piece of malt loaf as a last resort seemed to settle his stomach and he battled on.

The two of us rode for a while with three other Pirates: Muffin Top, who was training for her Ironman debut; and my good friends Mr and Mrs Silent Assassin. The ladies were gearing up for the Outlaw, which Mrs Assassin had completed in 2011 to emulate her husband. A house with one Ironman is bad enough, but imagine the strength of your relationship if you had two given the stresses that you experience on your journey?

Silent Assassin had picked the easy option and opted for Ironman Wales with its tsunami swim, nosebleed-inducing bike ride and leg-breaking run. It was a good job he was as tough as they come. The three of them were all going really well, and it was great to catch up with Mr Assassin and chew the fat. We had not done that since the morning after the Outlaw in 2010 when we shared a fry-up. With great company in our little peloton of five the miles just melted away.

Unfortunately though the road surfaces were shocking, and this would be my downfall. Heading downhill into Northwich I hit a deep pothole at speed and was horrified to hear a loud snapping noise. I instantly knew what had happened. I had blown a spoke out on my rear wheel. As I started up the hill a booming voice shouted "come on Holgs, think of Lanza, and put the effort in".

The not so Silent Assassin, who had been delayed by a red traffic light, was approaching from behind, but Lanza couldn't have been further from my mind. All I could think about was my wheel, as the metallic clang of the loose spoke resonated against its neighbour in a taunting manner. B*****s.

With the hill behind me I pulled up alongside Andy H, and although I knew the answer, asked anyway: "What are the chances of me riding 60 hilly miles with a broken spoke?" The look on his face said it all. I decided to battle on though, hoping that things wouldn't deteriorate.

A gap started to open up between Andy H and myself. He was part of the Pirate train with the other three and I was blown out the back. It was a like a chain gang Tuesday. The clanging noise was driving me mad and although I felt physically strong, the bike wasn't responding.

As a last-ditch attempt to save the day, Andy H taped the spoke to its neighbour. I would never have thought of carrying gaffer tape in my saddle bag, but since that day I always do. It weighs next to nothing and could be that little piece of magic that gets you home from the middle of nowhere. The taping offered my ears relief at least, and I guess in a way cleared my mind as I could keep up again.

But approaching 50 miles I started to feel the back of the bike moving all over the place, and the screech of the tyre as it rubbed on the frame was awful. Real fingernails down a chalkboard kind of stuff, dogs all over Cheshire winced each time it happened.

Andy H dropped back and assessed the situation from behind as I climbed up a hill. His conclusion as we arrived in Macclesfield was that it was game over. I told him to keep riding and I would find my own way back, but he stayed with me, worried that I might total the wheel and smash my face and body up.

Those last ten miles were probably the scariest of my life, especially the last climb of the day where I had no choice but to get out of the saddle. I tried to climb as gingerly as possible, keeping my weight from the pedals, and just hoped that the wheel wouldn't jam in the frame. Thankfully it didn't.

We rolled back into HQ having done 60 miles, so all was not lost. These were decent training miles, but it was frustrating to have to cut short when I physically felt so good. Still it was best to live to fight another day rather than risk face-kissing the tarmac and losing my front teeth again. I had my natural ones kicked out aged nine while playing rugby and I now have implants.

I suppose you could say that I don't have much luck with the bikes, what with Saddlegate, but this was just one of those things. Potholes are tougher than bike spokes, and British roads are littered with them. The way I looked at it, it was better to get my run of bad luck out the way, rather than have it travel to Lanzarote with me.

Luckily the local bike shop managed to fix the wheel a couple of days later which meant that the big training day that I had been instructed to do was a goer. When I first got the e-mail from my coach Richard Mason, I blinked in disbelief. He wanted me to ride for five hours, rest for an hour and then run for two hours. That was going to be tough, especially as I was streaming with cold. But telling myself to man up that's what I did – well almost.

The alarm went off at 4.30am. I'd laid my gear out in the spare bedroom the night before, so as not to disturb Em. I looked out of the window, and surprise surprise it was pouring down. Compression top, bib-tights, long sleeve cycle jersey, two pairs of socks, neoprene overshoes, fluro waterproof jacket, sunglasses (yellow lenses to enhance light), buff, helmet and Goretex gloves and I was ready to go. Can you see why I got up half an hour before I set off?

I grabbed a load of gels and stuffed my pockets. I deliberately didn't eat and decided that I wouldn't consume anything but water for the first two hours to try and tap into my plentiful fat reserves.

I was running two lights on the back of the bike, each at half a watt and giving visibility up to a mile and on the front I had a 1200 lumen flashing light and then just for good measure another 1000 lumen torch on my helmet. I looked like a rider from the movie *Tron*. It was overkill really but I was about to hit unlit country lanes, and I both needed to be seen and to see where I was going. You know you are out early when all you see for the first hour or so is roadkill – rats, rabbits, pheasants and loads of toads as it was their mating season. The only living creatures I saw were sheep on the fell roads, and they did their very best to crash into me. They aren't the brightest of creatures. How the hell can lambs, which are full of energy and enthusiasm, turn into sheep which are dull, stupid and always look thoroughly bored? Maybe I should ask the IronFarmer about that.

I was never more than five miles from home, riding loop after loop repeating all the big hills that I could find. It was pretty boring, so I decided to spice things up by playing road kill bingo. The first to reach five sightings would win, and then I would start again. The rabbits put up a good show but the poor unfortunate toads won. It was slightly grim but the macabre game kept me going. Try it some time, it will certainly take your mind off your cold and tired legs. The rain and mist eventually blew away which meant I could turn off the illuminations. My legs felt good climbing. I wasn't fast, averaging just over 12 mph, but I did climb just shy of 3,900 feet – only about a third of the climbing in Lanza. Most of my climbing was done seated. I only got out of the saddle climbing Littledale, a beast of a hill which rises 478 feet in just over a mile.

I had forgotten what a tough climb that was, although I wasn't helped by all the mud and crap on the road either. That climb was quickly followed by the Tower, 650 feet in 1.2 miles. I took great satisfaction from the fact that for the first time ever I had managed to stay seated and grind it out.

To be honest the five hours went by a lot quicker than I thought they would. I drank one bottle of water, and one of Nuun, an electrolyte sports drink. I also consumed six gels, one every half an hour in the last three hours and I don't think I suffered for not having eaten in the first two hours.

I got off the bike, cold and wet but not feeling as trashed as I thought I would. I stripped off in the garage, remembering to close the door so as not to alarm my new neighbours. I put my running gear on and away I went plodding down the street. I couldn't afford the luxury – or pain – of an hour's rest in between the bike and the run as instructed because I had family commitments.

The run was a straight out and back, flat route, trying to mimic Lanza. I had two gels on the run and again the two hours flew by. I took that to be a good sign. I made it home just after noon, and was rewarded with a cuddle from Charlotte, who didn't seem to mind that her daddy was dripping in sweat. That was the best part of the day.

I really felt like I was on a roll, I was beginning to peak at just the right time. Full of enthusiasm and wanting to erase the disappointment of cutting Jodrell Bank short I put a last minute entry in to the Kendal Sportive. The very hilly 75-mile ride would be the perfect test of my legs and my desire.

The day started off as I expected. I set off with a group of my fellow COLTs and I was dropped on the long climb out of Kendal towards Kirkby Lonsdale. It wasn't a vicious climb, more of a "this is going to take a while" sort of climb, you know – seated and sustained. I wasn't disappointed to get dropped as I had my own agenda, it was going to be a long day, and I wasn't interested in beasting myself to save some overrated male pride.

After all, in Lanza, I didn't expect to see any club-mates on the bike, they would all be way up the road ahead of me. Kendal was great practice for the big event as it is all about "me, myself and I" as De La Soul would say.

I felt strong in myself and climbs of Barbondale and Dent felt comfortable. Turning out of Dent and heading towards Kingsdale Head I was joined for a few minutes by Chris Lawson, my club-mate and fellow nutter who like me was doing both Lanza and the Outlaw. We passed a sign at the side on the road that said "Don't Look Up", and the climb up Kingsdale Head had started.

Other than Hardknott Pass I'd never seen anything so evil in all my time on a bike. It made the torturous Tow Top from the Tour of Staveley look like a speed bump. The 25 per cent gradient climb was a leg-breaker, it went on and on and on. Every time I turned a corner and hoped for some respite, the road just ramped up again.

Chris blew me away on the climb but I just paced myself, passing people who had shot past me at the bottom and were now walking, bent double, holding on to their bikes for support. My lungs were bursting, my quads were popping and to be honest I couldn't even pedal squares, but somehow I kept on my bike and kept moving forward at an average pace of between two and three miles per hour. The relief at the top was sublime and the view was simply stunning as I looked back down at the valley that I had just come up. The sense of achievement wasn't bad either.

The long descent towards Ingleton was fun, spinning the legs out to get rid of the poison that had just engorged the muscles. I was joined by a guy also training for Lanzarote and he reassured me having done it last year that there was nothing as evil as that. Phew. After a quick feed stop to replenish the bottles I started the long climb out of Ingleton towards the North Yorkshire town of Hawes. Approaching the wonderful Ribblehead viaduct, a monument to the great age of steam, I heard a familiar sound that I'd hoped I'd never hear again.

Ping! clip,clip,clip...

I pulled over and swore, kicking the grass verge in frustrated disbelief. My back wheel had lost a spoke. I was 30 miles into a 75-mile event and I was in the middle of nowhere. The wheel had been repaired and trued, getting me through a hilly five-hour ride on it the weekend before yet it was knackered. I stood there feeling like I was cursed. Learning from Jodrell Bank I had some gaffer tape with me and taped the spoke to its neighbour and jumped back on, fuming in silent rage.

I rode on at half pace until the village of Dent, passing through it for the second time that morning. Dent features a 500-metre stretch of cobbles. This was the final nail in my coffin. PING. Another spoke had gone, and the wheel lost all shape as the rubber of the tyre jammed against the frame. The wheel locked solid but luckily I managed to unclip.

I was 50 miles in, there was no short cut, no support car and no mobile signal. S**t! Luckily a guy that I'd been riding with on and off caught me back up. His wife was in Dent with the car and a bike trailer. They took pity on me, he agreed I couldn't ride on the wheel and his wife drove me back to Kendal and race HQ for my second DNF in two weeks and a sobering piece of déjà vu pie.

Poor Em must have been expecting a right moody git to walk through the door, especially after I'd given her the news of my failure, or should I say my bike's failure, over the phone. By the time I got home though I was fine, what was the point as after all it was nothing I'd done wrong, just bad luck. Despite not finishing, I had still ridden 50 miles and climbed 4,500 feet, so it wasn't a complete waste of time. The following day I ordered a cheap pair of wheels that were reviewed as being "bomb proof" and so far thankfully they have been.

I must have blinked because the year had flown by. I was stood in my office staring at the image looking back at me. On my wall I had just flipped over my triathlon calendar to May, and there was a timely reminder of what I was about to face. Several toned warriors on carbon steeds battled through a desolate landscape darkened by centuries-old fire.

It was Timanfaya, "The Fire Mountain", one of the iconic hills from the Lanzarote bike course and it seemed to go on for ever. I gulped and just stared. In 19 days I had a date with the god of Fire Mountain. It suddenly all seemed very real and very near.

My head got a massive boost a couple of nights later after meeting up in the pub for a COLT Lanza seminar led by coach Richard Mason, John Knapp and Mr Lanzarote, Chris Wild. Between them they could give the Lanzarote tourist board a run for their money. They talked us "newbies" through the course, gave us tips and advised on what to do in the days before and on race day.

I listened more intently than I ever had at any lecture, absorbing it all as though my life depended on it, and at that point I really thought it did. I learnt that as long as I paced myself correctly, took on enough fluids, and didn't attack the hills early I should survive the bike. I started to formulate my race plan in my head. Walking home in the dark my mind was racing with excitement and healthy fear. To me Lanza had always been about the bike. If I got off the bike inside the 11 hours and 30 minutes cut-off allowed for the swim and bike sections, I knew I would complete the marathon despite the prospect that the tarmac could be touching temperatures of 50 degrees by mid-afternoon on race day.

Stepping though the puddles my mind envisaged 19th May at around 6pm. I had just reached T2 and handed my bike over. I had a huge grin on my face. My vision disappeared as I waited for a bus to pass before I crossed the road and I couldn't help but smile wryly as I thought: "It will probably fade within a mile but hey what the hell, it's Ironman, it's supposed to hurt."

24

SLOW COOKING IN LANZAROTE

I looked at my watch. It was eight in the morning and I'd been up for a few hours and for once training wasn't on the agenda. A restless night had been followed by a few hours of triple checking that I had my passport, travel documents, money, bike shoes etc. It was hard to believe at the ripe old age of 39 that I would be flying on my own for the first time.

I had spent the last couple of days packing all my gear, taking the bike apart, packing it in its box. That caused a major stress when I couldn't remove one of the pedals, but luckily it was solved by a mad dash to the local bike shop and two mechanics jumping on the bike spanner to loosen it. At least it wasn't me being a numpty for once.

I was a prize numpty a couple of days beforehand when I had taken the bike in to get serviced. The mechanic told me that my cassette was worn and that I would need a new one. This was the Giant. I had decided at the last minute to leave the ROO at home as the Giant had more gears and suited my climbing style better than the built for speed triathlon bike. "Do you want me to put a 25 on like the one that's already on?" asked the mechanic. I thought I was hearing things. "A 25? It's a 32 on the back," I answered, looking down at the cogs on the cassette. He smiled the sort of smile that Jeremy Clarkson would give an owner of a Vauxhall Vectra. "It's a 25."

"Yeah, why not," I laughed and then explained what a prat I'd been. I had ordered the new cassette online about three years previously. It arrived and I fitted it, ever so proud of myself. I never counted the teeth on the largest cog, if I had I would have found out that the shop had sent me a 25 instead of a 32.

I should have realised as a 32 is the size of a dinner plate and a 25 is more of a bread roll plate for the sophisticated among you. What a muppet. However I was a happy muppet because it meant that I wasn't as crap a climber as I thought, I was getting up the hills with a harder gear. This little quirk actually gave me a boost considering I was about to face a lot of climbing. That was the last of the drama. I made it to the airport on time, sailed through customs, and best of all the plane didn't crash. I stepped off the flying metal tube and the heat hit me full on. I had waited 12 months for this. Welcome to Lanzarote Holgs.

Ironman Lanzarote is somewhat of an enigma among the triathlon community, and having experienced the race first hand I can fully understand why. It is tough, hot, desolate and hilly and yet at the same time stunning, inspiring, rewarding and fun. It rightfully deserves the respect that is given to it as the toughest Ironman on the circuit, it's not a race you can turn up to and just 'wing' it, you need a plan and you need to stick to it. Here's how my time on the island went.

The Build-Up

I'll be honest with you, this race really scared me, unlike any other I'd ever attempted before. Most people enter races that play to their strengths, but I had chosen to enter one that played to my weaknesses.

For those who read my previous book you'll know that I died on my arse in the heat of Frankfurt, destroyed my legs climbing the hills of Le Terrier and pretty much moaned about how much I hated cycling in the wind. So entering Lanzarote probably wasn't my most sensible move.

Last year when I got excited at the prospect of doing it and got a pass out from Em, I took advice from three people who were veterans of this race; Richard Mason, John Knapp and Chris Wild. They all 'green lit' my idea and it then became reality.

The enthusiasm from Chris was contagious; he's practically a tax exile who is part of the furniture at this race. And throughout the year he had reassured me that I could do it. On the Tuesday before the race, I was cursing him as I thought I'd made the biggest mistake of my life.

Team COLT met in Puerto del Carmen for a training session on the swim course. Everyone was excited. This was to be my first ever sea swim and the water was amazingly clear and warm. But it was unbelievably salty. Halfway round the loop I had been dropped by the others (which I'd expected) and suddenly I found myself throwing up, a combination of the saline intake and the choppy waves.

After I'd made a chum line for any sharks in the area I was less than confident when I got out of the sea. All the good work and progress I'd made with my swimming was forgotten. I now had doubts about the swim, bloody hell I might not even get the chance to ride up any hill if they had to fish me out of the drink on race morning. The day only went from bad to worse.

After the swim Team COLT headed for coffee and cake at the wonderful German Bakery, and judging by the queues of toned, hard bodied Scandinavians and Bavarians this little gem of a place wasn't much of a secret among the triathlon community. The coffee and walnut cake took away the taste of the salt and made for some great team bonding but we all had an eye on the thermometer on the table. It read 110 degrees and it was only 10.30am. We all laughed and joked but you could sense the undercurrent of doubt amongst those that were about to race.

Later that afternoon a small group of us did a 90-minute bike ride and a 20-minute run really just to test that the bikes were working after the flights out. We did a little climb but nothing serious and within ten minutes I couldn't feel my throat, the heat was drying everything up. Andy Ley got a hell of a shock when one of his tri bars came lose as we descended back down into town. However that would be the least of his problems once we started out on the run.

He nipped back into the hotel to change out of his bike shirt telling us that he was too hot. I waited patiently with Kel Hirst, the blonde mother of two, who being ex-navy fitted in really well with essentially a group of blokes on a foreign holiday. She was an Ironman, and a good one despite being diabetic. Andy emerged wearing his new tri top that he'd bought earlier that afternoon. He was resplendent in powder blue, it really brought out the colour of his eyes. We set off plodding past the bars and tourist shops selling the usual tat that Brits seem to buy on holiday, plastic buckets, cuddly donkeys, sombreros.

"Andy you do know you are wearing the ladies' version of that top don't you? I was in the shop earlier and the blokes' is a black version," I asked as I gasped for air. Kel dissolved into fits of laughter. Unknown to me, earlier Kel and her husband Matt had said the same thing. "Did she put you up to this?" growled Andy as he too broke into laughter. We must have looked a right trio dodging through the tourists laughing like loons.

"I think a little wee just came out," confessed Kel. Well that was it, we were done and had to walk. Luckily we were about 100 metres from the hotel. Poor Andy had the p**s taken out of him for the rest of the trip, and to be honest he still hasn't lived it down.

It was a good job we had the laughter because that run was a real eye-opener. How the hell would we be able to bike/run the huge distances in those conditions? I got back and over the next hour drank four litres of water and Gatorade, and I was still dehydrated. That was after only an hour and ten minutes of light exercise. I was worried to say the least.

The day after worry turned to all-out fear. Chris Wild took myself, Andy Ley, Kel Hirst and Chris "IronHobbit" Clarke for a drive around the bike course, and then onto La Santa to register. His expert commentary was brilliant, and come race day I would pretty much remember all that he said as I had concentrated on his every word, looking for ways to make the ride easier. His invaluable hints on gearing, where to push and where to hold back were all stored mentally and used on race day and for that I can't thank him enough.

However seeing my nemesis the bike course up close and personal scared the s**t out of me. It was all that I'd feared and worse. The hills were monsters, the hills that no one considered hills were long and relentless and the hairpin descent off Haria was like nothing I'd ever seen before. Think Lombard Street in San Francisco, you know, the one that's bendier than a Russian gymnast.

Then add in sheer cliff face-type drops with a safety wall about 30 centimetres high and you'll get a feel for it. When the IronHippy quipped, "This is where Marc Herremans crashed and became paralysed," it didn't help matters either. In fact although I now realise his comment was a veiled warning to be careful on that stretch, it actually gave me nightmares that night.

I felt physically sick at the prospect of riding down that hill. It was ironic that I'd spent all year worried about riding up the hills of Lanzarote and now I was having an actual nightmare about coming down one of them. The further into the course we drove the quieter the car got.

That night I passed on going out with my club-mates for dinner and just sat in the apartment on my own. I was scared, and I was torn. My texts home were very negative, I've never doubted my ability or resolve as I did that night. If someone had offered me a flight home in those few hours of turmoil I may have taken them up on it.

The texts of support from my parents and Em made me feel so much better. My spirits climbed further when my mate Diane Scholey got in on the motivational act as well. I worked with Diane, and she loved the island and knew just what I would be facing in terms of the conditions. She had no interest in triathlon but she said all the right things in those messages. I will forever be grateful for the texts I received that night as they really brought me back from a dark place and got me to man up.

The next day, another club-mate who is a comparable cyclist to me, Christine Gardner, blew my fears away. The Outlaw Lady told me that she had completed most of the climbs on training camps and that if she could do it then so could I. It was the confidence boost I needed.

I was so happy that I could have kissed her but I dialled back my enthusiasm as I didn't want to upset her husband Paul, who was sat next to her. Mind you in that particular moment I would have quite happily kissed him as well.

The afternoon before the race I was sat by the hotel pool with a few of the team: Pete Denness, the youngster who the following morning would get out of the sea ahead of the female pros in a display of pure raw talent; Chris "IronHobbit" Clarke who, true to form, was relaxing with a pint of ice cold beer and joked: "I'm tapering, and just having the one." I think in his eyes beer and cakes are performance enhancing substances, and in reality on the evidence from his results you couldn't argue against him; Richard Mason, who had invested so much in using this race to qualify for Kona, was brooding in the knowledge that he wouldn't finish the race.

A few weeks back in training Richard had crashed with John Towse and his knee was a mess. It looked like John Hurt's stomach in *Alien* right before the pop. He had promised his wife, Sarah, and everyone else who was concerned about him that he would run out of T2 and then stop. It must have been awful for him to sit there knowing what was ahead. I for one was over the moon for him when he eventually recovered and qualified for Kona at Ironman UK a few months later.

The last person in the group was my good mate Chris Lawson. Because of work commitments he had only arrived late the night before, and in reality he probably shouldn't have been there at all. Several weeks earlier we had all been at a COLT training camp in the Lake District and poor Chris had caught a nasty infection while swimming in Derwentwater.

Unfortunately his ankle and lower leg developed cellulitis, causing his sympathetic team-mates to nickname him "Iron

Kebab Leg". He couldn't train, and it was touch and go if he would be allowed to fly. His leg was still swollen, and his sandals cut into his puffy skin. We all wondered how he would get his cycling shoes on the next day.

He wasn't in the best of moods because Kel, who was a nurse, had advised him not to race. His coach Richard had also just done the same. Both of them had his health and best interests at heart but I could see how upset he was to be told this. I think he wanted reassurance and the no-nonsense ex-military psyche of those two just wasn't cut out for that.

I on the other hand had no such training, and told him: "You've come this far, you've defied everyone to actually get here and it would be a shame to stay in bed tomorrow morning. No one here expects you to finish, so go swim, if you have to pull out after that then there's no shame. We all know that if you were fit with two good legs you'd storm this race.

"If I was you and I was here, no one would stop me from at least having a go. Kel and Richard make more sense than me and I agree with them to be honest but only you know if you can do it or not. I have faith in you mate, as do they, the question is do you have faith in yourself. If the answer is yes then that is all that matters."

We sat silently looking down at our three good legs and a kebab cooling in the pool. He came back to me later, a smile back on his face, and before he even told me I knew we would be racing together at first light the next day.

In a flash the six days of acclimatising had gone by and I was sat alone in my hotel room eating my pre-race meal of pasta in bolognese sauce, a simple, high-carbohydrate dish that was easy on the stomach but would also top up my energy reserves for the massive day to follow.

My phone buzzed and I looked at the photo of Charlotte holding a sign saying "Good Luck Daddy." I had a lump in my throat, I just about had time to compose myself when the phone started ringing. It was great to hear Em's voice. This was the first time I would be facing an Ironman without my rock but she assured me that she would be following all day online and Sarah Patterson would be texting her updates from the side of the course.

She said: "I've got someone here who wants to talk to you," and when Charlotte came to the phone and said "hiya Daddy" I almost burst into tears. It was the first time she had put those two words together. It was time to make them both proud, it was time for Daddy to do it for his little girl.

Race Day

I was up before 5am having slept unusually well to eat my porridge, washed down with a coffee and some Imodium. I didn't fancy any bowel explosions on the course so took the extra precaution, having read the tip on an online forum.

I met the others and we walked the 15 minutes to the transition area, passing clubbers on their way home to bed. We were about to start the longest day of the year and they were about to sleep through it. Transition was abuzz with an air of nervous energy as I put the gels on the bike and pumped the tyres.

We got into our wetsuits and exchanged handshakes of luck like First World War officers about to go over the top of the trenches. We were off to battle; unlike those poor souls we would make it back.

The Swim

The faster lads headed towards the front of the crowd and Chris Lawson and I headed for the back. We looked up and noticed the COLT flag flying from the balcony of John Knapp's room. The black and white Union Jack had never looked so powerful, and I felt compelled to give it a nodded salute of respect. I took it as a good omen for what was to come. I was a COLT and I was immensely proud to be one.

Minutes before the off Chris and I embraced and wished each

other luck. He planned to stay in touching distance as open water isn't his favourite thing and we usually swim together in training. The countdown began. I felt the hot sand moving beneath my toes as I inched closer to the water, desperate to get going.

I closed my eyes and thought of everything I'd been through and how lucky I was to have the opportunity to slay some demons. This was my moment, this was my time and nothing was going to stop me. THREE, TWO...

Chaos.

The swim is a beach start so basically the gun goes and you run into the sea, 1,600 people all legging it into the water at once. The jockeying for position among the swimmers was worse than the Boxing Day sales on Oxford Street. Pent-up aggression, nerves and adrenaline just came flooding out. You hit the water and you have to be strong or you get destroyed.

The first stretch out to the turn buoy was carnage. I was kicked full on in the face twice and got a few licks of my own in. The congestion at the turn was suffocating and we were like moths drawn to a light. There was just no space at all but once around the turn I kicked hard and pulled away from those around me, finding my own little bubble to swim in.

People would later comment about how much diesel there was in the water from the flotilla of boats and jet skis but I didn't notice it at all. My mouth was probably numb with all the salt I was taking on board. I figured it would do me good for later when I started to lose my body's salt in the oppressive heat.

Before I knew it I was coming into the shallows, ready to run up the beach through the baying crowds and back into the water for lap two. A time of 41 minutes 30 seconds for the first lap meant that I was bang on target. I had been worried that I would be lapped by the elite swimmers but thankfully that hadn't happened.

There was a lot more room on the second lap, with a bit of argy bargy at the first two turn buoys. I started to enjoy the swim. The salt was awful but thankfully there was no repeat of my chumming for sharks. The wind started to create a bit of a swell which probably slowed me down as I turned into it after the final buoy for the long home straight parallel to the beach.

The highlight of the lap was seeing two dinner plate-sized jellyfish ascending from the depths. I just kept thinking "don't you bloody dare" as the last thing I needed was to start the bike covered in stings. Chris Wild had been stung in a practice swim a few days before and luckily for him none of his team-mates offered to pee on his wounds, not even Kel.

I reached the bottleneck and the huge arch which marked the end of the swim and lunged out of the water in 42.34 giving a total swim time of 1.24:04. My legs pushed me through the cheering crowd, on through the showers for the long run across the beach into T1.

As the helicopter swirled overhead, dance beats boomed from unseen speakers and the crowds went wild, I grabbed my cycling kit bag from its peg and headed into the huge change tent.

I ran straight into the back of Andy Ley, who had his wetsuit stripped off and was about to head out. We were both buzzing, high on endorphins. In seconds he was gone and I wouldn't see him until the run. I didn't sit down. I washed the sand from my feet and took great care to dry them as I would be on them a long time. Sand in the wrong place could wreck my day.

Next I applied Savlon to my undercarriage, giving my skin a protective barrier from the chaffing of the saddle. Finally and most importantly I allowed one of the many volunteers to smother me in factor 50 sun cream.

Having run up the steep path from the sand to the road that doubled as the bike holding area I dived into a perfectly clean Portaloo for a pee, as it would be almost nine hours until I went again. Emerging back onto the street filled with lycra warriors I put my helmet, glasses, gloves and shoes on and began the very long run to my bike.

Once I'd picked the bike up I still had about 300 metres to run to the mount line. T1 took me 12.47 and I really didn't mess about, and contrary to popular belief I didn't do a crossword.

The Bike

I soon cleared the immense crowds on the prom, and began a very lonely section of the day. Hundreds of people flew past me as it was a fairly flat start. I knew this would happen and I'd left my ego at home. I wasn't bothered how many people beat me, this day was about me not beating myself by being silly.

My race plan was to just sit and pedal, keep the heart rate down as much as I could and just pace myself so that I beat the bike cut-off 11 hours and 30 minutes after the race started. My ultra-running buddy Gobi had drilled it into me over the past few months that I had to race with my head and not my heart, and that's exactly what I set out to do. I wore both my Garmin and my watch, the latter integral to my nutrition plan. It beeped every 30 minutes to let me know it was time for gel. I had 16 High-Five gels either in my little box on the bike's top tube or in the back of my tri top.

I stuck to the same apple flavour that I'd used throughout my training. There was a certain comfort and reassurance as each one glided down my throat, a taste of home not quite on a par with the egg and chips that most of the island's visitors were eating every day but I guess it followed the same principle: I was a Brit abroad and I was eating British food.

I stuck to this religiously, also drinking the Powerbar drink that was on offer at the feed stations and it seemed to work. I didn't feel dehydrated, didn't bonk and my stomach didn't go bang.

Luckily the temperatures had dropped and although it was still much hotter than I felt comfortable with it wasn't the searing inferno that we'd experienced in the days before. If it had been then it would have been deadly.

Almost as soon as you leave Puerto del Carmen you are climbing. It doesn't feel like a big climb, and it kind of messes with your head that you are only doing seven miles per hour, but when you reach the top and look over your left shoulder, the sea is a long way down.

The course is littered with those sorts of climbs, mostly uphill, long drags into strong headwinds. They sap your energy and your mental resolve. Everyone knows about the big climbs of Haria and Mirador del Rio, but I found that the unnamed climbs were the worst. I was mentally ready for the biggies, not so for the pesky little ones.

On the fast descent to El Golfo, you pass the fast racers coming back the other way. I got a boost as I saw John Knapp and we exchanged waves. It's amazing how seeing a familiar face really lifts your spirits.

The loop round El Golfo was probably my favourite part of the course, the contrast of the harsh, jagged, black volcanic wasteland with the crystal azure waters of the ocean was something no HD camera could ever capture. I have been lucky to see some of nature's wonders like barrier reefs, Table Mountain, rainforests and Niagara Falls, but El Golfo rivalled them all. Another boost came when I saw my name and those of my club-mates chalked on the road. That was unexpected and worth some free speed.

The climb back from the south of the island was long and hard, and a sustained effort was needed on a road that seemed to constantly be disappearing over the hazy horizon. My reward for making it to the top? A left turn off the highway and I was experiencing what my triathlon calendar had not done justice to.

The climb of Timanfaya, the Fire Mountain, was underway. By the time I reached the infamous climb, the sun was high in the sky and the headwinds had arrived. If you want to recreate this at home here's what you need to do. Set your turbo trainer up in a sauna at the local gym, on your left have a friend throw a bag of sand in front of the industrial sized fan that they've just switched on and pointed at you, while your other mate holds a fan heater on full about an inch from your nose.

I actually found this bit to be the toughest climb of the whole course and yet of the biggies on paper it looks the easiest. It just sapped my energy. Passing through the jagged lunar landscape this was the first point where I had a word with myself, reminding my mind and spirit that I had a little girl at home who'd missed out on one too many breakfasts or bedtime stories with her Daddy because of this. I didn't need telling twice.

I think I was at the 75km mark when I heard "aren't you that bloke that wrote that book?" to which I instantly replied with great affection: "Aren't you that crap swimmer?" It was Chris Lawson, who true to my taunt had experienced a torrid swim but he'd made it.

I've never been so happy to be overtaken by a club-mate. He was flying, I had a new hero. I wouldn't see him again until the run, but again it was a boost. If he could do it with a leg that looked like spam, then I had no choice but to soldier on.

The climb up to Haria past the windmills seemed to go on forever, although somehow I found the energy to join in with a Mexican wave performed by the race's mobile mechanics that had stopped their van at the top and were blaring out Queen's We Will Rock You, just what I needed. Apparently when Chris had sailed past them earlier he'd been treated to Another One Bites The Dust which didn't quite have the same motivational effect.

At the top of the monster climb that seemed infinite I stopped at the special needs station as days before I'd left them a bag with my race number on it 'just in case'. Mine, like all the others, was taken to the top of the mountain and placed in a cotton musset bag, the kind you see the Tour riders deftly emptying on Alpine descents.

I took out the Ibuprofen and an energy bar, placing the tablets in my back pocket as they weren't needed. I munched my first solid food of the day while admiring the view and stretching my back. I wasn't in a rush and I didn't fancy the hairpin descent with a musset bag.

I composed myself and then set off down the stretch of road that had given me vivid nightmares of my death. Approaching each bend I grasped my brakes in plenty of time, and rode sensibly in a controlled manner. To my relief the descent had been scarier in a car than on two thin wheels, which wasn't a reflection on the

IronHippy's driving skills. What was fun was hitting the cobbles at the bottom and having to change gear again to begin the huge climb up Mirador. Yes, the two biggest climbs are immediately after one another.

I had expected to have to dismount and walk up both Haria and Mirador but I never did. I just sat and pedalled, never once rising out of my saddle. In fact I sat for the whole of the course, only standing to stretch my back and hamstrings. I conserved energy that would help me on the run.

The views at the top of Mirador were out of this world. Way below the crystal clear turquoise water of the Atlantic offered a warm contrast to the harsh, dark, volcanic wasteland of the central part of the island, a wasteland that I'd just cycled across. That view made everything seem worthwhile.

Just Google "Ironman Lanzarote Mirador" and marvel at the images that appear, and I defy any of you to not want to just jump on a plane with your bike and go and experience it for yourself. Go on, you know you want to. That view was worth the 400-euro entry fee alone. Granted, on any other day that same view would have been free, but you know what I mean.

Now most people say that once you get over Mirador it's all downhill back to transition, and to a certain extent they are correct as there are a fair few long descents. However the course has a final sting in the tail to catch those that may have overcooked themselves on the big climbs – you still have over 800 metres of climbing to do.

The road took me back towards Teguise, the town that lay in the centre of the island that I'd already passed through on the climb towards the wind farms of Haria. I was beginning to suffer, being slowly cooked in the afternoon sun, I could feel patches of my skin crisping where the sun protection had failed to cover.

Periodically around the course the COLT support crews had leant out of car windows or stopped in villages to shout much-needed support. Unlike other Ironman races I'd done this really was a lonely bike course. Other than the huge goat farm towards the end there weren't even any cows or sheep to look at. At times it would be almost an hour of perfect silent isolation, with only the sound of my breathing and the turning chain for company.

As I pedalled alone I presumed that the COLT supporters would have headed for the run as our fast boys would be well into the marathon. I knew I was the last COLT out on the bike. In front of me all I could see was desert and the dual carriageway winding for miles through it.

As I crested a small rise I had to blink, was that a mirage? I raised my hand above my eyes and squinted. No, it was the COLT support. The noise was deafening. "There's only one Andy Holgate, one Andy Holgate."

I grinned like a kid at Christmas, high-fived them all and shouted "I bloody love you lot" and boy did I mean it. That was the final boost I needed to get home. They were brilliant for waiting for me, I can't thank them enough. A few moments later they sped past frantically beeping the car horn, I couldn't help but fist pump the air, and scream my lungs out: "Yeahhhhhhhhhhhhhhh."

Despite my giddiness my head wasn't done messing with me though. As I headed down the infamous "goat track", a single winding road, I glanced at my watch and my brain went into overdrive. I was well within the bike cut-off, with only five of the easiest miles to go, yet for some reason I didn't believe it. I was convinced I wouldn't make it. Maybe I'd had too much sun.

It was thankfully short-lived as I soon glimpsed a runner ahead and I knew I had almost beaten the beast. My demon was in trouble, all that stood between me and victory was the small matter of 26.2 miles of running. I couldn't contain my joy and all along the prom as I passed runners on my bike I didn't stop grinning. I had made it, I had completed the bike course in eight hours and 40 minutes, 20 minutes ahead of the schedule I had in my head. I had raced to the plan, I had raced with my head and not my heart.

I waddled into T2, dumping the bike with a volunteer. It had served me well and had come through relatively unscathed, but not intact. It had lost the handlebar ends on the notorious section of rough road that would rival the pavé of Paris-Roubaix, but given my recent run of bike luck I was happy with such small insignificant damage.

I grabbed my run bag and went into the change tent. Almost ten minutes later, covered in more sunscreen and after another pee I headed out onto the marathon.

The Run

I was just so happy that I'd made it to the run, I really wasn't arsed that I was about to run a marathon in temperatures of 30 to 40 degrees Celsius. I had beaten the bike course and I knew that I was going to get a Lanzarote Ironman medal. Nothing could go wrong now and if it did I had enough time left to walk/limp and still finish in time. I was one happy bunny.

About 300 metres from the finish I shouted out to Chris Wild. Drenched in sweat and hidden behind mirrored shades, the man partly responsible for me being on the island was about to finish. I was just setting forth.

He had spent all year telling me we would see each other on the run, and thinking I would still be cycling as he crossed the finish line I'd never believed him. I should have done. We high-fived and I congratulated him as he headed for a PB of 10.33:18 on his "home" course.

The support along the prom was something else, and again the COLT following topped it all. I ran to Sarah Patterson, who had been in touch with Em all day, and said: "Tell Em I'm going to do it." I was drunk with the emotion of it all.

Further high-fives with COLT buddies IronHobbit and John Knapp raised me up again. John shouted "you are going to do it" with a huge grin on his face. Then the endless procession of COLTs continued with Andy Ley and Kel Hirst. "Wahoo, we've all made it," shouted Andy. What a feeling. Of course we still had a way to go but I knew what Andy meant.

The long first lap got pretty lonely out past the airport, and I was almost blown off my feet as a Thomson jet landed 100 metres away. I met Chris Lawson. "If you catch me you need to rethink the name of the next book," he said. "There's no chance of me catching you," I said. He was a good six kilometres in front of me and moving well. He knew the provisional title was "last COLT standing".

Although my Garmin was beeping at me after every mile, I don't think I looked at it. I wasn't interested to be honest. I was just having so much fun, shouting encouragement at club vests that I recognised: Mersey Tri, Cumbrian Tri Aragon's, Rochdale Tri and acknowledging those who wished this slow-moving Pirate well.

The only downside to the marathon course was that we had to run past a fish restaurant, and I can't stand the smell of fish being cooked. It took all of my self-control not to empty the contents of my stomach on the white concrete floor of the esplanade. Mind you the only food in my stomach was the gels that I had been consuming like clockwork.

I continued to take one at each aid station. I kept cool in the heat by taking on as much fluid as possible. At each aid station I would take a cup of isotonic drink and wash it down with a cup of water, switching to cola in the latter half of the run as I tried to get a final energy boost.

I also grabbed the cold sponges that were on offer and stuffed them inside my tri top, following a great tip from Richard. He had told me that I had to keep not only my head cool but more importantly my core. The water from the sponges trickled down my chest and back with each step. I didn't care that I looked like Quasimodo's twin brother.

After receiving the brilliant advice from Richard I had asked him about ice on the run course. I intended to put it under my cap to cool my head as I had done in Germany, and I knew that the organisers provided ice because the IronHippy always ran this race with a cube in each hand to help with his concentration. Richard just laughed and replied in his own unique style: "No offence Andy but all the ice will have melted by the time you get to the run." I hadn't thought of that and he was probably right.

I was delighted however when I reached the third aid station and was offered the frozen little gems, greedily stuffing them under my cap. I smiled as I ran off, Richard's words echoing in my ears. For once coach you were wrong.

By the second and third lap the COLT support was bolstered by those who had already finished, medals hanging proudly from their necks, I desperately wanted to earn one of those treasures. The swollen numbers meant that the atmosphere went up another notch. I saw my team-mates for the last time on the course running in the opposite direction to me, heading for a finish that I was over an hour away from.

Andy Ley stopped and told me he was suffering having stopped to throw up. He was also having trouble peeing which both was worrying and a sign of dehydration. I congratulated him on his imminent finish and we went our separate ways, me into the darkness and him to a finish line of joy swiftly followed by a medical tent and a syringe.

Not 400 metres behind him strode the blonde bomber Kel. I just got a grunt as I called her name, she would later have no recollection of seeing me. She crossed the line celebrating a wonderful achievement with her two amazing kids, Amelia and Alex.

Moments later she had a 'hypo', a diabetic crash that saw medical staff come running from everywhere and chocolate bars being forced down her throat. Thankfully after being on a drip she made a full recovery. Andy and Kel are both bloody tough athletes, and it just goes to show how demanding this race could be.

By now it had gone dark as I headed out for the last few miles away from the crowds. None of my fellow stragglers appeared to be on their own, each had a chaperone so I accepted Jack Billingham's offer of some company. Jack was a Barrow lad like me and we had formed a friendship over the previous months as we ran together on Wednesday nights. He was just getting into triathlon and had flown out to support his club-mates and to see what all the fuss was about. I think he was almost as excited to be there as I was.

His enthusiasm helped me to pick my feet up. He was a great

help, taking my mind off the last lonely part of the race away from the frenzied crowds of the finish.

I met Sarah Patterson for the last time on the side of the road. I gave her a big sweaty hug as she handed me my COLT top to put over my Pirate one. I had thrown it to her as I ran past on my first lap. I'd decided to race in the Pirate one because it didn't ride up exposing my back to the blistering sun. In the days beforehand I was worse than a girl trying to decide what to wear on a night out.

So I had raced as a Pirate but I wanted to finish as a COLT. I pulled on the white top over my soaking yellow one and turned for home thanking Sarah for everything and Jack for sharing those last miles with me. I had the last one to do on my own. That was Sarah's cue to text Em to say that I would be finished in ten minutes, knowing that she was up late in Lancaster watching the live video feed.

I'd always said that Lanzarote was about just getting the job done but in my mind I had always harboured the ambition to finish in under 16 hours. I ran through the crowds of holiday-makers spilling out of the pubs after watching Chelsea win the Champions League. Glancing down at my watch I knew that if I pushed hard I might just achieve that sub-16 finish.

A grinning Paul Gardner emerged from the crowd, congratulated me, and raced ahead to tell our club-mates at the finish that I was on my way. The atmosphere was mind-blowing, every person along the prom either clapped or offered encouragement, and language was no barrier as the victory of an Ironman cut across national borders.

Moments later I was amazed by the sight of the COLTS at the start of the finish tunnel creating a guard of honour with the club flags. They were a sight for sore eyes. I grinned with pride at their final act of support. The noise from the crowd and the PA system made a night in Ibiza seem quiet but I swear I heard every one of my friends' voices. Maybe it was the Lancashire accents.

I was 50 metres from finishing the one race I had promised Em that I would never do because it would kill me. I was alive, I

WAS ALIVE. COME ON. I high-fived them all, and grabbed a flag. I was so proud to be a COLT, I was lucky to know these wonderful people and I was so relieved to finally be in touching distance of my impossible dream. I punched the air and roared like a Spartan going into battle and sprinted for the line.

Something primal snapped inside me. I was no longer a librarian, I was the quintessential alpha male. The flag that I had grabbed was waving above me and I spotted an outstretched arm. It was Chris Wild, the friend partly responsible for me being there was at the finish. We high-fived, and I screamed as I became a Lanzarote Ironman in 15 hours, 50 minutes and 30 seconds.

The Aftermath

I never stopped grinning. I shook the race director's hand, had the medal placed around my neck and waited to be medically assessed. That bit didn't happen as I was moved to one side to be interviewed for *Ironman.com* by Mike Cliffe-Jones. I had met up with Mike earlier in the week. A fellow triathlete, he was very supportive and just as excited as I was at the finish.

He knew he was sharing one of the best moments of my life. My euphoria is evident for all to see on YouTube – just search for my name. During that interview I uttered a phrase that I have never lived down: "Marathons don't bother me."

What I should have said was: "This particular marathon didn't bother me as I'd beaten the bike course." I sounded like such an arrogant t**t but it really was just a moment of pure unadulterated joy. I was so proud of myself for slaying my demons, and it tasted so much better than anything I had achieved before in triathlon. I was drunk in the moment of victory.

Suddenly Chris Wild was by my side, we embraced and I just babbled at him. I knew that all year, and especially all race week he'd felt like a nervous parent about to send his kids off to school. I was the last of his kids to make it through the school gates. I had made him wait but he could now relax and enjoy the party. What a journey, a truly magical experience.

As soon as I could I phoned Em as I wanted to reassure her that I was alive and well and not on a drip. She told me that she could tell by the video of me crossing the finishing line that I would be fine, maybe the smile had given it away. I didn't stop smiling for days. I told her that I loved her and Charlotte and headed for the beer tent with my mates. We were and forever will be Lanzarote Ironmen.

25

I LOVE TRIATHLON

I think one of the hardest things to deal with in the days immediately after completing a race that has been your primary focus for almost a year is the sense of "what do I do now?" OK, you also have to deal with the sore legs, ribs, blistered feet, and in the case of Lanzarote the blistered sunburn.

My sunburn was pretty bad on my forearms, and on my knees in the gap between my tri shorts and my calf guards. I wasn't even aware of it until I got into bed after the race. I didn't sleep much because I was drunk on adrenaline, but also every time I moved it hurt like hell as my damaged skin bristled and throbbed. No amount of after-sun lotion was going to help my nuclear glow.

After getting back to the UK I went to the chemists in London and then to the doctor and the use of hydrocortisone cream helped me heal, making me look like someone had attacked me with a cheese grater.

I was in London for the British Sports Book Awards. It was Sod's Law that the ceremony would take place only two days after the race. A consequence of that was that I had to rearrange flights, as I was originally coming home on the Monday.

I was gutted to be missing the club party in the infamous Route 66 bar, and apparently by the end of the night there were some serious shapes being thrown. Instead I caught a flight back to Manchester and drove home, falling into bed just after 3am.

My alarm went off at 6am so that Em and I could catch the train to London.

I wore my black finishers' shirt with pride as I limped through Covent Garden to the hotel. My feet were blistered, my legs ached, I couldn't feel the toes on my left foot, and I looked like I'd been badly spray-tanned. The last thing in the world I wanted to do was put on leather dress shoes and a tuxedo. I just wanted to go to bed. Em looked stunning, a beauty that easily matched the grandiose setting of the Savoy, where the awards were taking place. In contrast I was very much an uncomfortable beast, wincing every time I moved as my starchy shirt grated my burnt skin. I was nominated in the category of Best New Writer, and was honoured to achieve such recognition. I was the only non-journalist or sports star to be shortlisted, which was good enough for me. I never expected to win, but it was a highlight when my name appeared on the big screen and some of the great and good from the world of sport and literature such as David Millar, Paul Kimmage, Nick Hornby and Sebastian Faulks applauded me.

I know they were just being polite and they had no idea who I was but just let me have that moment. Of course I came away empty-handed, the quite brilliant *Ghost Runner* taking the prize as I had predicted.

Over dinner, which was actually our first night out together since Charlotte was born, Em asked me if I was upset not to win. "This isn't real," I replied as I looked around the room of household names. "It's amazing to get to experience this but if anyone had said last week, you can only have one trophy, a Lanzarote Ironman medal or this award. I wouldn't have hesitated. I wanted that Lanza medal more than anything."

I surveyed the room of superstars, household names and faces, there was only one Lanzarote Ironman in the room and he was anonymous, knackered and happily content.

I took a complete week off from training after the race. I stretched, I used my foam roller to unknot my muscles and I wore my compression clothing like it was going out of fashion. Hang on, was it ever in fashion?

I only had 33 days until I put my body through hell all over again. It was going to be an interesting experiment to see if I could do it. Those days flew by and the hardest part of Outlaw preparation wasn't physical but mental. I was back running, cycling and swimming and it all felt fine.

That was the problem, fine wasn't great, fine wasn't exciting, fine wasn't motivating. It was so difficult trying to raise my game again after the emotional high of that night in May. I had left my triathlon heart in Puerto del Carmen, and the Outlaw by comparison was an ex who wouldn't go away. I had planned to be in peak form and chase a PB in Nottingham but I just couldn't rise to the occasion. I was an impotent Ironman.

And then just from nowhere I woke up and like in *Dallas*, it was all a bad dream. I was excited and couldn't wait to race. In all honesty I think I'd just gone through a post-race downer and come out the other side feeding on the excitement of the many others I knew that were going to be racing.

Actually my renewed enthusiasm hadn't come from nowhere, it had materialised one Wednesday night when I was running with The Outlaw Ladies and Chris Lawson. The ladies were so excited and yet so nervous. Chris and I spent the whole run talking about what to expect in an Ironman. The sounds, the feeling, the pain, the euphoria, and it was then that I realised as I span the tales that I was as excited and nervous as they were. In that moment I knew I was no longer impotent, my desire had returned. I wanted to be an Outlaw again.

"Lift your head up Andrew, it will make running easier." I knew as soon as I heard the words from my Dad that he was correct. He walked alongside me in the early evening sunshine, slowing his walking pace to fall in line with my running.

"I know Dad, but I just don't have the energy to lift my head," I whispered in defeat from under my sweat-stained green cap, a cap that I hoped hid my pain and disappointment. We had been here before, but unlike Frankfurt there would be no second wind along the banks of the Trent. That's the thing with Ironman, your day can go from dreams of glory to the depths of despair in an instant. I had seven miles to go, I hated Ironman, I hated triathlon but most of all I hated myself for being in that moment. It was light years away from how I felt at 7.19am that morning.

"Andy Holgate, what the bloody hell are you doing here?" was the shocked response from my mate Chris Wild as he pulled me from the rowing lake. I laughed as I looked down at my watch, 1.19:45 blinked at me from the screen. I had done it, I had finally got under 80 minutes for an Ironman swim. I had worked so hard at my swimming this year, and this was just reward.

The swim had been quite violent, more so than any other I'd done. It struck me as strange as there was plenty of room for everyone. After halfway the water became more violent than my fellow competitors, the waves crashed into me, making me work that much harder as the wind became my enemy.

I stripped my wetsuit off in seconds and headed into the change tent, which for once wasn't too crowded. I found a vacant spot on the extreme edge of one of the benches and sat down to put my shoes on. Thirty seconds later I was in the lap of a fellow Pirate, and I didn't even know his name, hadn't taken him to dinner or even a movie.

Three guys had all stood up at the same time, creating a see-saw effect that catapulted me into my fellow shipmate. I was glad he cushioned my fall. Can you imagine explaining to people that after a swim PB you couldn't continue because you were injured by a bench in transition? People probably would have believed me given some of the things that have happened to me before in triathlon.

I was out on the bike and pedalling my way along the banks of the lake when I looked down to see what my heart rate was. I don't know if it had been the shock of the fall or my excited desire to get out of T1 as soon as possible that caused me to leave my Garmin behind. I'd trained all year in my heart rate zones, and now I would be racing blind, not knowing if I was pushing too hard. There was nothing I could do other than put it out of my mind and pedal.

The bike course had changed since I did this race back in 2010.

There was a different approach into Southwell which took in the only climb of the day at 20 miles. Oxton Bank didn't live up to the hype as I crested it smoothly without leaving the saddle. Yes it raised my heart rate (not that I had any data on that) but it didn't have me blowing and huffing like a Whinlatter or a Mirador.

The descent into Southwell was pure fun, a moment of aerobar pleasure, and not the chocolate variety. After that though the bike became a war of attrition as I battled the strong headwinds that swept across the open countryside like a scythe, cutting into my speed and energy reserves with an evil howl of delight.

The new lower loop would be very fast on a clear calm day – this was not one of those days. The rain hammered against my aero helmet as I struggled to stay on my aerobars, the ROO wobbled as the crosswinds tried to tear it from under me. One of the many Pirates that passed me, Muffin Top, chirped that she was "enjoying the wind as it was making it interesting".

I certainly didn't share her enthusiasm for it. But it was small pockets of banter like that which made that southern loop more manageable. The Pirate feed station was a highlight and especially seeing my mate Silent Assassin and his son Jordy, they always raised a smile from me.

The mobile COLT support was something else. Andy Ley, David Pattinson, Paul Gardner – The Outlaw Husbands – seemed to be popping up everywhere offering vocal encouragement.

The highlight of the bike course was when I heard a now mandatory and familiar retort from Chris Lawson. "Aren't you that bloke that wrote that book?" "Aren't you that crap swimmer?" was my tongue in cheek reply.

Chris had caught me much earlier in Lanzarote, but without the hills to use to his advantage this time around I'd stayed in front until just shy of 80 miles. A few seconds later, good wishes exchanged, he had gone out of sight.

I ploughed on, getting slower as the wind got stronger. I came up behind a lone figure in white and made to pass him on a single track road almost at the end of the second loop when I noticed the name Sid on the back of the shirt. I was so pleased to see him and my enthusiastic "hey Sid" made the poor sod jump a mile.

Sid Poppyfields Sidowski was doing his first ever triathlon. My book had helped water a small seed that he had in his head that he could do an Ironman. What followed for him were the familiar months of hard training, injury, and more worries than he had ever thought he would have.

We exchanged tweets and e-mails, and I among others tried to keep him positive especially in the last month before the race when serious doubts set in. So I was over the moon that he'd made it through the swim. He had one last lap to go and I told him confidently that I would see him on the run and he would be an Outlaw. I don't think he believed me as I rode away, heading for T2.

I slowed to come into T2 and was so happy to see my mate Chris Wild again that I didn't notice the speed bump. I had unclipped ready to dismount and my pedal was in the six o'clock position. It hit the concrete and my saddle nose bounced up and caught me hard, which was a pain I could have done without.

I handed my bike to Petal and then shook hands with the now retired 2010 Donut Champion, Fat Buddha. The pair were two more Pirates helping out, they were everywhere. I was off the bike in six hours and 48 minutes, about ten minutes ahead of schedule. This time there were no comedy mishaps in transition. I quickly spoke to my Dad, and got the location of where the rest of the family were so I could wave at them later.

Unlike two years ago I headed out on to the run full of confidence, even joking with Viking, who was part of a relay team that I'd make him work hard to catch me. The first lap of the lake was fine, my legs worked and I was actually enjoying it. I stopped as I passed the boathouse to wave at the family, removing my cap so that Charlotte could recognise me. She waved and shouted "Dadeee". I set off for the river bank in a great mood.

I've never seen so much yellow and black. Nearly every other competitor was a Pirate and I acknowledged them all. What was bizarre was that several people recognised me and spoke to me about the book. I had no idea who they were. I also spoke to people that I'd been offering advice to on Twitter and forums, appropriate I guess that we had met for the first time during an Ironman. High-fives and handshakes continued throughout the run with friends old and new alike.

I was so pleased to see my fellow COLTS, all of whom raced brilliantly. I was the only one not to get a PB. Graham Hodgson won his age group, a great achievement in his first Ironman, and missed a sub-ten-hour finish by seconds. Chris Lawson, despite having Lanzarote in his legs, took over an hour off his best ever time.

The "Outlaw Girls" as they had christened themselves were brilliant. Sarah, Christine and Mandy had seen their loved ones complete Ironman races and thought they would like a go at it. They had trained like demons all year, and it was so uplifting to meet them all coming the other way down the path, smiles contagiously radiating from the three of them. They made the race look easy as they joined the Ironman club.

Shortly after 13 miles my day fell apart. My left calf muscle was on fire. That combined with the pain in both feet caused by the rough surface of the lake path saw me slow to a pedestrian pace. Viking caught me, we hugged, and he offered to wait with me and pace me home. I told him he'd do no such thing as he was running so well.

As I ran past the boathouse again I could hear the cheers from the crowd, but I just didn't have the energy to acknowledge them. I feel bad about that. I did manage to wave at my family, and shout to Em that I had a lap to go. This was so she could hand Charlotte to me as I came into the finish. I made it to the other side of the lake where the conversation with my Dad took place, and cut a lonely figure as I shuffled past.

I have no idea how long that last lap took me, all I know is every step hurt. I couldn't even lift my feet off the floor. I said "well done" to every competitor that I met on that final loop, and thanked every marshall. I was so pleased to see Sid again, and he would make it home with about 13 minutes to spare before the 17-hour time limit expired.

It seemed like the whole world came past me on that last loop. I was convinced that my Pirate mate Dave the ex-Spartan and my COLT friend Christine were going to catch me at any minute. They too however had slowed down. One person who did pass me was Brian Kinsella from Carlisle. The man who I'd become friends with after the race at Ely was about to become an Ironman. Once again he had seen me at my worst, but one day I'll make sure he sees me at my best.

Apart from my desire to get the job done the only thing that kept me moving forward was the thought of holding Charlotte. She was my inspiration. It was almost as if I could feel her little heart beating with every painful step that I took around that lake. With each step it got louder, with each step I was closer to her, with each step I was less of an athlete and more of a Daddy.

I'd had enough of being an athlete for one day. I was about to experience the proudest moment I'd ever had in triathlon. I wouldn't have swapped what was about to happen for a PB, hell not even for a world record. I limped into the finishing chute and there she was, my inspiration, my gorgeous 19-month-old daughter and her beautiful mum, Em.

Charlotte was wearing a Pirate headscarf, a surprise touch that Em had kept from me. I couldn't help but laugh, she looked so cute. I was afraid that after not seeing me all day she would be scared when I picked her up but I needn't have worried. A hug and a kiss were followed by a very enthusiastic "Daddeee".

Our journey was almost over. I loved triathlon. We posed for photos and then Charlotte rather graciously let her knackered old man share in her moment of glory as she became an Outlaw in 14 hours and 29 minutes.

26

ANYTHING IS STILL POSSIBLE

"Every day in Africa a gazelle wakes up and knows he must run faster than the fastest lion or be eaten. Every day in Africa a lion wakes up and knows he must run faster than the slowest gazelle or starve. It doesn't matter whether you are the lion or the gazelle when the sun comes up, you'd better be running."

The words above inspire me, they motivate me and keep me training on days when I lack motivation and inspiration. I ended my first book with that African proverb and I still read it most days although I've now figured it out and it does actually matter if you are the lion or the gazelle.

I'm a lion. Quite simply the lion can afford to make mistakes, there will be other gazelles, a warthog, hell even a zebra or two. If the gazelle screws up, it's dead. Over the last few years I've made loads of mistakes yet I'm not dead, I have the opportunity to keep hunting, to keep living and to keep on roaring.

I have been extremely fortunate to have become a parent and an Ironman, something that I share with many people around the globe. Neither journey so far has been smooth, and at times I've felt weaker than a new-born kitten, but the lows make the highs that much sweeter when you get to taste them.

I have come to realise that becoming an Ironman is like becoming a new parent. You can read all the books that have been written, you can attend classes, you can buy the magazines, you can watch videos online, you can listen to your friends' stories of love and pain and you can buy every piece of kit available.

The reality of it all is, you just need to find what works for you. There isn't a plan that fits everyone. Desire, love, nurturing, listening, watching, developing, realising your limitations and failings are essential skills needed by parents and athletes alike.

There are many paths to becoming a successful parent, we all choose different ones and likewise there are many paths to becoming an Ironman, but whichever path you choose it will always be eventful and ultimately rewarding. Don't get hung up on the little details, embrace your inner athlete, get your arse off the sofa and just enjoy life.

We are human, we learn from our mistakes. I watched as my toddler spent hours falling over, smiling and then eventually walking on legs that were stable. She fell down, she learnt and she succeeded. I have made many mistakes on my journey and had countless falls. I've not always learnt straight away, my weaknesses sometimes overtake me and I'm transported to a place I don't wish to be.

One such place is my fat life, one that I thought I'd left behind for good. It's kind of ironic that I started down the path to revisiting that dark place when I was writing my first book. When I raced this summer in Lanzarote and Nottingham I weighed over 17 stones. I had failed to hit any of my weight loss targets, BUT I had changed for the better. In darker days I would have been miserable, I would have been immobile and I would have been staring a heart attack in the face.

Now I focus on the positive, the lights have come on making that dark place a thing of the past – if I could finish two Ironman races five weeks apart while weighing more than 17 stones, just what the hell am I capable of when I lose weight? I am no longer repulsed by my body when it is fat. I am more amazed at what it can do, what punishment it can take and still survive.

Now I'm not advocating being overweight and since the Outlaw I have started to chip away at my fat reserves by following a sensible eating plan. I've lost two stones in three months and

I'm feeling the benefits. I'm faster, I'm now capable of running a six-minute mile which for a bloke of my size is pretty good. I've swum 400 metres in the pool in under eight minutes, something I never even dared to dream was possible. And suddenly those hills on the bike don't seem as daunting or painful. I'm still no mountain goat but I'm no longer a heffalump.

I'm loving the improvements but the point I'm trying to make is that if your heart is really in it, and your desire is strong it really doesn't matter what you weigh. With any triathlete as with any car it's the quality of the engine and not the condition of the bodywork that counts. So if you are reading this and thinking "I couldn't do an Ironman because I'm too fat" think again.

If my fat self is capable of finishing one of the toughest races on the planet then so are you. I'm not special, I'm just like you, flesh and blood and plenty of padding. You just have to want it badly enough, work hard and keep moving forward. Throw away whatever excuses you are clinging to and just go for it.

People in their 80s, people missing limbs, even people from Warrington have become Ironmen. There is no excuse. As Ironman world champion Chrissie Wellington rightly says, you can "live a life without limits".

My desire to succeed now mirrors that of my daughter. I have embraced my 'inner toddler'. I suggest that whatever goal you are striving for that you do the same. It doesn't have to be an Ironman, it doesn't have to be a triathlon, just something that you want, an achievement that calls your name.

Take yourself back to a time when your innocence and enthusiasm were all that mattered, you didn't care if people laughed, you didn't care if you failed, you didn't care what you looked like, hell you didn't care if you wet yourself, all that mattered was having fun. Now I'm not suggesting that we all start wetting ourselves again, I don't have shares in Tena, but sport and therefore triathlon is about having fun and I think sometimes we can forget that.

We get fixated on weight, speed, and distance, always asking more of ourselves, always pushing and pushing, and that is great.

I am as guilty of that as the next middle-aged man in lycra. As much as I want to push myself to the limits I wouldn't be able to do so if I didn't enjoy it. I think I'm an endorphine addict, a fun junkie, a triathlete who just can't stop.

The moment it stops becoming fun, and I don't mean mid-race when nothing is fun, I mean when I no longer want to train, to push, to succeed, I'll walk away. The funny thing is, I can't ever see that happening. To think that this whole triathlon malarkey for me started with a dare from my colleague and now it's an integral part of my life. Triathlon has given me so many opportunities and I love it.

I've lost count of how many people have told me how inspiring I am. It's great to hear but I just don't see it. I'm just Andy Holgate, a husband, a dad, a librarian, an author and a not very good triathlete. I've not won races, not set records, not saved lives and not put my life on the line for others.

I'm proud of my achievements, I'm happy to share my thoughts, my fears, my loves, my failings and my successes with each of you. I'm not unique, there are plenty of people out there like me blogging and doing similar things, doing them better than me.

People like Cortney Martin with her *Cort the Sport* blog, showcasing how she went from a sedentary mum of two to representing her country at the world championships. People like Corrine Ellison who recovered from open heart surgery to complete Ironman Austria. There are plenty of people out there to draw inspiration from, you could become one of them. We all inspire in our own ways.

So where do I go from here? I want to continue to better myself as a person and a triathlete, following John Knapp's mantra of always moving forward. I have begun working with Kevin Foster-Wiltshire, one of this country's top trainers. He is kicking my arse into shape, which can only be a good thing. I have begun to mentor several people that are making their Ironman debuts in 2013, offering advice and thoughts on their training, quashing their fears and generally just keeping them sane, or as sane as would-be Ironmen can be. It's great fun and very rewarding. I almost entered a double Ironman race for 2013, and I'll be honest in saying that it's still on my agenda but for once I reined in my enthusiasm. After the Outlaw I travelled to Wales to watch my younger brother take part in the United Kingdom 100km road running championships.

Craig is supremely fit and earlier this year he had won his debut 100-mile race (yes, you read that correctly) in 15 hours and 11 minutes to beat a quality field by almost an hour. In Wales he would take the silver medal. As I watched him do justice to the England vest he wore so proudly I also noticed his suffering and I realised that I would be in a much worse state if I were to take on 4.8 miles of swimming, 224 miles of cycling and 52 miles of running.

His body was that of a serious athlete, mine by comparison was that of a bloke who played at being an athlete. I decided that if and when I went down the stupidly long route I'd be ready and prepared to my physical limits. I'm working towards that goal.

I'm very lucky that I have such a supportive structure around me, both with training partners and club-mates. I'm also extremely fortunate to have a wife that understands my addiction and my need to train and race, although I've not read her chapter yet and I may be mistaken.

Just how lucky I am was brought home to me early this year when one of my mates who was training for an Ironman had to be, shall we say, economical with the truth. His wife was a bit sick of Ironman taking over their family life and had been vocal about it while still being supportive.

Gentleman X, as I shall refer to him, didn't want to rock the boat further but needed to get in a seven-hour brick session. He left for work that morning suited and booted but hid around the corner and waited for his wife to go to work. He then returned home to get changed into his lycra uniform and headed out on the bike. So you see just how lucky I am that I don't have to hide from my wife (not yet anyway).

I have said it before but it needs saying again: Ironman is a time-consuming and often selfish pastime. You have to be selfish to get the training done. If your partner doesn't support you then you have two choices. The cheapest and less emotional choice would be to take up another hobby. The rewards however of this hobby far outweigh the penalties and I hope that I've managed to get that across to you.

I guess in reality there are three types of Ironman. The first is the type that just stops at one, they've ticked that box and moved on. I thought I was the second type and to a certain extent for me Lanza shows that I am, the one that ticks the box and then moves on to a harder challenge, a Celtman, a Norseman or the double, triple or even the deca Ironman. In time I know that I will move on. I really fancy taking on the Scottish mountains, the icy fjords of Norway and the mind-numbing laps of the 281.2-mile monster.

But for now I'm the third type of Ironman, the one I've been all along, the one who chases a time. I have so far failed in my attempts to break the 12-hour barrier. I want to achieve that so badly. Chris Wild also falls into this category and has warned me that once I've achieved it I'll chase 11 hours, then ten and eventually nine. I don't think I'm that good but who knows what my body is capable of given the right structure, preparation and the alignment of the planets on a race day in the future.

I am hoping that my day will come in Nottingham as I have unfinished business with the Outlaw. It's kicked my arse twice but in 2013 I won't give it the opportunity to do so again. I will follow my destiny, make my own luck, train harder than ever before and turn up with my race face on. I also have unfinished business with Chris Lawson. Just for once I would like to have him still chasing me when we get to the run, just to make him suffer a little. We will resume our battle in Nottingham.

Unfortunately my Mam won't be there to physically witness it as she passed away in September 2012. I miss her deeply as do all her family and friends. She was my biggest supporter, she believed that I could achieve great things and encouraged me in every endeavour I undertook. She was a great inspiration to me, and one that I will constantly draw on as I go through my life. She watched me complete three of my five Ironman races and I firmly believe that she will be watching down on me next summer, smiling and saying her favourite phrase "it's all fun and games". Hopefully I'll make her proud.

We make our own destinies. The less you focus on the end result, the quicker you will achieve it. If you have one eye fixed on the destination, you are not focusing clearly on the journey. Don't look beyond what is directly in front of you as the path will constantly change.

Ironman is a journey, and you need to go into it with both eyes open. I'll leave you now, lord knows I've rambled enough. I just want to wish you all the very best with your own journeys, enjoy them wherever they may take you. If it's a similar journey to mine then the words below might keep you moving forward to your goal.

It is a journey of 140.6 miles that begins for many, months, maybe years ago. It is a journey that doesn't begin on the start line. It is a journey that will see each individual ask themselves more questions than they ever thought they would ask. It is a journey that will hurt, a journey that will inspire. It is a journey that requires sacrifice, dedication and love. It is a journey that will be over in the blink of an eye, regardless of the time taken. It is a journey of thrills and hopefully no spills. It is a journey that will be shared with loved ones and strangers alike. It is a journey that will be celebrated. It is a journey that may redefine who you are. It is a journey that will be remembered for the rest of your life. It is a journey that will teach you that anything is possible.

And when that journey is done my friends you will be an Ironman.

27

EMMA'S VERSION

Before writing this, I asked Andy "what is it worth?" and he laughed, nervously. But, for once in my life, I'm going to keep it brief, and I'll be kind (unless he drops any more bombshells on me before it's published!).

If I had a pound for every time someone has asked me if I'm interested in triathlon, or if I've ever considered entering an event I would be a very rich lady and I wouldn't be with Andy anymore because I'd have bought the rights to marry George Clooney (that's legal, right?).

My answer is simple – no. Not for the reason that people expect (and it is true) – because I'm lazy. But my reason is – murder. If two people with the same level of interest in triathlon that Andy has lived in the same house, and tried to complete all of their training; and enter all the events that interested them, one of us would commit murder (and I have a sneaky feeling it would be me).

Everything that drives Andy – his motivation, energy, determination, and yes, his stubbornness, all the things I admire about him and everyone else I have met at the many triathlon events over the years, if I had the same qualities (although I don't always call them that!), we would be like two bulls clashing horns in a china shop. So, in my defence, being lazy is a good thing for once.

I can't imagine there are many 'breeds' of people with the same level of enthusiasm for talking about the varying benefits of different types of running shoe, or the material and style of wetsuit, or for trying on many versions of kit to see which one works best – these are the scenarios where I now put on my "yes dear" face. Many times I have nodded and said "hmmm" to Andy telling me the results of people I have never met (don't get me wrong, I'm pleased for you, but I liken it to me telling Andy the plotlines of soaps even I don't watch!). And Andy is still mystified that these things are not scintillating to everyone! In summary, you definitely CAN hear too much about lycra.

In terms of being a supporter, Andy has told me many times that without the support of his family and friends, he would not have become a triathlete in the first place and there are times when, without support, he would have quit. I think that sums up how important both the physical and emotional support is. But, in case you had any delusions – it's not a glamorous job.

When I first met Andy, his main interest was in running. The idea of running for enjoyment was completely alien to me, and I was further shocked that he, and the original crew of Viking, Min and Dave among others, voluntarily entered events too.

My first experience of watching him run has probably determined my rules for being a spectator now – I had orders barked at me to "stand there", "hold that", "watch my bag", "make sure you take pictures of me" – I told him that if that experience was repeated, I wouldn't be going to spectate again.

He has mellowed out a lot more now, and has learned to tame the adrenaline, which makes spectating a lot more enjoyable, although it is surprisingly hard work (even Andy has confessed to this!).

I think my 'favourite' memory of watching Andy was at the Cleveland Steelman, when myself and his Mam and Dad stood in a field in absolutely torrential rain for three hours (yes, we are probably dafter than Andy!). Needless to say, the car journey home ended up with Andy in his clean, dry change of kit, and the rest of us in t-shirts and travel blankets. Reading that back, we are definitely nuts.

My worst experience supporting is something I blame on

pregnancy hormones. Waiting for Andy and his cousin Mike at the Outlaw in 2010, the time when I expected to see them both finish had long passed. I was an emotional wreck in floods of tears, with visions of them in an ambulance due to the heat that day.

Luckily, Andy's friends around me were not victims of hormones, and were fully confident that he would appear soon – which he did. It turned out that Mike had finished a couple of hours ago, none of us had seen this, and he was quite happily tucking into the finishers' buffet.

For any partners new to supporting a triathlete, my cheat's tip would be (and you probably won't have much choice in this either) to become very familiar with upcoming triathlon events in your area because you can be fairly certain you can block those dates out on your calendar! Oh, but maybe I should also mention that you may not be told about these dates, and it is assumed they will telepathically communicate themselves to you...

Life with triathlon in it isn't always rosy. We have had our fair share of fallings out about triathlon, and that's without me wanting to take part in it. Many of those fallings out have happened over the last two years, with the arrival of Charlotte.

As anyone will tell you, the arrival of your first child is everything you expect and much much more, but you also have to think about proper grown-up things that you've never (well, I hadn't!) considered before, like domestic arrangements – for example if one of you goes out, the other person inevitably has to stay in – this had not occurred to me before Charlotte arrived.

So with the amount of training Andy has put in in 2012, it's a good job I don't mind being at home. He has also confessed (with not too much torturing) that triathlon is the top priority in terms of planning his time, and arranging annual leave – this year I had to nag him to book two weeks off to spend with me and Charlotte, whereas his dates for Lanzarote and Nottingham had been booked months in advance.

This isn't a deliberate neglecting of the other parts of his life, or a selfishness, but it is how much influence triathlon has over his life. I can certainly understand that for a lot of triathlon widows this is too much to take, and causes problems. Also, my admiration goes out to any families where both partners are triathletes, and no murders have been committed.

The truth is that I can't imagine Andy without triathlon in his life. Firstly, he would get under my feet too much. Secondly, I don't know what would replace triathlon as his addiction I suppose you would call it. What would become his focus, his drive, his motivation? Again, without even being a participant, I can see that there is nothing else like it, nothing could come close to that type of challenge (if anyone dares suggest ultras or doubles here, think about how much you value your life first).

As I said before, I am full of admiration for everyone I have met at events over the years. I think you either have the drive to be a sportsperson, no matter what type of sport it is, or you don't. To wake up at 6am on a cold, wet day and have the drive to go out and run or get on the bike, is alien to me – if I saw it was raining, I would decide to just stay in bed.

I have met some wonderful people and made some very good friends through Andy's interest in firstly running, and then triathlon. I think this is another of the reasons for the appeal of triathlon to him, and the people I have met – the comradeship and the support for each other. If it was every man/woman to him/herself then people wouldn't return to triathlon but the level of support is unbelievable.

Yes, there is the desire for a good time, but there is also the willingness to help somebody who is struggling reach the finish line. I have always believed that life is not black and white, that there are many shades of grey (I'll have to change that phrase now won't I?!). Life has certainly thrown many events at us this year, and to many other people we know – and I know that the support between triathletes extends to life outside of triathlon (yes, it does exist!).

An often-heard comment from Andy is that he feels bad for having missed a training session, or because he's tired and hasn't got the energy to go out – because of things that have happened in 'real life', and I tell him that life goes on, and so will triathlon despite having missed a training session. Unless you're a professional triathlete being paid to train and compete, there will always be that battle for time, that conflict between the desire to train and everything else that you have to fit into life.

Each year my 'opinion' is asked for when he is deciding which event to enter next (although he has usually already made his decision, I'm not daft), and I will consider the terms and conditions that he has to agree to first.

I'm still thinking of them for next year's event, so any suggestions are welcome!